POLITICAL CAMPAIGN STAMPS

MARK WARDA

The information provided in this book is strictly for the use and enjoyment of collectors.
The opinions expressed on the collectible materials listed in this book are not necessarily those of the publisher.

Published by

krause
publications

700 E. State Street • Iola, WI 54990-0001
Telephone: 715/445-2214

Please call or write for our free catalog of publications. Our toll-free number to place an order or obtain a free catalog is 800-258-0929 or please use our regular business telephone 715-445-2214 for editorial comment and further information.

Library of Congress Catalog Number: 98-84100
ISBN: 0-87341-616-3
Printed in the United States of America

Acknowledgments

No book of this type would be possible without the help of many collectors who shared their knowledge and collections.

I am especially grateful to Andy Adkins, John Denune, Mark Evans, Tom French, Ed Mitchell, and Charles Schmidt for going out of their ways in helping with the compilation of information for this catalog.

Also deserving of special thanks are the following people who helped make this catalog possible: Randy Christensen, Tim Coughlin, Arthur R. Critchfield, Jack Crowder, Robert Cutter, Robert J. DuBois, Frank G. Edmiston, Lon Ellis, Warren Ellis, Peter Fisher, Jerry Grigaitis, W. William Hanneman, U. I. "Chick" Harris, David Holcomb, Esbjorn Janson, Philip S. Jones, Dave Lemon, Tom Maeder, James McNaughton, Paul A. Melnick, Larry Melton, Henry Michalski, John Miskevich, Bruce Mosher, Jay Nesbitt, Dr. Edward Novick, Christopher D. Olmstead, Steve Pauler, Donald Pirtle, Robert M. Platt, Sterling Rachootin, Don Reuter, Richard Roberts, Guy Rossi, Henry B. Scheuer, Walter E. Schmidt, Paul Schumacher, Eugene Spaziani, Ewald van Elkan, Joseph D. Ward, Jr., Rob Washburn, Eugene Wolosiewicz, and David Yount.

Contents

Chapter 6 Patriotic, War, and Peace

Chapter 7 Miscellaneous Causes

Addendum

Index

Introduction

This is the most comprehensive catalog of political campaign stamps, seals, and labels ever published. It includes all political campaign and cause items from 1856 through publication known to the author after three decades of collecting and research. The author self-published a book of 500 presidential campaign stamps in 1990. In 1962 R. C. Mosbaugh compiled a mimeographed loose-leaf catalog of fund-raising seals which included many political causes; it was updated between 1976 and 1984 by the Christmas Seal and Charity Stamp Society. This book, *Political Campaign Stamps*, includes all political cause items listed in both of the above mentioned works for which pictures were available, plus many new items discovered in the years since.

Organization. The items in this book are organized by subject matter, unlike the Mosbaugh system which organized them by source. This is in keeping with the trend among stamp collectors in recent decades. For many years people collected stamps by country. In recent years more and more collectors are collecting by topic, and catalogs and lists are being published consolidating those topics.

The basic organization in this book is by the design and text on the face of the stamp. For example, all stamps with the word "peace" are in the anti-war section. Where the design is generic or not political, the stamp is listed under the subject which the issuing organization was supporting. For example, a stamp picturing running children and a Christmas tree, which was issued by a school for black children, is in the section for blacks.

Stamps which are opposed to a political candidate are usually listed under that candidate. Our initial preference was to list them under the opposing candidate, but this is often difficult to determine. An anti-Nixon sticker could have been issued by supporters of Kennedy, Humphrey, or McGovern, or by Republicans who opposed his nomination. This system is helpful to collectors who collect anything pertaining to a particular candidate, whether it is for or against him.

One exception is "No Third Term" stamps. Several of these items also mention Willkie and must be included in the Willkie section. To keep them all together we have included all of the rest under Willkie as well. We are aware that some of them may have been issued by Democrats.

Inclusions and exclusions. In compiling a catalog of this type, many logistical decisions must be made. Should we only list items which came in sheets with perforations between them, or should we also include "stickers" which were issued singly and in pads? What about "peel and stick" items? What are the largest sized items that we should include? What about window stickers and bumper stickers? Should we include every item mentioning a candidate, or only those proven to have been used in their campaign?

It would be impossible to make everyone happy. There are no clear distinctions, so all decisions must be arbitrary. Here is what we decided and why. Items issued individually and in pads and booklets (as opposed to being issued in sheets) were included because it is not always possible to determine how an item was printed and because many of these items are as nice or nicer than those produced in sheets. Also, they served the same purposes. The size limit was set at three inches because larger items served a different purpose, such as window stickers or bumper stickers. However, a few items over three inches, because they were part of a set or especially interesting, have been included. No peel and stick items were included because the glue on these is not stable and most of them self-destruct in a very few years. However, ways are being found to preserve them and perhaps a future edition may include them.

This book includes every item known to the author which appears to have been used in a politically-related campaign. The campaigns range from presidential elections to local referenda and peripheral causes such as censorship and AIDS funding.

There are many other types of items in which collectors of this material may have an interest. For example, various veterans groups have issued fundraising seals over the years and collectors of patriotic items may wish to add these to their collections. Also, many countries have issued stamps featuring U. S. presidents, and collectors of a particular one may wish to collect those stamps. However, because these items do not promote a political cause we have not included them. Material of this type is mentioned in sidebars throughout the book.

Some collectors seek out any items picturing their specialties, such as John F. Kennedy, but to keep this book at a reasonable size we have included only material which was issued during the life of the person and could have supported their candidacy. For those interested in collecting material from any period of time, the American Topical Association and other organizations may have listings of material issued which could be helpful.

Sets of stamps picturing all of the presidents have been issued for many years, and are not normally used in a campaign. However, the last stamp in each set was issued during the term of the sitting president and could have been used to support his reelection, so these are included.

Terms and abbreviations. Stamp collecting is very specialized and different meanings are attached to the words "stamp," "seal," "label," and similar words. To a stamp collector the word "stamp" can only mean something issued by a government body. However, because the material in this catalog is of greatest interest to political specialists we have used the common meaning of the word "stamp" to cover the little paper items with glue on the back which look like postage stamps. To a political collector a label would be something used on a jar or can.

Some terms and abbreviations used in this work are:

Perf.: perforated with little round holes (in some cases the number of holes per inch may vary between stamps)

Imperf.: issued with no perforations

Roulette: perforated with little knife slits rather than round holes

Hopeful: candidate who sought a party's nomination but did not receive it

MI: margin inscription, the text printed on the margin of the sheet

SE: straight edge, when the edge of a sheet of stamps has no margin and no perforations

T: top   **L:** left   **R:** right   **B:** bottom

MIT: margin inscription at the top of the sheet

SE:LBR: straight edge at the left, bottom, and right edges of the sheet

Values. Because there has never been a comprehensive catalog of this material before, there are not consistent prices in the market for the material in this book. Unlike government postage stamps, quantities printed are unknown and demand is elastic. For the same item you can check with five dealers and get five different prices ranging from $5 to $200. What is the true value of such an item? Hopefully this book will correct that disparity by showing relative scarcity of the material listed.

Typically, material of this type is valued much lower by stamp specialists than by political specialists. Stamp specialists concentrate on government-issued material which has a fixed cash value. Political cause stamps, printed by private companies, are of much less interest to such collectors. One philatelic columnist even went so far as to describe such material as "album weeds" and said that he routinely threw it in the trash after purchasing a collection. Too bad—he probably threw away a fortune. A nickname for this material is "cinderella" labels. This is because it is thought of by most stamp collectors to be a worthless step-sister to stamp collecting.

Political specialists place a much higher value on this material. Campaign stamps are as much a part of campaigns as buttons and posters and are very easy to store and display. While they are not as popular as buttons, better items routinely sell for over a hundred dollars.

If only one copy of a stamp has been seen in the collecting community in recent years and many people collect the candidate pictured, the price can rise to unbelievable levels at an auction. This is especially true if each collector thinks that it is the only one he or she may ever see and is intent upon owning every item related to his or her specialty. Needless to say, if you come across several sheets of a stamp valued at $50, you will not get $50 for each stamp. There may be only a few dozen collectors willing to pay that price for that stamp, and once they all have it the price will drop.

The values in this book are expressed in a high-low range. These are the prices at which a collector can expect to pay for a single item from a dealer. In most cases the minimum price is 50 cents because few political dealers bother with items at less than that price, but some stamp dealers who specialize in cinderella labels may have this material available at lower prices, especially when filling a large order.

On any items of which only one or a few copies are known, the value is listed as "R" for Rare. The value of such items cannot be predicted until some come to market.

A few weeks from now a stamp listed in this catalog might sell for many times the listed price because several people wanted it badly, or it might sell for a fraction of the listed price because several sheets came onto the market. Stamp collectors will probably be surprised by some of the prices in this book. Because most stamp collectors consider political labels as cinderella material they assume they are worth only a few cents a piece. Therefore a stamp listed in this catalog at $25 or $50 will often be considered a 10- or 50-cent item by a stamp collector. Happy hunting!

Condition. Unlike postage stamps, which were printed by the hundreds of millions, distributed throughout the country, and saved by many thousands of people, political stamps were usually printed in small quantities, available in limited areas, and ignored by most collectors. While there are stamp dealers in nearly every community which can supply virtually any U.S. postage stamp, some political labels may take years to locate. Most stamp dealers do not keep this material in stock but sell it as soon as it comes in the door. The best sources of material like this are the few cinderella dealers in the stamp hobby and some political collectibles dealers, but their stocks are not deep and usually they have a waiting buyer for any good item they come across.

For these reasons condition is usually of little importance to political collectors for most items. The large quantities of postage stamps allow collectors to discriminate and collect only perfectly centered copies with undisturbed gum (glue) on the back (mint, never hinged). For stamp collectors, value is diminished for hinge marks on the back, missing gum, and straight edges (no perforations on one or more of the edges), if examples are available with perforations on all four sides.

But with political stamps, most collectors are happy just to find a copy of a long-sought item and are not as concerned about condition. For this reason, although perfect copies are of course preferred, defects or lack of glue on the back of an item does not usually detract much from the value.

Christmas seals which have been used on an envelope and are "tied" to the envelope by falling under the postmark (proving that they were used when the envelope was mailed) are usually much more valuable than unused Christmas seals. That is because most Christmas seals are still available by the millions but those used on envelopes are much harder to find. Stamp collectors therefore also put more value on political stamps tied to envelopes, but political collectors seem to prefer unused copies which do not have postmarks on them.

Numbering System. Because the total number of items which can be included in this catalog will never be known, it would be impractical to number the items with numerals starting with number 1. Therefore the items are numbered separately for each candidate or category using their initials or an abbreviation of the cause. (For example the 8 Abraham Lincoln stamps are numbered AL-1 to AL-8.) However, Alfred E. Smith is designated merely AS to differentiate him from Adlai E. Stevenson who is AES. Also, Woodrow Wilson's stamps are prefixed TWW- (for Thomas Woodrow Wilson) to differentiate them from the World War stamps prefixed WW-.

Where the stamps can be broken into subgroups or types, we have broken up the numbering starting with 1, 101, 201, 251, etc. to allow future addition of newly-discovered material without completely renumbering the section.

Colors. Colors specified for each item are according to the list below. A slash mark "/" separates an ink color from the paper color. For example, Bk/Gd means black ink on goldenrod paper. The abbreviation s.c. means surface-colored paper. This means that the paper is colored only on the front. The colors are of the inks used to produce the stamp. Sometimes shading with black ink appears gray, or red and blue may make a purple color, however, we have listed only the inks used.

Color List

B: Blue	**Bk:** Black	**Br:** Brown
Cm: Carmine	**Cr:** Cream	**Dk:** Dark
Gd: Goldenrod	**Go:** Gold	**Gr:** Green
Gy: Gray	**Lt:** Light .	**Ma:** Maroon
MC: Multicolored	**Or:** Orange	**Ol:** Olive
Pk: Pink	**Pu:** Purple	**R:** Red
Ro: Red-orange	**Se:** Sepia	**Si:** Silver
Tn: Tan	**Tu:** Turquoise	**Y:** Yellow

Help! All of the stamps, seals, and labels issued in this country to support political causes will probably never be known, but we would like to keep updating this book to make it as comprehensive as possible. If you have any material not pictured in this book, please send photocopies to Mark Warda, c/o Krause Publications, 700 East State Street, Iola, WI 54990-0001. Your help will be acknowledged in a future edition.

Chapter 1

Presidential Stamps

This chapter contains all material which was issued for presidential candidates, vice-presidential candidates, and their wives during their lifetimes.

Memorial items have not been included because they are so much more numerous and not nearly as popular as those issued during the candidate's campaign or lifetime.

Sets of stamps picturing all of the presidents have been issued since the nineteenth century. While they were not necessarily meant for campaigns, they were issued during the term of a sitting president and could have been used to promote his reelection, and are therefore included at the end of this chapter.

Presidential Campaign Stamps

John C. Fremont, 1856

JCF-1	Bk/Pk (1856)	20.-40.
JCF-2	Bk/Cr (1856)	25.-50.

JCF-3	RB	20.-50.

This is by the same manufacturer as AL-9 and GMC-1. There are matching stamps picturing Gen. Winfield Scott, George Washington, a text message, and there may be others. See CW-1, CW-2, and CW-3 in Chapter 6.

JCF-4	Br/Cr	R

"Our Jesse" refers to Fremont's wife.

JCF-5   R
Same design with "Free Land, FREE LABOR, FREMONT!"
JCF-6   R
Same design with "FREMONT will prove the *buck*wheat chaff."

JCF-7   R
Same design with "Freedom's Pioneer, the brave FREMONT!"
JCF-8   R
Same design with "No 'Old Bach' wanted at the White House"
JCF-9   R
Same design with "Give 'em Jessie"
JCF-10   R
Same design with "Freedom's Pathfinder, FREMONT!"

John C. Breckinridge, 1860

JCB-1	Pu (1860)	R

This stamp is a mate to AL-1, AL-2, and SD-1. The picture came from a 1934 auction catalog and is the only one available.

Stephen A. Douglas, 1860

SAD-1	(1860)	R

This stamp is a mate to AL-1 and 2 and to JCB-1.

Abraham Lincoln, 1860, 1864

Picture shown at 90%

AL-1	DkPu (1860)	R
AL-2	B (1860)	R

AL-4   AL-7

AL-3	2¢ Bk/Ro s.c. (1864)	25.-50.
AL-4	3¢ Bk/G s.c. (1864)	25.-50.
AL-5	4¢ Bk/Pk s.c. (1864)	25.-50.
AL-6	5¢ Blue (1864)	25.-50.
AL-7	10¢ Bk/Y s.c. (1864)	25.-50.
AL-8	12¢ Bk/dkG s.c. (1864)	25.-50.

AL-9	RB	25.-50.

This is a mate to GMC-1 and is by the same

Presidential Stamps • 9

manufacturer as JCF-3. There are matching stamps picturing Gen. Winfield Scott, George Washington, a text message, and there may be others. See CW-1, CW-2, and CW-3 in Chapter 6.

AL-10   RB   25.-50.

AL-11   RB   25.-50.

George McClellan, 1864

GMC-1   RB   15.-30.
This is a mate to AL-9 and by the same manufacturer as JCF-3. There are matching stamps picturing Gen. Winfield Scott, George Washington, a text message, and there may be others. See CW-1, CW-2, and CW-3 in Chapter 6.

Rutherford B. Hayes, 1876

RBH-1   MC   10.-20.
Die cut. Might be from a presidential set.

James A. Garfield, 1880

JAG-1   MC   25.-50.
Die cut. Distributed on cards of thirty-two (4x8). Shows Garfield with Vice President Arthur.

JAG-2   MC   10.-20.
Die cut.

Picture shown at 85%
JAG-3   MC   10.-20.
Die cut.

Winfield S. Hancock, 1880

WSH-1   MC   25.-50.
Die cut. Shows Hancock with vice-presidential candidate English.

Chester Arthur, 1880, 1884

CA-1   Multicolored   10.-20.
Die cut.

James G. Blaine, 1884

JGB-1   25.-50.

JGB-2   MC   25.-50.
Mate to JL-1. More valuable as a set.

John Logan, 1884

JL-1   MC   25.-50.
Mate to JGB-1. More valuable as a set.

Grover Cleveland, 1884, 1888, 1892

GC-1   Se   R

Picture shown at 67%
GC-2   MC   10.-20.
Die cut.

Picture shown at 67%
GC-3   MC   10.-20.
Die cut.

Picture shown at 67%
GC-4   MC   10.-20.
Die cut.

Picture shown at 67%
GC-5   MC   10.-20.
Die cut.

Picture shown at 67%
GC-6   Multicolored   10.-20.
Die cut.

William McKinley, 1896, 1900

WMK-1   Gr   8.-15.
WMK-2   Tn   8.-15.
WMK-3   DkBr   8.-15.
WMK-4   Ol   8.-15.
WMK-5   Cm   8.-15.
These are mates to WJB-1 through WJB-3.

WMK-6   Gy   5.-10.

WMK-7   Go/Bk   5.-10.
Sheets of nine (3x3) MIR: "TABLET & TICKET
CO. —Manufacturers of— Campaign Stickers,
Seal Marking Tickets, Willson's Gummed Let-
ters and Figures, Advertising Stickers, &c. CHI-
CAGO AND NEW YORK."

William J. Bryan, 1896, 1900, 1908

WJB-1   Cm   10.-20.
WJB-2   Tan   10.-20.
WJB-3   Gr   10.-20.
These are mates for WMK-1 to 5, and there may
be other colors.

WJB-4   B (perf. 12) (1908)   5.-10.
WJB-4a   B (perf. 10) (1908)   5.-10.
These are part of a set which includes Taft,
Debs, and Chafin.

WJB-5   Bk   10.-20.
Mate to WHT-1.

WJB-6   MC   10.-20.
WJB-7   MC   10.-20.
WJB-7 has "Schuneman & Evans..." as the text.

WJB-8   10.-20.

WJB-9   10.-20.

WJB-10   10.-20.
The Single Tax Party supported Bryan for president.

Theodore Roosevelt, 1904, 1912

TR-1   Bk on thick paper   10.-20.

TR-2   RBY   10.-20.

Alton B. Parker, 1904

ABP-1   Bk/Pk   R

William H. Taft, 1908, 1912

WHT-1   Bk (1908)   10.-20.
Mate to WJB-5.
Booklets of two or four panes of six (2x3). SE: RBL; MIT: "COPYRIGHT, 1908, BY PHOTO STAMP CO."

WHT-2   B (perf. 12) (1908)   5.-10.
WHT-2a   Blue (perf. 14) (1908)   5.-10.
Sheets of 100 (10x10) SE:RBL MIT. This is part of a set which includes Bryan, Debs, and Chafin.

Picture shown at 80%
WHT-3   R

WHT-4   Bk   10.-20.
Booklets of two or four panes of six (2x3). SE: RBL. Mate to TWW-5.

Front   Back
WHT-5   B   10.-20.

WHT-6   R   10.-20.
WHT-6 and JSS-1 (below) are a set and collectors will pay a premium for the set.

CAMPAIGN STICKERS

Can be used as Letter Seals, Envelope Corners, on Postal Cards, Parcels, Letter Paper, Etc.

"VOTE FOR TAFT."

PHOTO COPYRIGHT, 1908, BY MOFFETT STUDIO, CHICAGO.

Booklet Cover for WHT-1

This is the cover of a booklet of WHT-1 stamps. It contains three panes of six stamps each. It is printed in black on thick red paper. The reason some of the stamps can be found on what looks like pink paper is that when wet the red from the booklet cover stained the stamps.

James S. Sherman, 1908, 1912 Vice President

JSS-1   R   10.-20.

JSS-1 and WHT-6 (above) are a set and collectors will pay a premium for the set.

Eugene V. Debs, 1904–1920

EVD-1   B (1908)   25.-50.+

This is part of a set which includes Bryan, Taft, and Chafin.

EVD-2   B   R

Picture shown at 85%

EVD-3   Br   40.-60.+

Panes of five (5x1) in booklets of twenty. SE:TRB

EVD-4   BkR/B   10.-20.

The wording "Carry on!" on this stamp suggests that it might have been issued after Debs' death. It is very similar to and was printed by the same printer as NT-3.

Eugene W. Chafin, 1908 Prohibition Party

EWC-1   B (1908)   15.-25.

This is part of a set which includes Bryan, Taft, and Debs.

James B. "Champ" Clark, 1908 Hopeful

JBC-1   R (roulette)   15.-25.
JBC-1a   R (perf.)   15.-25.

It is possible that JBC-1a was created from JBC-1 by adding perforations.

Thomas Woodrow Wilson, 1908–1916

TWW-1   BkY   R

TWW-2   RBBrT   10.-20.

Booklets of five panes of ten (5x2). SE: TRB

TWW-3   BkBrOrY   25.-35.

TWW-4   Bk   10.-20.

Copies which appear to be on pink paper most likely were changed by the dye in the red booklet cover.

TWW-5   Bk   10.-20.

Booklets of two or four panes of six (2x3). SE: RBL; MIT: "COPYRIGHT, 1912, BY PHOTO STAMP CO." Mate to WHT-4.

TWW-6   RB   5.-10.

Die cut.

| TWW-7 | Br | 5.-10. |
| TWW-7A | Gr | 5.-10. |

| TWW-8 | RB (1916) | 2.00 |

TWW-9	MC (1916)	10.-20.
TWW-10	MC (1916)	10.-20.
Complete set of twelve w/o Bryan		25.-40.
Complete set of twelve w/ Bryan		30.-50.

TWW-10 is the same as TWW-9 except text at bottom reads "Schuneman & Evans..." This stamp is part of a set of twelve featuring the vice president and the rest of the cabinet. There are at least these two different types, and probably more. The set including TWW-9 comes with either Robert Lansing or William Jennings Bryan as Secretary of State. See also TRM-1 and WJB-5.

TWW-11a	B	4.-8.
TWW-11b	R	4.-8.
TWW-11c	Gr	4.-8.
TWW-11d	Br	4.-8.

It has been suggested that these were issued in Czechoslovakia in the 1920s but this has not been verified or unproved.

Picture shown at 67%

| TWW-12 | R | 8.-15. |

Picture shown at 120%

| TWW-13 | MC | R |

Picture shown at 90%

| TWW-14 | MC | 10.-20. |

| TWW-15 | BrRGr | 8.-15. |

| TWW-16 | MC | 15.-30. |

| TWW-17 | Br | 8.-15. |

| TWW-18 | | 5.-10. |

Made in France. Single stamp in a sheet with other designs.

| TWW-19 | RBBk | 5.-10. |
| TWW-20 | RBBk | 5.-10. |

TWW-20 has text above and below the picture reading: "14 JUILLET 1919/FÉTE DA LA VIC-TOIRE."

TWW-21   RBBk   5.-10.

TWW-22   RBBk   5.-10.

TWW-23   RBBk   5.-10.

TWW-24   MC   10.-20.

TWW-25   MC   4.-8.

Thomas R. Marshall

TRM-1   Multicolored   5.-10.
TRM-2   Multicolored   5.-10.
TRM-2 has "Schuneman & Evans..." as the text.

Arthur E. Reimer,
1912 Socialist Labor Party

AER-1   Blue   15.-25.
This was used on a 1912 campaign envelope and is assumed to be from that election.

Charles E. Hughes,
1908-1916

CEH-1   RBBr   R
Copies are known with the date "1916" rubber stamped on the sides.

CEH-2   B (1916)   25.-35.

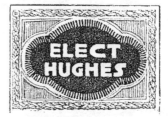

CEH-3   RB   15.-25.

The People's Governor
——— TO BE ———
The People's President
"TUESDAY
IS HUGHES' DAY"   VOTE

CEH-4   R   15.-25.

CEH-5   RBk   2.-4.

L. V. Sherman, 1916

LVS-1   BYBr   20.-30.

Allan L. Benson, 1916 Socialist Party

ALB-1   B   10-20.

Booklets of two panes of ten (5x2).

Warren G. Harding, 1920

WGH-1   B   10.-20.

WGH-2   RB   15.-25.

WGH-3   LtBBk   15.-25.

WGH-4   OrBk   10.-25.

WGH-5   15.-25.

> " * * * The torches of under-
> standing have been lighted,
> and they ought to glow and
> encircle the globe."
>   PRESIDENT HARDING.

Picture shown at 85%

WGH-6   Bk   2.-6.

> "Justice is better served in con-
> ferences of peace than in
> conflicts at arms."
>   PRESIDENT HARDING.

Picture shown at 85%

WGH-7   Bk   2.-6.

The last two Harding stamps may have been issued after his death.

James M. Cox, 1920

JMC-1   RBk   R
JMC-2   GrBk   R

> Keep Faith With
> our Sons
> Bring America into
> The League of Nations
> Vote For
> **Cox and Roosevelt**

JMC-3   RB   30.-60.

Gen. John Pershing, 1920

JP-1   RBBk   5.-10.

Leonard Wood, 1920

LW-1   RB   15.-25.

Calvin Coolidge, 1924

Picture shown at 67%

CC-1   Br   R

CC-2   RB   10.-20

CC-3   BkOrGyGr   10.-20
Blocks of twelve were distributed in envelopes
which had one stamp affixed to the front.

YOU CAN HELP

TO   KEEP

CALVIN COOLIDGE

By sticking these seals on
Letters and the back of
Envelopes, or by using
them on Billboards, Pack-
ages, Hat Bands, Etc.

Picture shown at 65%
Envelope containing CC-3

CC-4   Br   5.-10.
CC-4A   R   8.-15.

CC-5   RB   8.-15.

CC-6   RBGr   15.-25.

Picture shown at 75%
CC-7   BkTuOr   10.-25.

Picture shown at 75%
CC-8   RB   20.-30.
These were sold in rolls for 5¢ a roll by John W.
Little Co., Pawtucket, RI
Note: Fakes exist without the copyright symbol.

Picture shown at 85%
CC-9   RB   10.-20.
These were sold in rolls for 5¢ a roll by John W.
Little Co., Pawtucket, R.I.

John W. Davis, 1924

JWD-1   RB   R

JWD-2   RB   40.-60.

Herbert C. Hoover, 1928, 1932

HCH-1   RB   R

HCH-2   RBGo   R
Embossed and die cut gold foil.
Issued by F. E. Mason & Sons, Batavia, N.Y.

HCH-3   RB (1932)   5.-15.

HCH-4   R (1928)   5.-10.
Booklets of ten sheets of ten (5x2). Mate to
AS-1.

HCH-5   B (1928)   5.-10.
Booklets of ten sheets of ten (5x2). Mate to
AS-2.

HCH-6   BBk   6.-12.
Sheets of five (5x1) in booklets of twenty.

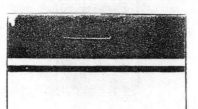

OFFICIALLY
APPROVED
REPUBLICAN
HOOVER
STAMPS

20 for $1.00
(5c. each)

Booklet cover of HCH-6.

HCH-7   Se (photo) (1932)   5.-10.
Mate to FDR-36.

HCH-8   RB   10.-20.

HCH-9   B   8.-15.

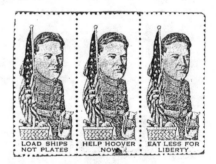

Picture shown at 75%

HCH-10   BkRBY   5.-10.
HCH-11   BkRBY   5.-10.
HCH-12   BkRBY   5.-10.
These appear to have been issued during World
War I when Hoover was United States Food Ad-
ministrator.

HCH-13   Bk/Or (1932)   5.-10.
Mate to FDR-45.

HCH-14   B/B   5.-10.
Sheets of four (2x2). SE:TRBL

HCH-15   RB   3.-6.

HCH-16   RBY (perf.)   4.-8.
HCH-17   RB (imperf.)   4.-8.

HCH-18   RB   8.-15.

Picture shown at 85%
HCH-19   RB   10.-20.

HCH-20   B   2.-4.
Panes of five (5x1) in booklets of twenty similar
to booklets of HCH-6.

Picture shown at 85%
HCH-21   R   6.-12.

Picture shown at 67%
HCH-22   RB   2.-4.

HCH-23   RB   2.-4.

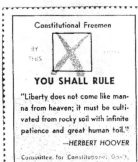

HCH-24   RB   2.-4.

Alfred E. Smith, 1928

AS-1   R   6.-12.
Panes of ten (5x2) in booklets of 100. SE: TRB
Mate to HCH-4.

This catalog only includes
stamps which were produced
during a president's lifetime.
For popular presidents such
as Lincoln and Kennedy there
are thousands of stamps
which were made after their
deaths. If you specialize in a
particular president you can
add these to your collection.

Picture shown at 55%
Booklet cover of AS-1.

AS-2   R   6.-12.
Panes of ten (5x2) in booklets of 100. SE: TRB
Mate to HCH-5.

Picture shown at 70%
AS-3   RBk   20.-30.

Picture shown at 70%
AS-4   BkR   20.-30.
Note: It appears that the colors on this stamp run
when wet.

AS-5   MC   10.-20.

Picture shown at 80%
AS-6   10.20
Because Smith's Catholicism was an issue in
some areas of the country, this is believed to be
an anti-Smith item.

William Z. Foster, 1928 Communist Party

WZF-1   RBkGr   R

WZF-2   RBkTu   R

Norman Thomas, 1928, 1932, 1936, 1940, 1944, 1948 Socialist Party

NT-1   R   5.-10.

NT-2   Bk/Pk   3.-6.

NT-3   BkR/B   8.-15.

NT-4   R "Vote for..."   3.-6.

I have not attempted to collect "peel and stick" labels for this book, but they have been used since the 1940s and have gotten even more popular with campaigns in recent years. In some cases they are used in place of campaign buttons to save money. If you collect campaign stamps you may want to add thse to your collection. One problem with such items is that with age the glue may migrate into the paper, discoloring it. To avoid this the glue can be removed with a solvent. Be sure to test the solvent before cleaning a valuable sticker and to only use the solvent in a well-ventilated area.

NT-5	R "Vote to forever..."	3.-6.
NT-6	R "The profit system..."	3.-6.
NT-7	R "Work for..."	3.-6.
NT-8	R "Join the..."	3.-6.
NT-9	R "The whole..."	3.-6.
NT-10	R "Your vote and your..."	3.-6.
NT-11	R "Your vote and mine..."	3.-6.
NT-12	R "Capitalism has..."	3.-6.
NT-13	R "I'm tired of..."	3.-6.
NT-14	R "A dog may..."	3.-6.
NT-15	R "Be a SOCIALIST..."	3.-6.
NT-16	R "Unemployment..."	3.-6.
NT-17	R "If you love..."	3.-6.

This set is on thin paper with round perforations.

NT-4a	R "Vote for..."	3.-6.
NT-5a	R "Vote to forever..."	3.-6.
NT-6a	R "The profit system..."	3.-6.
NT-7a	R "Work for..."	3.-6.
NT-8a	R "Join the..."	3.-6.
NT-9a	R "The whole..."	3.-6.
NT-10a	R "Your vote and your..."	3.-6.
NT-11a	R "Your vote and mine..."	3.-6.
NT-12a	R "Capitalism has..."	3.-6.
NT-13a	R "I'm tired of..."	3.-6.
NT-14a	R "A dog may..."	3.-6.
NT-15a	R "Be a SOCIALIST..."	3.-6.
NT-16a	R "Unemployment..."	3.-6.
NT-17a	R "If you love..."	3.-6.

This set is on thick paper with roulette perforations.

Picture shown at 70%
Full sheet of NT-4a to NT-17a.

Franklin D. Roosevelt, 1932, 1936, 1940, 1944

FDR-1	B (1932)	10.-15.

Booklets issued by the Democratic National Committee with text inside and out, sold for $1. Panes of six (2x3). SE: TRB

FDR-2	RB	5.-10.

FDR-3	Br/Y (1932)	4.-8.
FDR-4	Without union bug (1932)	3.-6.

Panes of ten (2x5). SE:RBL Top two stamps have union bug, other eight do not. A page in the

booklet carries a reproduction of one stamp in black ink.

FDR-5	Pu (1932)	2.-4.

Sheets of forty or fifty. SE:TRBL

FDR-6	Br (1932)	2.-4.
FDR-7	Bk (1932)	4.-8.
FDR-8	Se (photo) (1932)	5.-10

FDR-6 is known in sheets of 100 consisting of two groups of fifty (5x10) with a gutter between. There are no perforations in the gutter or between outer stamps and outer margin.

FDR-9	Se (photo) (1936)	10.-25.

FDR-10	Tn (1940)	3.-6.

Picture shown at 80%
Coupon contained in booklets of FDR-3 and FDR-4.

FDR-11   Bk (photo) (1940)   8.-15.

FDR-12   Se (photo) (1936)   5.-10.

FDR-13   50¢ RB/Y (1944)   R
FDR-14 $1 value RB (1944)   R
ILGWU stands for International Ladies' Garment
Workers Union.

FDR-15   3.-6.

FDR-16   (1932)   8.-15.

FDR-17   B (1932)   2.-4.
FDR-18   Br (1932)   2.-4.
FDR-19   Gr (1932)   2.-4.
FDR-20   Or (1932)   2.-4.
Sheets of twenty (5x4). SE:TRBL

FDR-21   Bk (photo) (1940)   3.-6.

FDR-22   Bk (photo) (1940)   3.-6.

FDR-23   Se (photo) (1940)   3.-6.

FDR-24   RB   3.-5.
Sheets of fifty (10x5). SE:TRBL

FDR-25   Gr   3.-6.
FDR-26   Ma   2.-4.

FDR-27   RB   4.-8.

FDR-28   RB   4.-8.

FDR-29   4.-8.

FDR-30   RB   4.-8.

FDR-31   B/B   8.-15.
FDR-32   Br/Y   8.-15.
Sheets of twenty (5x4) MIB: "Artist, John Bob Payne, Payne Advertising Co./Engraving Brand Engraving Co./Printing Sunset Printing Co./ Originator and Sales, Geo. S. Cabbell/San Antonio, Texas"

FDR-33   Tn   4.-8.

FDR-34   MC   3.-6.
Part of a set of at least forty-eight patriotic stamps issued in 1942. See Chapter 6.

Note: The item with Arabic text pictured as FDR-34 in the earlier catalog by this author turned out to be a piece of plastic and not a stamp. Therefore it has been replaced by a newly-discovered stamp.

FDR-35   RB   3.-6.

FDR-36   Se (photo) (1932)   3.-6.
Mate to HCH-7.

Picture shown at 67%
FDR-37   RB/Si   4.-10.

FDR-38   GrBk (1936)   8.-15.
FDR-39   GrBk (1936)   8.-15.
FDR-40   GrBk (1936)   8.-15.
FDR-41   GrBk (1936)   8.-15.
FDR-42   GrBk (1936)   8.-15.
Believed to be a sheet of fifty (5x10) SE:TBLR

FDR-43   RB   3.-6.
Sheets of ten (2x5) SE:LBT

FDR-44   RB   3.-6.
Sheets of ten (2x5). SE: TBLR

FDR-45   OI   4.-8.
Mate to HCH-9.

We Want Roosevelt

FDR-46   RB   .50-2.
Sheets of four (1x4) in pads.

Don't take the Pitcher out
When he's winning the game
KEEP ROOSEVELT

FDR-47   2.-4.

FDR-48   B/T   2.-4.

Keep the NEW DEAL—it's a GOOD DEAL

FDR-49   B/T   2.-4.

LABOR says: Return WILLKIE to WALL Street

FDR-50   B/T   2.-4.

AMERICA FIRST
RIGHTEOUS GOVERNMENT
ROOSEVELT GARNER
VOTE NOV. 8
EMPLOYMENT   PROSPERITY
REPEAL

FDR-51   RB   3.-6.
Possibly in the same sheet as FDR-62.

FDR-52   RB   4.-8.
Round die cut.

FDR-53   3.-6.

FDR-54   RB   3.-6.

FACTS, NOT FAVORS SHOULD GOVERN LEGISLATION
Franklin D. Roosevelt

FDR-55   R   3.-6.

All Natural Resources For The Benefit Of All The People
Franklin D. Roosevelt

FDR-56   R   3.-6.

FDR-57   Ma   3.-6.
FDR-58   Or   3.-6.

FREE ENTERPRISE
NO. 4th TERMITES

FDR-59   4.-8.

America's Fastest Growing Club
FDR FOR EX-PRESIDENT
Join Now—No Dues—Just Remember in November to Vote for
FDR FOR EX-PRESIDENT
THOS. F. OGILVIE, SEC'Y, ATLANTIC CITY
1,000 LABELS LIKE THIS $1 POSTPAID

FDR-60   3.-6.

FDR-61   Gr   3.-6.

AMERICA FIRST
RIGHTEOUS GOVERNMENT
ROOSEVELT GARNER
1933 1937
EMPLOYMENT   PROSPERITY
REPEAL

FDR-62   RB   3.-6.
Possibly in the same sheet as FDR-51.

DON'T FORGET THE BIG
DAUPHIN COUNTY DEMOCRATIC RALLY THURSDAY NOV. 3
MADRID BALLROOM
VISIT CAMPAIGN HEADQUARTERS
14 North Market Square
PHONE 4-4108

FDR-63   B/Pk   3.-6.
November 3 fell on Thursday in 1932 and 1960.
This appears older than 1960, so it is probably a 1932 FDR item.

Picture shown at 95%
FDR-64   Gr   3.-6.

It is up to you to insist that this pledge is kept:

"Your boys are NOT going to be sent into any foreign wars."

Pres. Franklin D. Roosevelt
Oct. 31. 1940

Picture shown at 90%
FDR-65   RB   2.-4.

KEEP THIS PROMISE!

"We made it clear that ships flying the American flag could not carry munitions to a belligerent; and must stay out of war zones."
F.D.R. 10/28/40

Picture shown at 95%
FDR-66   R   2.-4.

Say it again, Mr. President!!!
PLEASE, *won't you say it again?*
"We will not participate in foreign wars and we will not send our Army, Naval or Air Force, to fight in foreign lands outside of the Americas except in case of attack."
F. D. R. 10/23/40

Picture shown at 90%
FDR-67   B   2.-4.

IT IS UP TO YOU TO INSIST THAT THIS PLEDGE IS KEPT:

"Your boys are not going to be sent into any foreign wars."

PRESIDENT FRANKLIN D. ROOSEVELT
Oct. 31, 1940

FDR-68   RB   3.-6.

President Franklin D. Roosevelt.
The White House,
Washington, D. C. ......*Right now, 194..1...*
Dear Sir:
Get U. S. Out of War and
KEEP U. S. OUT OF WAR!!
Sincerely yours,
John Q. Public

Picture shown at 67%
FDR-69   Bk   2.-4.

"I say most Earnestly, that the People of AMERICA and the government intend to remain at PEACE with all the World." — Franklin D. Roosevelt.

FDR-70   RB   3.-6.

"HOSTILITIES exist. There is no blinking at the fact that our people, our territory, our interests are in grave danger.
"WITH confidence in our armed forces, with the unbounding determination of our people-- we will gain the inevitable triumph - - so help us God."
—Franklin D. Roosevelt, Dec. 8, 1941.

Picture shown at 70%
FDR-71   3.-6.

DO NOT OPEN
UNTIL
PRESIDENT ROOSEVELT
SAYS
IT'S CHRISTMAS

Picture shown at 95%
FDR-72   3.-6.

ON TO WASHINGTON
AUGUST 21-30, 1935

At the Invitation of
PRESIDENT FRANKLIN D. ROOSEVELT
30,000 Scouts Will Be Camped at the Nation's Capital for Ten Days to Celebrate the 25th Anniversary of the Boy Scouts of America
SPECIAL RAILROAD RATES

FDR-73   MC   5.-10.

FDR-74   Br/B   3.00

FDR was on the ballot of the American Labor Party as its presidential nominee.

FDR-75   RB (1942)   3.-6.

Picture shown at 95%
FDR-76   RB (1942)   4.-8.

FDR-77   (1932)   8.-15.

FDR-78   RB   4.-8.

Ask the steward for a coin card to fill with money. When filled, mail it to the address below. Your money will be used to Fight Infantile Paralysis.

COMMITTEE for the CELEBRATION of the PRESIDENT'S BIRTHDAY
KEITH MORGAN, National Chairman
50 East 42nd Street, New York, N. Y.

FDR-79   3.-6.

FDR-80   3.-6.

FDR-81   B   3.-6.

FDR-82   RB (1944)   3.-6.
Panes of ten (5x2) in booklets of 100. SE: TRB.

Picture shown at 90%
Booklet cover of FDR-82.

WE ARE DEVOUTLY GRATEFUL FOR THIS

★ **PLEDGE** ★

"I HAVE SAID THIS BEFORE, BUT I
SHALL SAY IT AGAIN AND AGAIN.
YOUR BOYS ARE NOT GOING TO BE
SENT INTO ANY FOREIGN WARS."

PRESIDENT ROOSEVELT
OCT. 30, 1940

NATIONAL LEGION MOTHERS OF AMERICA

Picture shown at 62%
FDR-83   RB   3.-6.

William H. Murray, 1932

WHM-1   20.-40

WHM-2   RB   20.-40.
WHM-2a   RoB   20.-40.
Panes of ten (2x5) in booklets. SE:LBR

John N. Garner,
1932, 1940 Hopeful

JNG-1   BkBr   3.-6.

JNG-2   Se (photo)   3.-6.

JNG-3   B   3.-6.

James Farley,
1940 Hopeful

VOTE FOR HONEST
JIM FARLEY
FOR PRESIDENT

JF-1   5.-10.
Note: This is a mock-up of the stamp because a
photocopy was unavailable at press time.

Earl R. Browder, 1936, 1940

ERB-1   50¢ RBk   10.-20.
ERB-1 $1 RBk/Y   10.-20.
Panes of two (2x1) in booklets containing one
pane of $1 stamps and three panes of 50¢
stamps. Plain brown paper booklet covers.

Alfred M. Landon, 1936

AML-1   Se (photo)   15.-25.

AML-2   Se (photo)   8.-15.

AML-3   BrOr   3.-6.

AML-4   Bk/Y   3.-6.

Sheet of fifty (10x5). SE:LBR; MIT: ABC PRINT-ERS, CHICAGO

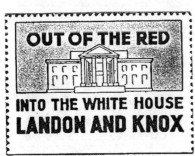

AML-5	DkBPk	8.-15.
AML-6	DkBPk	8.-15.
AML-7	DkBPk	8.-15.
AML-8	DkBPk	8.-15.
AML-9	DkBPk	8.-15.

AML-5 through AML-9 printed together on one sheet. Believed to be sheets of fifty (5x10). SE:TRLB On the bottom two stamps in the left corner is the following: "COPYRIGHT 1936 -

PERMAC LABEL CO., 126 MAIDEN LANE, NEW YORK." Other stamps in the sheet do not contain this legend.

AML-10   Bk   10.-20.

Picture shown at 90%
AML-11   Bk   10.-20.

Picture shown at 90%
AML-12   Bk   10.-20.

Picture shown at 90%
AML-13   Bk   10.-20.

Picture shown at 90%
AML-14   Bk   10.-20.
AML-10 through AMI-14 were printed together on one sheet.

Picture shown at 90%
AML-15   Bk   10.-20.

Picture shown at 90%
AML-16   Bk   10.-20.

Picture shown at 90%
AML-17   Bk   10.-20.

Picture shown at 90%
AML-18   Bk   10.-20.

Picture shown at 90%
AML-19   Bk   10.-20.
AML-15 through AML-19 were printed together on one sheet.
SEE PAGE 29 FOR ILLUSTRATION OF AML-20 TO AML-29

AML-20	BkY	5.-10.
AML-21	BkY	5.-10.
AML-22	BkY	5.-10.
AML-23	BkY	5.-10.
AML-24	BkY	5.-10.
AML-24	BkY	5.-10.
AML-26	BkY	5.-10.
AML-27	BkY	5.-10.
AML-28	BkY	5.-10.
AML-29	BkY	5.-10.

AML-20 through AMl-29 printed together on one sheet.

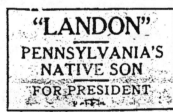
AML-30   Br/Y   5.-10.

AML-31   RBY   4.-8.

Round die cut. Other names are Massachusetts local candidates.

AML-32   RB   3.-6.
AML-33   RB   3.-6.
AML-32 has union bug and round-hole perforations. AML-33 has no union bug and roulette perforations.

AML-34   RB   3.-6.
AML-35   RB   3.-6.
AML-34 has union bug and round-hole perforations. AML-35 has no union bug and roulette perforations.

Wendell L. Willkie, 1940

WLW-1   RB   6.-10.
Panes of ten (5x2) SE:TRB.

WLW-2   RB   8.-15.
WLW-2 says "ERIE COUNTY, N.Y." at top, WLW-1 does not. Panes of ten (5x2) SE:TRB.

WLW-3   RB   4.-8.
WLW-4   RB   30.-50
WLW-4 is a 4-inch by 6-inch version of WLW-3. Sheets contained eight rows of ten of WLW-3, but the sixteen stamps in the center are replaced with one copy of WLW-4. SE: TRL; MIB

WLW-5   MC   2.-4.
Sheets of fifty(?) SE: TBRL

WLW-6   Pu   2.-4.
Sheets of 100 (10x10) MI: "COPYRIGHT 1940 - PROMOTIONAL STAMP CO. 1353 THIRD STREET RENSSELAER, NEW YORK"

WLW-7   Bk (photo)   8.-15.
Mate to FDR-11.

Picture shown at 95%
WLW-8   B   2.-4.

AML-20

AML-21

AML-22

AML-23

AML-24

AML-25

AML-26

AML-27

AML-28

AML-29

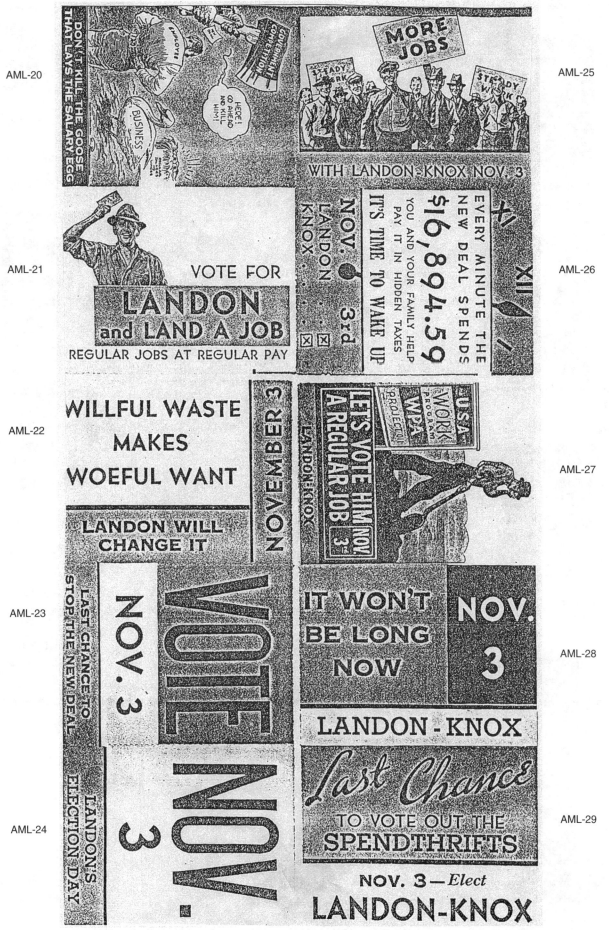

Picture shown at 95%

Sheets of twenty (5x4) SE: TLR MIB: "R.W.B. Label Co. 210 West 7th St. Los Angeles"

Picture shown at 75%
WLW-9   BBk   5.-10

Picture shown at 75%
WLW-9A   BBk   5.-10.

Picture shown at 75%
WLW-10   BBk   4.-8.

WLW-11   Bk (photo)   3.-6.

WLW-12   Bk (photo)   3.-6.

WLW-12a   Bk (photo)   3.-6.
WLW-12a has a darker frame around the photo.

WLW-13   Se (photo)   3.-6.

WLW-14   Se (photo)   3.-6.

WLW-15   RB   1.-2.

WLW-16   RB   1.-2.

WLW-17   RB   1.-2.

WLW-18   WLW-19
WLW-18   RB   1.-2.
WLW-19   RB   1.-2.
Sheets of 100 (10x10) (twenty sets of five dif. WLW-15 through WLW-19)
MI:B "CANTURBURY PRESS, INC., BROOKLYN, N.Y." SE:LTR

WLW-20   RB   3.-6.

WLW-21   Bk (photo)   3.-6.

Picture shown at 70%
See color plates for complete set of twenty-five.
WLW-22   MC   3.-6.
WLW-23   MC   3.-6.
WLW-24   MC   3.-6.
WLW-25   MC   3.-6.
WLW-26   MC   3.-6.
WLW-27   MC   3.-6.
WLW-28   MC   3.-6.
WLW-29   MC   3.-6.
WLW-30   MC   3.-6.
WLW-31   MC   3.-6.
WLW-32   MC   3.-6.
WLW-33   MC   3.-6.
WLW-34   MC   3.-6.
WLW-35   MC   3.-6.
WLW-36   MC   3.-6.
WLW-37   MC   3.-6.
WLW-38   MC   3.-6.
WLW-39   MC   3.-6.

WLW-40	MC	3.-6.
WLW-41	MC	3.-6.
WLW-42	MC	3.-6.
WLW-43	MC	3.-6.
WLW-44	MC	3.-6.
WLW-45	MC	3.-6.
WLW-46	MC	3.-6.

Stamps are numbered consecutively from left to right across each row.

Sheets of twenty-five different. MIR: "Set of 25 for 25¢/Use One IN Your Mail/Robinson Posterettes, 303 4th Ave., New York" SE:TLB

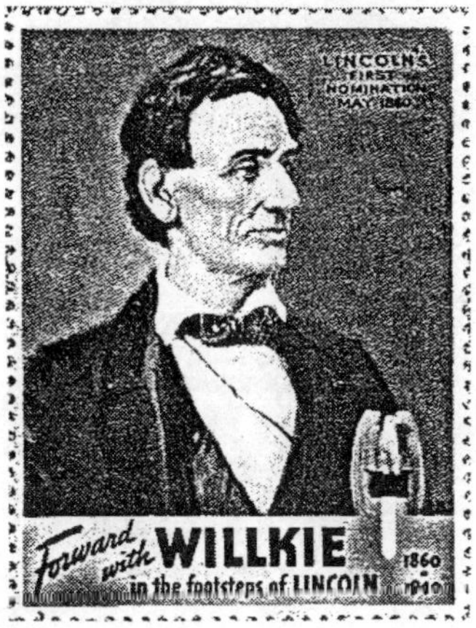
LINCOLN'S FIRST NOMINATION MAY 1860
Forward with WILLKIE
in the footsteps of LINCOLN
1860
1940

See color plates for complete set of twenty.

WLW-47	MC	3.-6.
WLW-48	MC	3.-6.
WLW-49	MC	3.-6.
WLW-50	MC	3.-6.
WLW-51	MC	3.-6.
WLW-52	MC	3.-6.
WLW-53	MC	3.-6.
WLW-54	MC	3.-6.
WLW-55	MC	3.-6.
WLW-56	MC	3.-6.
WLW-57	MC	3.-6.
WLW-58	MC	3.-6.
WLW-59	MC	3.-6.
WLW-60	MC	3.-6.

WLW-61	MC	3.-6.
WLW-62	MC	3.-6.
WLW-63	MC	3.-6.
WLW-64	MC	3.-6.
WLW-65	MC	3.-6.
WLW-66	MC	3.-6.

Sheets of 100 (10x10) (five sets of twenty dif.) MIT: "Published by Historic Prints & Poster Stamps, Inc. Times Bldg., Chicago, Ill./HELP WILLKIE WIN!/Copyright 1940, Historic Prints & Poster Stamps, Inc., 211 West Wacker Drive, Chicago, Ill." (repeats)

These stamps are identical to a 1938 set of Lincoln stamps except that the words "LINCOLN Immortal American" are replaced with the Willkie slogan. See below.

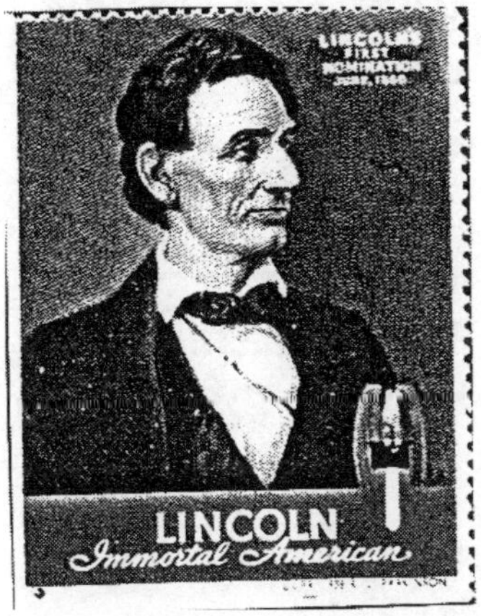
LINCOLN'S FIRST NOMINATION JUNE, 1860
LINCOLN
Immortal American

The following stamps are imperforate versions of the above set. They were affixed to post cards used as publicity for the sets. Post card specialists will pay $50 or more for intact post cards. Prices listed are for stamps alone.

WLW-47A	MC5.-10.
WLW-48A	MC5.-10.
WLW-49A	MC5.-10.
WLW-50A	MC5.-10.
WLW-51A	MC5.-10.

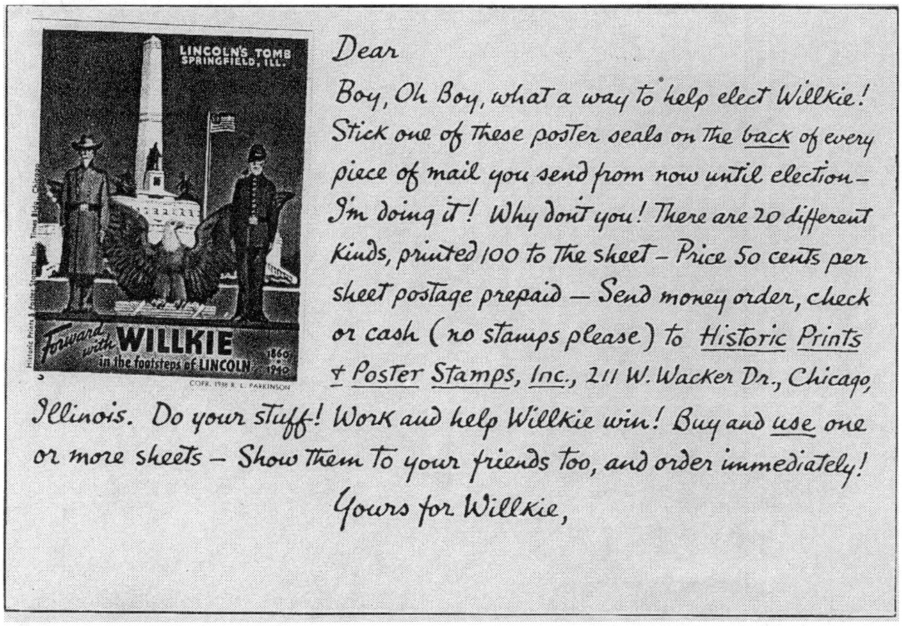
LINCOLN'S TOMB SPRINGFIELD, ILL.
Forward with WILLKIE
in the footsteps of LINCOLN
1860
1940
COPR. 1938 R. L. PARKINSON
Dear
Boy, Oh Boy, what a way to help elect Willkie!
Stick one of these poster seals on the back of every
piece of mail you send from now until election –
I'm doing it! Why don't you! There are 20 different
kinds, printed 100 to the sheet – Price 50 cents per
sheet postage prepaid – Send money order, check
or cash (no stamps please) to Historic Prints
+ Poster Stamps, Inc., 211 W. Wacker Dr., Chicago,
Illinois. Do your stuff! Work and help Willkie win! Buy and use one
or more sheets – Show them to your friends too, and order immediately!
Yours for Willkie,

Picture shown at 87%

Postcard containing WLW-60A.

WLW-52A	MC5.-10.
WLW-53A	MC5.-10.
WLW-54A	MC5.-10.
WLW-55A	MC5.-10.
WLW-56A	MC5.-10.
WLW-57A	MC5.-10.
WLW-58A	MC5.-10.
WLW-59A	MC5.-10.
WLW-60A	MC5.-10.
WLW-61A	MC5.-10.
WLW-62A	MC5.-10.
WLW-63A	MC5.-10.
WLW-64A	MC5.-10.
WLW-65A	MC5.-10.
WLW-66A	MC5.-10.

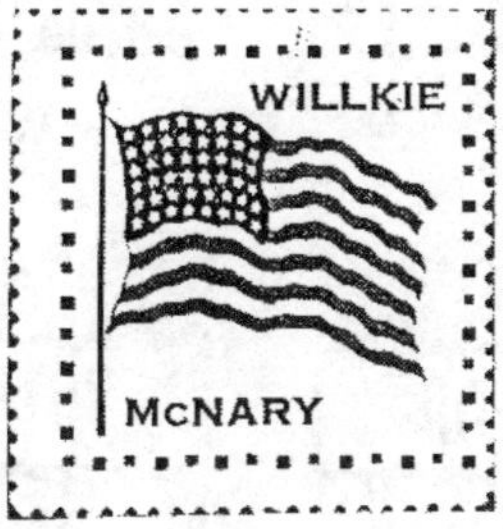
WILLKIE
McNARY

WLW-67 RB 3.-6.

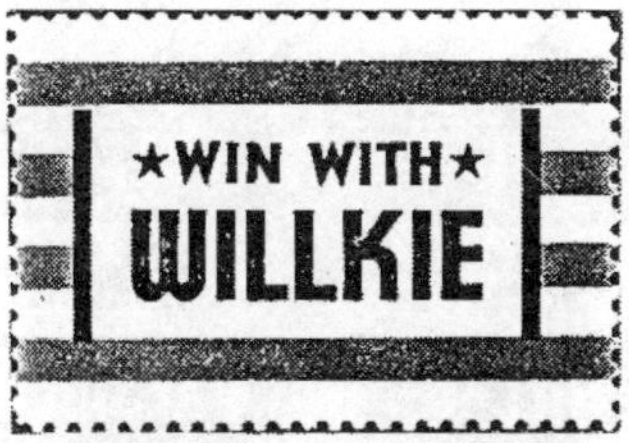
★WIN WITH★
WILLKIE

WLW-68 RB 3.-6.

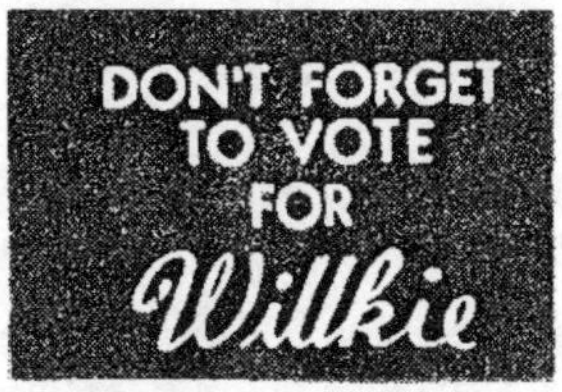
DON'T FORGET
TO VOTE
FOR
Willkie

WLW-69 B 3.-6.

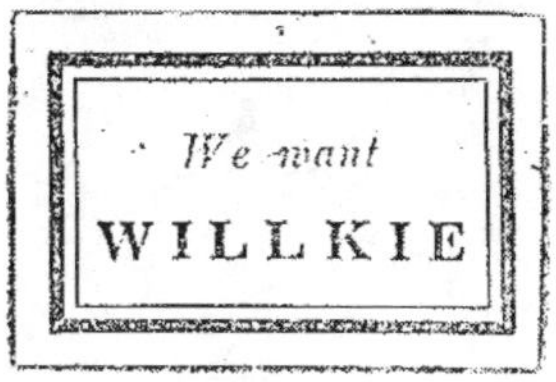
We want
WILLKIE

WLW-70 3.-6.

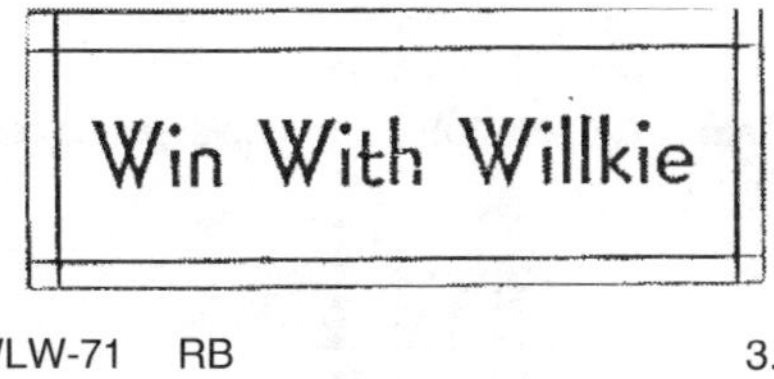
Win With Willkie

WLW-71 RB 3.-6.

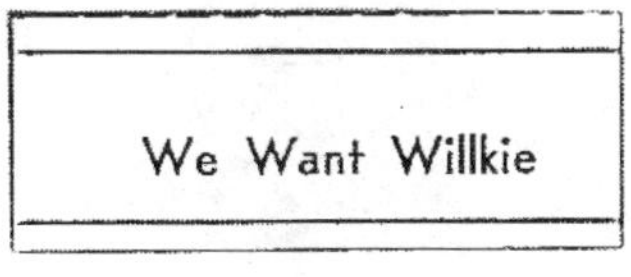
We Want Willkie

WLW-72 RB 1.-2.

WLW-73

WLW-74

WLW-75

WLW-76

WLW-77

WLW-78

WLW-79

WLW-80

WLW-81

WLW-82

WLW-73	RB	1.-2.
WLW-74	RB	1.-2.
WLW-75	RB	1.-2.
WLW-76	RB	1.-2.
WLW-77	RB	1.-2.
WLW-78	RB	1.-2.
WLW-79	RB	1.-2.
WLW-80	RB	1.-2.
WLW-81	RB	1.-2.
WLW-82	RB	1.-2.

Sheets of 100 (10x10). One complete set is contained in each row.

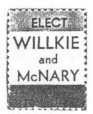

WLW-83   RB   1.-2.

WLW-84   RB   1.-2.
Sheets of 100 (10x10). MIB: "Issued by the New Jersey Republican Finance Committee, 744 Broad St., Newark, N. J., Joseph A. Bower, Chairman"

WLW-85   RB   2.-4.
WLW-86   Bk   2.-4.

WLW-87   RB   2.-4.

WLW-88   B   2.-4.

WLW-89   RB   2.-4.

Another Democrat FOR WILLKIE

WLW-90   RB   2.-4.

WILLKIE

WLW-91   RB   2.-4.

WLW-92   RB   2.-4.

WLW-93   RB   3.-6.

WLW-94   R   3.-6.
WLW-95   B   3.-6.

One For All -- All For One
We Will Win With WILKIE

Picture shown at 80%
WLW-96   Br   3.-6.
Note: This stamp is a new discovery since the author's previous catalog. The stamp that was numbered WLW-96 has been renumbered WLW-142.

STOP THIRD TERMITES

WLW-97   RB   3.-6.
Note: This stamp is a new discovery since the my last book. The stamp previously numbered WLW-97 has been renumbered WLW-137.

WLW-98   R   3.-6.
Sheets of six (3x2) SE:TLBR

WLW-99   RB   3.-6.
Round die cut.

WLW-100   RB   3.-6.
Round die cut.

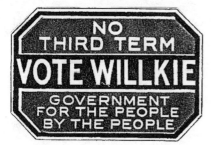

WLW-101   RB   3.-6
Die cut and embossed.

Picture shown at 85%
WLW-102   MC   3.-6.
Sheets of twenty (5x4) SE: TBLR

Picture shown at 85%
WLW-103   Bk/Y   3.-6.

WLW-104   Bk/Y

WLW-105   RB   3.-6.

WLW-106   RB   2.-4.

WLW-107   RB   3.-6.
WLW-107A   RB   3.-6.
WLW-108   RB   3.-6.
WLW-109   RB   3.-6.
WLW-107 is imperforate with union bug and "7"
as shown. WLW-107A is the same but with larger "7". WLW-108 is the same but has the "7" in a
circle. WLW-109 has no union bug and is perforated on at least 1 side.

WLW-110   RB   3.-6.

WLW-111   RB   1.-3.

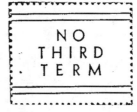

WLW-112   Bk/B   2.-4.

WLW-113   RB   2.-4.

WLW-113A   RB   3.-6.
WLW-113 and WLW-113A may have been
printed on the same sheet. There may be other
varieties as well.

WLW-114   WLW-115

WLW-116   WLW-117

WLW-118

WLW-114   RB   3.-6.
WLW-115   RB   3.-6.

WLW-116 RB   3.-6.
WLW-117 RB   3.-6.
WLW-118 RB   3.-6.

WLW-119 RB   1.-3.

WLW-120 RB   2.-4.

WLW-121 RB   2.-4.

WLW-122 RB   2.-4.

WLW-123 RB   1.-2.
WLW-124 RB   1.-2.

Sheets of 100 (10x10) with alternating designs. SE:LTR, MIB: "© Russell Branch—Boston, Mass." MFWRO might stand for Massachusetts Federation of Women Republican Organizations.

"Yoo Hoo, Mr. Willkie!"
From the Republican Party platform of 1940: "The Republican party is firmly opposed to involving this nation in foreign wars." AND SO ARE THE PEOPLE!!

Picture shown at 90%
WLW-125 B   3.-6.

Picture shown at 95%

Picture shown at 95%

Picture shown at 95%

Picture shown at 95%
WLW-126 RB   2.-4.
WLW-127 RB   2.-4.
WLW-128 RB   2.-4.
WLW-129 RB   2.-4.

SE: LBR; MIT: "PLACE THESE GUMMED STICKERS ON THE ENVELOPES OF ALL LETTERS MAILED. FOR ADDITIONAL STAMPS CALL DEARBORN 0035, SUITE 320, HOTEL LA SALLE COPYRIGHT REGISTERED 1938-SX PTG. CO." Note: Address believed to be Chicago.
WLW-126A RB2.-4.
WLW-127A RB2.-4.

WLW-128A RB2.-4.
WLW-129A RB2.-4.
WLW-126A through WLW-129A are imperforate versions of the above set.

WLW-130 RB   2.-4.

WLW-131 RB   2.-4.

WLW-132 RB   2.-4.

WLW-133 RB   3.-6.

WLW-134 BkRB   4.-8.
WLW-135 through WLW-166 and WLW-167 through WLW-198 are shown on the next page.

WLW-135 through 166 were printed in blue. They are numbered consecutively from left to right across each row. They are priced as follows:
Full sheet   60.-90.
Single stamps   2.-3.
WLW-167 through 198 were printed in red. They are numbered consecutively from left to right

After seven years—our problem still is JOBS. Vote for **WILLKIE!**	For our defense!—put a real administrator in the White House. Vote for **WILLKIE!**	Willkie has respect for the people—the people respect **WILLKIE!**	Your life is your own. Keep it that way. Vote for **WILLKIE** and democracy!
Britain doesn't regret changing horses! Vote for **WILLKIE!**	There is no indispensable man in a democracy!	The New Deal would rather see the people *dependent* on relief than *independent* in jobs.	Our first task: unity and recovery at home. Vote "WILLKIE"!
"It is not Big Business we have to fear . . . it is Big Government" —WILLKIE	"Who nominated Roosevelt?" —Roosevelt "Who nominated Willkie?" —THE PEOPLE	Don't let war scares scuttle American democracy. *Kill the Third Term!*	"Who got us into the middle of the stream?" Let's get out with **WILLKIE!**
Production is the one way to prosperity. Vote for **WILLKIE!**	If Roosevelt saw what was coming why didn't he prepare? Put our defenses "on hand" with **WILLKIE!**	What good is collective bargaining if you haven't got a job? Vote for **WILLKIE!**	Power doesn't belong to one man. It belongs to the people. Reclaim it with **WILLKIE!**
We can't borrow our way to prosperity. We've got to work for it. Vote for **WILLKIE** and jobs!	Is democracy "washed up"? Shout "NO" with **WILLKIE!**	"My pop can't make me a Captain"	Let's decide our own destiny! Vote "NO" on Third Term and War!
Vote for a man who *believes* in democracy— **WILLKIE!**	A leader should prevent panic, not promote it. Elect **WILLKIE!**	This is a *real* emergency. Elect **WILLKIE** our next President!	Government Your Master— Roosevelt Government Your Servant— **WILLKIE**
What deal has the New Deal made with Kelly, Hague and Flynn?	A margin of only 5½ million votes elected Roosevelt in '36. Landslide for **WILLKIE** in '40!	Get off that fence! Vote for the American Way with **WILLKIE!**	Keep state socialism "over there." Vote for **WILLKIE!**
Our vast reservoir of money and savings is idle. Put it to work making jobs. Vote for **WILLKIE!**	If a third term, why not a fourth? a fifth? Let's stick to democracy with **WILLKIE!**	Roosevelt is "talking" us into certain war. Stop—think first—with **WILLKIE!**	Not "Heil" but farewell to the New Deal. Vote for **WILLKIE!**

Picture shown at 97%
Full sheet of WLW-135 through WLW-166.

across each row. They are priced as follows:
Full sheet   60.-90.
Single stamps   2.-4.

WLW-199   Bk   2.-4.

WLW-200   Bk   2.-4.

WLW-201   RB   2.-4.

WLW-202   B   2.-4.
Appears to have been issued in rolls.

WLW-203   2.-4.

WLW-204   3.-6.

WLW-205   3.-6.

Thomas E. Dewey, 1944, 1948

TED-1   RB (1948)   R

TED-3   RB (1944)   2.-4.
TED-4   RB (1944)   2.-4.
TED-5   RB (1944)   2.-4.
TED-6   RB (1944)   2.-4.
TED-7   RB (1944)   2.-4.
TED-3 to 7 are also known with the word "SPECIMEN" overprinted in red.

TED-8   B   2.-4.

TED-2   B (1948)   2.-4.
Sheets of 100 (10x10). Blank margins.

TED-9   RB   3.-6.

Harry S. Truman, 1948

Picture shown at 80%
HST-1   Red   4.-8.
Sheets of thirty-three (3x11). This slogan was used by both sides in the election so it is unknown if this stamp was produced by the Truman or Dewey camp.

HST-2   RB   1.-2.
Sheets of 100 (10x10). SE: LTR

HST-3   RB   3.-6.

Henry Wallace, 1948

HW-1   BOr   5.-10.

John W. Bricker, 1948, 1952

Picture shown at 85%
JWB-1   BrOl   8.-15
Panes of eight (2x4) in booklets. SE:TRB

Douglas MacArthur, 1948, 1952

See also JWB-1 above.

DMA-1   RBk   4.-8.
Sheets of twenty-five (5x5) SE:TRBL

DMA-2   Bk   4.-8.

DMA-3   RB   3.-6.
Sheets of fifty-four (9x6). SE:TLRB

DMA-4   RBBr   3.-6.
In a sheet with patriotic labels of other designs.
See PAT-54.)

DMA-5   MC   3.-6.
From a 1942 set by Hearst Pubs. Inc.

DMA-6   RBk   4.-8.

DMA-7   3.-6.

DMA-8   RB   3.-6.

DMA-9   BY   3.-6.

DMA-10   3.-6.

Picture shown at 65%
DMA-11   BkYPk   4.-8.
Printed as a single stamp with margins all
around containing patriotic text.

Estes Kefauver, 1952, 1956

EK-1   BrB   6.-12.

Picture shown at 90%
EK-2   RB   3.-6.

Collectors looking for all types of items for a particular president can add matchbox labels to their collections. While these have not been used in many years in this country, foreign countries still produce them and some use U.S. presidents.

Robert Taft, 1948, 1952

| RT-1 | RBk | 3.-6. |
Sheets of thirty (6x5). No MI.

| RT-2 | B | 3.-6. |
Individual imperforate.

| RT-3 | RB | 2.-4. |

WE NEED SENATOR TAFT For President

Picture shown at 90%
| RT-4 | Bk | 3.-6. |

| RT-5 | RB | 1.-3. |

| RT-6 | R | 3.-6. |

Picture shown at 65%
| EK-3 | RB | 6.-12. |

| EK-4 | RB | 1.-3. |

Henry Krajewski, 1952, 1964 Poor Man's Party

| HK-1 | RB | 8.-15. |
Individual die cut.

Joseph McCarthy, 1952

I'M FOR McCARTHY

| JMcC-1 | RB | 3.-6. |

Stamps just like this one were also used during the 1968 election so it is possible that this was issued for Eugene McCarthy but the slogan makes it most likely that this was for Joe.

ALL COMMUNISTS, REDS AND RADICALS HATE JOE McCARTHY. I AM FOR HIM

Picture shown at 78%
| JMcC-2 | B | 3.-6. |

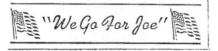

Picture shown at 78%
| JMcC-3 | | 3.-6. |

CO-EXISTANCE ?
"You can't make covenants with hell!" ---Senator Joe McCarthy--

| JMcC-4 | RB | 3.-6. |

McCARTHYISM is AMERICANISM

| JMcC-5 | RB | 3.-6. |

RT-7   B   4.-8.

Picture shown at 65%
RT-8   R   3.-6.

Dwight D. Eisenhower, 1952, 1956

VOTE FOR YOUR FUTURE

Picture shown at 90%
DDE-1   MC   4.-8.
Mate to RMN-1. Worth more as a pair.

DDE-2   MC   1.-3.
Sheets of fifty (10x5). Mate to RMN-6. SE: TBLR

DDE-3   RBBk   1.-3.
SE:LBR MIT: "FOR VICTORY IN 1956 WITH EISENHOWER HERMAN JAFFE, Publisher, 55 West 42nd Street, New York 36, N. Y. USE THESE STAMPS ON ALL YOUR MAIL HELP SPREAD THIS VITAL MESSAGE TO ALL AMERICANS COPYRIGHT 1956 L. RAY FOWLER HERMAN JAFFE RICHARD MARDUS DESIGNED BY L. RAY FOWLER NEW YORK, N. Y. REGISTER AND VOTE EISENHOWER IN 1956 PRINTED IN THE U.S.A."

DDE-4   BBk   3.-6.
DDE-5   Bk   3.-6.
DDE-6   Br   2.-4.

Front   Back
DDE-7   Green and black   1.-.2
Sheets contain forty of DDE-5 and forty of AES-5. On the right half of the center of the sheet is the following: "Like IKE or ADLAI? In an election year everybody's ads are 'messages' or slanted. We're being different. Here are 40 advertisements for 'the man of your choice.' Put them on your mail...packages...on your water cooler, if you like...any place. But remember: when you need true-to-life reproduction in labels, displays, postcards or 24-sheets, and service at its best, call Crocker...of course!" along with addresses of the company. AES-5 is known without the ad on the back and this stamp may also have been issued without the ad.

DDE-8   Se (photo)   3.-6.

DDE-9   RB (text blue)   2.-4.
DDE-10   RB (text red)   2.-4.
Individual imperforate.

DDE-11   Gr   2.-4.
DDE-11a   Gr   2.-4.
DDE-11 is solid line artwork and DDE-11a is a halftone with a background pattern of dots.

DDE-12   RB   2.-4.

DDE-13   RB (1952)   .50-1.
Sheets of 100 (10x10). SE:TRB

DDE-14   RB (1956)   1.-2.
SE: TBLR. On the bottom edge of the first three stamps in the bottom row is the text: "COPYRIGHT 1956, ATLAS ADVERTISING BROOKLINE 46, MASS."

DDE-15   RB   1.-2.

Sheets of forty (4x10). SE: LBR MIT: FOR USE ONLY ON THE BACK OF ENVELOPES CARRYING FIRST CLASS MAIL

DDE-16   1.-2.
Sheets of five (1x5). SE:LBR

DDE-17   RB   1.-3.

DDE-18   BkOr   2.-4.
DDE-19   BkOr   2.-4.
DDE-18 is an individual imperforate and DDE-19 is perforated in sheets of sixteen (4x4). SE:TLRB

DDE-20   RBBk   2.-4.
DDE-20A   RBBk Larger (3"x3")   2.-4.

DDE-21   RBBk   .50-1.
DDE-22   RBBk   .50-1.
DDE-22 has "©" under the "x" but DDE-21 does not. DDE-22 has MIB: "©Mrs. Glenn Balch, Republican Miniature Billboard Stamps, Send order to Republican Women's Club —Box 1158, Boise, Idaho, Every Stamp You Send Proclaims We'll Win in 1956"

DDE-23   RB   2.-4.

DDE-24   RB   3.-6.

DDE-25   3.-6.

DDE-26   3.-6.

DDE-27   Gr   1.-3.

DDE-28   Se (photo)   3.-6.

DDE-29   Se (photo)   8.-15.

The only known source for this stamp is a campaign button which can be taken apart to remove the stamp.

DDE-30   BkTu   3.-6.
Map of Michigan is in background.

DDE-31   BkGr   2.-4.
Sheets of thirty (3x10). SE:TLRB

DDE-32   RPu   5.-10.

DDE-33   MC   3.-6.

DDE-34   RB   2.-4.

DDE-35   Bk   2.-4.

DDE-36   RB   1.-3.
Distributed in coil rolls.

DDE-37   MC (Medal)   .50-2.
DDE-38   MC (Elephant)   .50-2.
Sheets of seventy (10x7) with alternating rows.
SE: LTR, MIB: "OFFICIAL REPUBLICAN CEN-
TENNIAL SEALS, ORDER ADDITIONAL
SHEETS FROM YOUR LOCAL REPUBLICAN
ORGANIZATION OR REPUBLICAN CENTEN-
NIAL COMMITTEE"

DDE-39   B   3.-6.

DDE-40   B   3.-6.

DDE-41   B   3.-6..

DDE-42   B   3.-6.

J. W. Fulbright, 1952

FULBRIGHT
for
PRESIDENT

JWF-1   RB   2.-4.

Harold Stassen, 1940-1988

STASSEN
FOR
PRESIDENT

HS-1   B   1.-3.
Individual imperforate in pads.

Adlai E. Stevenson, 1952, 1956, 1960

AES-1   R

VOTE FOR
STEVENSON

AES-2   RB (perf.)   3.-6.
AES-2a   RB (roulette)   3.-6.
Sheets of twenty-one (7x3). SE:TLB, MIR:
(union bug #91).

AES-3   RB   3.-6.

AES-4   4.-8.

Front   Back
AES-5   BBk   1.-2.
Sheets contain forty of DDE-5 and 40 of AES-5.
On the right half of the center of the sheet is the
following: "Like IKE or ADLAI? In an election
year everybody's ads are 'messages' or slanted.
We're being different. Here are 40 advertisements for 'the man of your choice.' Put them on
your mail...packages...on your water cooler, if
you like...any place. But remember: when you
need true-to-life reproduction in labels, displays,
postcards or 24-sheets, and service at its best,
call Crocker...of course!" along with addresses
of the company.
AES-6   BBk   1.-2.
AES-6 is the same design as AES-5 but with no
ad on the back.
Sheets of 100 alike (10x10). SE: TBLR

AES-7   RB   2.-4.
Sheets of fifty (5x10). MIB: (five union bugs with
#100).

AES-8   RB   1.-3.

AES-9   MC   1.-3.
Sheets of fifty (5x10) SE: TLR MIB: "©1956 CO-
OPERATE FOR A DEMOCRATIC VICTORY -
DEMOCRATIC VICTORY ASSOCIATES"

AES-10   BGy   2.-4.
Numbers AES-13 through AES-19 are same
color and style but different subjects and quotes:
AES-11   "ON WORLD PEACE"   2.-4.
AES-12   "ON FREEDOM"   2.-4.
AES-13   "ON THE ATOM"   2.-4.
AES-14   "ON SOCIAL SECURITY"   2.-4.
AES-15   "ON THE 'PATRIOT'"   2.-4.
AES-16   "ON SOCIAL SECURITY"   2.-4.
AES-17   "ON INDUSTRY AND LABOR"   2.-4.

Picture shown at 55%
AES-18   Bk   3.-6.

William Knowland, 1964 Hopeful

WK-1   B   2.-4.

WK-2   B   2.-4.

T. Coleman Andrews, 1956 Independent Party Constitution Party States Rights Party, 1964

TCA-1   RB   4.-8.

```
        INSTRUCTIONS!
(1) Detach  ballot  below  from
    these instructions
(2) After closing curtain, FIRST
    PUSH UP Shutter in large
    opening in upper left corner
(3) PASTE sticker flat and firmly
    on paper in the opening.
    Make sure the LOWER EDGE
    is smooth and down TIGHT
(4) THEN pull down levers for
    Senator and Congressman of
    your choice.

Electors for:
  President—T. Coleman Andrews
  Vice-Pres.—Thomas H. Werdel
Samuel T. Bennett        (X)
Thaddeus Brzuchalski     (X)
H. Brinsfield Cook       (X)
Amos R. Koontz           (X)
Anna Dorsey Linder       (X)
Bessie L. Schneider      (X)
Everette Severe          (X)
E. Steuart Vaughan       (X)
Robert Leo Wiseman       (X)
```

TCA-2   BkY   5.-10.
There are perforations through the center of the
stamp to detach the bottom.

John F. Kennedy, 1960

JFK-1   RB   1.-2.
Sheets of 100 (10x10) SE:TBRL

JFK-2   RB   3.-6.

JFK-3   RB   2.-4.

JFK-4   RB   1.-3.

JFK-5   Bk (photo)   4.-8.

JFK-6   RB   2.-4.

JFK-7   RB   3.-6.

JFK-8   Ma   3.-6.

George Van Tassel, 1960

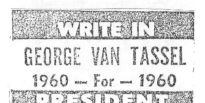

GVT-1	RB		2.-4.

Richard M. Nixon, 1960, 1968, 1972

Picture shown at 80%

RMN-1	Natural photo (1956)		4.-8.

Mate to DDE-1. Worth more as a pair.

Picture shown at 75%

RMN-2	Natural photo (1960)		4.-8.

Mate to HCL-1. Worth more as a pair.

RMN-3	MC		1.-2.

RMN-4	MC		.50-1.

RMN-5	MC		1.-2.

Sheets of 100 of which the first three rows are RMN-3, the next four rows are RMN-5, and the last three rows are RMN-4.
MIB: "FOR ADDITIONAL SHEETS WRITE OR CALL THE PENNSYLVANIA REPUBLICAN-MEDIA. PENNA." SE: LTR

RMN-6	MC (1956)		2.-4.

Sheets of fifty (10x5). Mate to DDE-2. SE:TBLR

RMN-7	RB (1960)		2.-5.

RMN-8	Se (photo) (1960)		2.-4.

RMN-9	RBBkOr (1968)		.50-1.
Full sheet			8.-15.

Sheets of 117 (13x9) SE: TBLR

RMN-10	Bk (1968)		1.-3.

Individual imperforate.

RMN-11	B		3.-5.
RMN-12	BR		2.-4.

RMN-13	Bk (1968)		2.-4.

Individual imperforate. Mate to HHH-1, GCW-4.

RMN-14	RLtB		1.-2.
RMN-15	RDkB		3.-6.

Note: Colors combine to make purple portrait. The dark blue ink was probably switched to light blue because the portrait looks so bad in the darker ink. Sheets of twenty-five (5x5) SE:LTR MIB: "THANK YOU FOR YOUR SUPPORT"

RMN-16   RB (1972)   1.-3.

RMN-17   RB (1972)   .50-1.
Sheets of 100 (10x10) imperforate. MIB: "Citizens to Re-Elect Richard M. Nixon/Use These Stickers on your Letters and Packages."

RMN-17a   RB (1972)   1.-2.
Center inverted.

RMN-17b   RB (1972)   2.-3.
Center inverted and too high.

RMN-18   RB   2.-4.
Individual die cut.

RMN-19   RB (1968)   .50-1.

RMN-20   RB   1.-3.

RMN-21 MC3.-5.
This stamp was included in a 1972 MAD Magazine. See also GCW-10 and STAX-1.

RMN-22   RB   1.-3.
Issued by the American Civil Liberties Union.
Sheets of forty-two (6x7) SE: TBRL

RMN-23   BkOr   1.-3.

RMN-24   Bk   1.-3.
Sheets of fifty (10x5).

RMN numbers 25 through 46 are pictured on the following three pages.

RMN-47   Bk/Or   2.-4.

Picture shown at 67%
RMN-48   Bk/Or   2.-4.

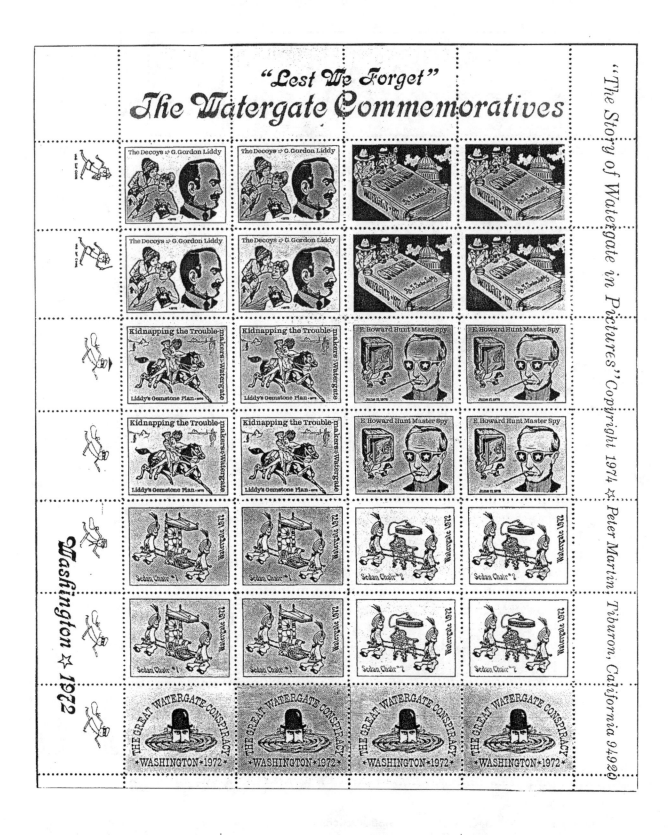

RMN-25	BkRBr (Liddy)	1.-2.	RMN-28	BkBrRB (Hunt)	1.-2.	RMN-31	BkRB (Derby)	1.-2.
RMN-26	BkRBBr (Book)	1.-2.	RMN-29	BkRBBr (Chair #1)	1.-2.	RMN-32	BkRBr (Derby)	1.-2.
RMN-27	BkBRBr (Kidnapping)	1.-2.	RMN-30	BkRB (Chair #2)	1.-2.			

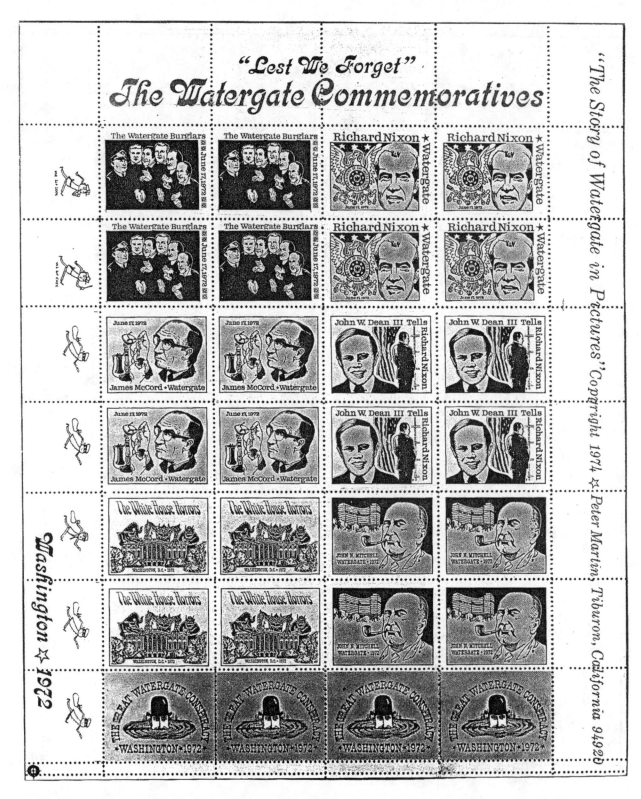

| RMN-33 | RBkBr (Burglars) | 1.-2. | RMN-35 | RBBk (McCord) | 1.-2. | RMN-37 | RBkBr (Horrors) | 1.-2. |
| RMN-34 | RBBkBr (Nixon) | 2.-4. | RMN-36 | RBkBr (Dean) | 1.-2. | RMN-38 | BkBrB (Mitchell) | 1.-2. |

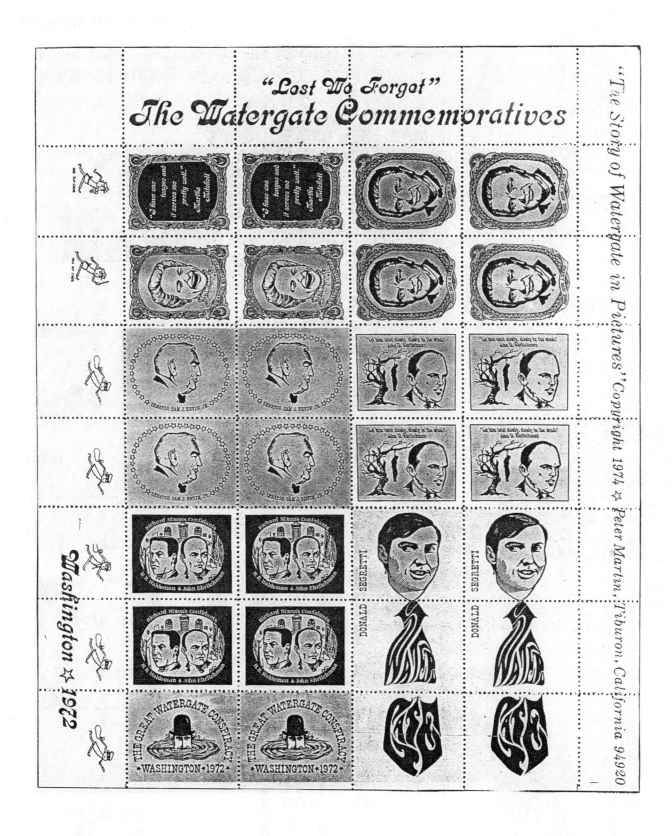

RMN-39	RBBk (Quote)	1.-2.	RMN-42	BRBk (Ervin)	1.-2.	RMN-45	BkRBr (Segretti)	2.-4.
RMN-40	RBBk (Mitchell)	2.-4.	RMN-43	BkBrR (Erlichman)	1.-2.	RMN-46	RBkB (Tie top)	2.-4.
RMN-41	RBrBk (Sirica)	1.-2.	RMN-44	BkBr (Haldeman & Erl.)	1.-2.	RMN-46A	RBkB (Tie bottom)	2.-4.

JOHN DEAN

MARCHED TO THE SOUND OF A DIFFERENT PLUMBER!

A MAD STICKER!

RMN-49   RBkY   2.-4.
Included in MAD Magazine.

THIS LICENSE PLATE WAS MADE BY A FORMER MEMBER OF THE WHITE HOUSE STAFF!

A MAD STICKER!

RMN-50   BkY   2.-4.
Included in MAD Magazine.

WE DID BUY A USED FORD FROM THIS MAN!

A MAD STICKER!

Picture shown at 67%
RMN-51   MC   3.-6.
Included in MAD Magazine.

WATERGATE WAS ENGINEERED BY ... **THIS STICKER WAS ACCIDENTALLY ERASED BY THE ADMINISTRATION!**

ANOTHER MAD STICKER

Picture shown at 43%
RMN-52   BkY   2.-4.
Included in MAD Magazine.

NIXON FOR PRESIDENT

RMN-53   Sepia (photo) (1960)   2.-4.

FOR PEACE AND ★ NIXON ★ PROSPERITY

RMN-54   RB (1960)   1.-3.
Sheet of fifty (5x10) SE:LR

WHEN NIXON ORDERED THE FREEZE-- I GOT LEFT OUT IN THE COLD!

RMN-55   Bk   1.-3.

Republicans can't seem to keep their heads above WATER gate!

RMN-56   Bk   1.-3.

AN END TO MANKIND

VOTE FOR NIXON

Picture shown at 55%
RMN-57   R   2.-4.

YOUR VOTE IS ALL HE NEEDS

RMN-58   Br   2.-4.

The MAN   The JOB

RMN-59   B/Go   2.-4.

NIXON'S THE ONE

RMN-60   B/Go   2.-4.

Re-elect the President

Picture shown at 90%
RMN-61   B   1.-2.
This is a square stamp with the corners printed to make it appear round.

HE'S TAN, RESTED AND READY

NIXON IN '92

RMN-62   MC   1.-2.

RMN-63   Bk   R

Supposedly these stamps were ordered by the Republican National Committee from a Swedish firm to commemorate the expected election of Nixon in 1960. When Nixon lost the election the committee allegedly refused to accept delivery and they were returned to Sweden. Most were destroyed but a few were distributed by Cseslaw Slania, the engraver of the stamps, to collectors of his work. Note his autograph on the edge of the stamp.

RMN-64   R   1.-3.

Stamp illustrated has a cancellation.

RMN-65   Gr   1.-3.
RMN-66   Bk   1.-3.

Stamp illustrated has a cancellation.

RMN-67   LtBDkB   1.-3.

RMN-68   Bk/B   1.-3.

IMPEACH MARTHA MITCHELL!

Picture shown at 90%
RMN-69   R   1.-3.
From MAD Magazine.

NIX-ON-DICK

RMN-70   Pu   1.-3.

RMN-71   RBBk (1968)   1.-3.
Sheets of fifty-six (8x7). SE:TLBR

We Don't Have Nixon To Kick Around Any More! That's Why We Need...
ALFRED E. NEUMAN FOR PRESIDENT
VOTE MAD

RMN-72   MC   2.-4.
From MAD Magazine, 1980.

Henry Cabot Lodge, 1960

VOTE REPUBLICAN

Picture shown at 90%
HCL-1   MC (1960)   3.-6.
Mate to RMN-2. Worth more as a pair.

George L. Rockwell, 1964 American Nazi Party

ROCKWELL FOR PRESIDENT!

Picture shown at 78%
GLR-1   RBk   5.-10.

Lyndon B. Johnson, 1964

LBJ FOR THE USA

LBJ-1   RB   .25-.50
Sheets of twenty (1x20). SE: TRBL

honouring LYNDON BAINES JOHNSON protector of the entire free world
100 CENTES ✳ POSTAGE
NEW ATLANTIS ✳ 1964

LBJ-2   B   2.-4.
Matches HHH-2.

Santa is Dead LONG LIVE Lyndon Claus

Picture shown at 78%
LBJ-3   RB   1.-3.

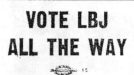

LBJ-4   RB   2.-4.

Picture shown at 67%
LBJ-5   1.-3.
From MAD Magazine.

LBJ-6   R   1.-3.
Picture shown has cancellation at top of stamp which is not part of the design.

Barry M. Goldwater, 1964

BMG-1   BkGo   1.-2.
Sheets of fifty (5x10). SE: LTR MIB: "COURAGE * PATRIOTISM * INTEGRITY"

BMG-2   RB   1.-3.
BMG-3   BkY   .50-1.
BMG-3a   DkYBk   .50-1.
Booklets of five panes of twenty (4x5). There are at least three different booklet covers for BMG-3.

BMG-4   3.-6.
From a sheet of stamps including twelve other candidates from Montana.

BMG-5   MC   1.-3.

BMG-6   Br   1.-3.

BMG-7   B (dull paper)   1.-2.
BMG-8   B (shiny paper)   1.-2.
Booklets of five panes of ten (5x2).

BMG-9   BBk   1.-3.

Picture shown at 67%
BMG-10   RBGo   1.-3.
Individual imperforate.

Picture shown at 77%
BMG-11   Bk/Gd   1.-3.

BMG-12   BkY   .50-1.
BMG-12a   BkDkY   .50-1.
BMG-12b Broken "O" in "VOTE" 1.-2.
Panes of twenty (5x4) in booklets of 100.

Picture shown at 73%
BMG-13   B/Y (s.c.)   2.-4.

Picture shown at 80%
BMG-14   B   1.-3.

BMG-15   RBk   3.-5.

BMG-16   RBk   3.-5.

BMG-17   RBk   3.-5.

BMG-18   RBk   3.-5.

BMG-19   RDkBLtB   .50-1.

GOLDWATER

BMG-20   B   .50-1.

BARRY GOLDWATER'S
address will be
1600 Pennsylvania Avenue

BMG-21   B   .50-1.

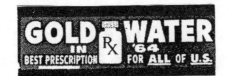

BMG-22   B   1.-2.

BMG-23   B/Gd   1.-3.
Sheets of twenty-five (5x5). SE: TLBR

BMG-24   Bk/Go   1.-3.
Individual die cut.

Artist's rendition. Photo unavailable.
BMG-25   Bk/Go   2.-4.
Individual die cut.

Picture shown at 50%
BMG-26   Bk/Go foil   2.-4.

Cherish Your Freedom?
THEN
Rediscover
YOUR
Responsibility!
VOTE REPUBLICAN!

BMG-27   BkY   .50-1.

BMG-28   1.-3.

GOLDWATER

Picture shown at 70%
BMG-29   Bk/Gd   1.-3.
Sheet of thirty-three (3x11)

William E. Miller, 1964 Vice-presidential Candidate

"Any government which gets so big
that it can give you everything you want
will also be so big that it can take everything you've got." — *William E. Miller.*

D. FOR A., P. O. BOX 600, SAN GABRIEL, CALIFORNIA.

Picture shown at 90%
WEM-1   1.-3.

"ANY GOVERNMENT WHICH GETS SO BIG THAT
IT CAN GIVE YOU EVERYTHING YOU WANT
WILL ALSO BE SO BIG THAT IT CAN TAKE
EVERYTHING YOU'VE GOT". WILLIAM E. MILLER

WEM-2   RB   1.-3.

Hubert H. Humphrey, 1960, 1964, 1968

HHH-1   Bk   1.-3.
Individual Imperforate. Mate to RMN-13, GCW-4.

HHH-2   R   2.-4.
Matches LBJ-2.

A change-yes. But to whom what. We aren't in doubt. The HUMPHREY-MUSKIE ticket means continued progress.

HHH-3   MC   3.-6.

Eugene McCarthy, 1968, 1972, 1976 Hopeful

EMC-1   RB   1.-3.

EMC-2   B   1.-3.

EMC-3   B   1.-3.

FOR PEACE & PROGRESS
McCARTHY
FOR PRESIDENT
VOTE APRIL 2

EMC-4   Bk   1.-3.

McCARTHY
not McCARTHYISM

EMC-5   RB   1.-3.

McCARTHY
For
Peace & Progress

EMC-6   RB   1.-3.

NOTE: There is a similar "I'M FOR Mc CAR-THY" stamp which was most likely issued in support of Joseph McCarthy in the 1950s. See under Joseph McCarthy.

Robert F. Kennedy, 1968 Hopeful

KENNEDY FOR PRESIDENT

RFK-1   Bk/Y   2.-4.

Robt F   Ethel
Kennedy

RFK-2   Bk   2.-4.

Robert Kennedy

RFK-3   2.-4.

KENNEDY
FULBRIGHT
1968

RFK-4   RB   2.-4.

VIVA KENNEDY

RFK-5   RB   2.-4.

R. F. K. 4 - '68

RFK-6   RB   2.-4.

George C. Wallace, 1968, 1972, 1976

WALLACE
FOR PRESIDENT

GCW-1   Bk   .50-1.
Sheets of 100 (10x10) SE: LBR

ALABAMA AND AMERICA NEED
GEORGE C. WALLACE

GCW-2   Bk   1.-2.

STAND UP FOR AMERICA!
GEORGE WALLACE

GCW-3   B   2.-4.

WALLACE FOR PRESIDENT

GCW-4   Bk   2.-4.
Mate to RMN-13, HHH-1.

Picture shown at 90%

GCW-5	RB	1.-2.
GCW-6	RB	1.-2.
GCW-7	RB	1.-2.
GCW-8	RB	1.-2.
GCW-9	RB	1.-2.

Panes of five different vertically, roulette between.

Let George do it!
WALLACE for President Committee
P. O. Box 263 ☆ Hialeah, Florida 33011

GCW-10   RB   2.-4.
Sheets of sixteen (4x4).

WALLACE

GCW-11   Bk   1.-3.
Imperforate sheets of sixteen. MIR: "ENV. STICKERS/cut apart small Wallace sheet Invisible glue on back Free assortment of all literature with self addressed stamped envelope. (Special $1.00 assorted pack) JOHN W. BIGGERT 413 Wagner St., Memphis, Tenn. 38103"

PASS THE WORD --
WALLACE - 68

GCW-12   1.-3.

WALLACE-72

GCW-13   Bk   1.-3.
Imperforate sheets of seventeen. MIR: "ENV. STICKERS/cut apart small Wallace sheet Invisible glue on back Free assortment of all literature with self addressed stamped envelope. (Special $1.00 assorted pack) JOHN W. BIGGERT 413 Wagner St., Memphis, Tenn. 38103"

★ GEORGE C. WALLACE ★
X¢   FMF   X¢
1968   Local Post   1976
PRESIDENTIAL CANDIDATE

GCW-14   B   1.-3.
Individual imperforate.

GCW-15   MC   3.-5.
Included in MAD Magazine, 1972.

Spiro T. Agnew, 1968, 1972 Vice President

STA-1   Bk/B   1.-3.

Picture shown at 67%
STA-2   MC   2.-4.
From MAD Magazine.

JOE McCARTHY IS ALIVE AND LIVING IN SPIRO AGNEW!

Picture shown at 67%
STA-3   1.-3.
From MAD Magazine.

★ 39th VICE PRESIDENT ★
1969   FMF   1973
X¢ Local Post X¢
★ SPIRO T. AGNEW ★

STA-4   B   1.-3.
Individual imperforate.
See also GCW-15.

E. Harold Munn, 1968 Prohibition Party

Prohibition Party
E. Harold Munn
PRESIDENT

Rolland E. Fisher
VICE-PRESIDENT

EHM-1   Bk   3.-6.

George McGovern, 1968, 1972

GMG-1   RBBk   1.-2
GMG-2   RBBk   3.-6.
Sheets of 100 (10x10). SE:TBLR
GMG-2 is the stamp in the bottom right corner of
the sheet.

Picture shown at 75%
GMG-3   B   1.-3.
Sheets of six (1x6) SE: LTR. MIB: Paid for by
Janice Loeb., Treas.,/Jeffersonians for McGovern-
/P.O. Box 128, Stoughton, Wis./53589.

GMG-4   B   1.-3.
Sheets of twenty (4x5)
These may have been issued during the senate
campaign, however they were distributed by the
presidential campaign, as were GMG-5 and
GMG-6.

GMG-5   B   1.-3.
GMG-6   B   2.-4.
Sheets of twenty (4x5). SE:TBRL
GMG-6 is the bottom right stamp in the sheet
which also contains nineteen copies of GMG-5.

GMG-7   Bk/Or   1.-3.
Individual imperforate.

GMG-8   Bk (photo)   3.-6.

GMG-9   Bk (photo)   3.-6.

GMG-10   Bk (photo)   1.-3.
Might be post-election.

Ronald W. Reagan, 1968, 1976, 1980, 1984

RWR-1   RBBk   3.-6
Sheets of fifty (5x10).

RWR-2   BrOr (1947)   8.-15.
RWR-2 is contained in a sheet of twelve movie
star stamps.

RWR-3   1.-3.

RWR-4   Bk   1.-3.

![Reagan again sheet]
Top row of RWR-5 to RWR-12 with top salvage.

Picture shown at 58%
RWR-5   RB   1.-3.
RWR-6   MC   1.-3.

RWR-7	MC		1.-3.
RWR-8	MC		1.-3.
RWR-9	MC		1.-3.
RWR-10	MC		1.-3.
RWR-11	MC		1.-3.
RWR-12	RB		1.-3.

Sheet of fifty-six (8x7). SE:RBL MIT: "My Country, My President. He works for me. I work for him. 56 STROKES FOR 56 FOLKS..." (lengthy text).

RWR-13	Br (1968)		2.-4.

RONALD REAGAN

RWR-14	Black (1980)		3.-6.

From a sheet of nine different 1980 hopefuls issued by YAF as part of a mail-in poll.

RWR-15	RBBk		2.-4.

RWR-16	RB		1.-3.

REAGAN FOR PRESIDENT ☒

RWR-17	RB		1.-3.

RWR-18	B		.5-1.

Sheet of fifty (5x10). SE: LTR MIT: "Republican Party of California." Some sheets (perhaps most) have no margin inscription.

RWR-19	BrOr		1.-3.

RWR-20	BrOr		1.-3.

RWR-21	BrOr		1.-3.

RWR-22	BrOr		1.-3.

Support President Reagan For A Better America.

RWR-23	Bk		.50-1.

Join The Reagan Revolution Vote Republican

RWR-24	Bk		.50-1.

RWR-25	Bk/LtB		1.-3.
RWR-25a	Bk/B		1.-3.

RWR-26	Bk/LtB		1.-3.
RWR-26a	Bk/B		1.-3.

RWR-27	Bk/B		1.-3.

RWR-28	Bk/B		1.-3.

RWR-29   RBBk   1.-3.

RWR-30   RBk   1.-3.

Picture shown at 80%
RWR-31   2.-4.
From MAD Magazine.

RWR-32   MC   2.-4.
From the book, *The 1990 Doonesbury Stamp Album* by Gary Trudeau. The book contains about 250 stamps, of which the above is one.

SEE ALSO GF-2 WHICH
PICTURES REAGAN WITH FORD.

Edward M. Kennedy, 1972, 1976, 1980 Hopeful

EMK-1   Bk   1.-2.
This stamp is included in a sheet of 36 different satirical political stamps.
See page 59.

John Schmitz, 1972 American Party

JS-1   Bk   1.-3.

Hopefuls, 1972

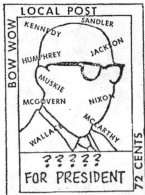

Picture shown at 80%

HPF-1	Bk/DkGr	1.-3.
HPF-2	Bk/Gd	1.-3.
HPF-3	Bk/R	1.-3.
HPF-4	Bk/LtY	1.-3.
HPF-4a	(hollow star printed UR)	1.-3.
HPF-5	Bk/Pk	1.-3.
HPF-6	Bk/Y	1.-3.
HPF-7	Bk/Gr	1.-3.
HPF-8	Bk	1.-3.
HPF-8a	(hollow star printed UR)	1.-3.
HPF-8b	(solid star printed UR)	1.-3.
HPF-9	Bk/B	1.-3.

These stamps were issued during the 1972 campaign and each stamp mentions nine of the possible candidates. They were affixed to envelopes and postmarked in various cities on the days of the presidential primaries. The star varieties listed were versions of the same stamp with an additional star printed under the "gn" in "Campaign."

Robert Byrd, 1976 Hopeful

RB-1   Bk   1.-2.
This stamp is included in a sheet of 36 different satirical political stamps.
See page 59.

Gerald Ford, 1976, 1980

GERALD
FORD

GF-1   Bk   2.-5.
From a sheet of nine different 1980 hopefuls issued by YAF as part of a poll. See page 58.

Picture shown at 80%
GF-2   Bk/Or   2.-4.

★ GERALD R. FORD ★
X¢   FMF   X¢
1776   Local Post   1976
BICENTENNIAL PRESIDENT

GF-3   B   2.-4.

Picture shown at 80%
GF-4   MC   2.-4.
From MAD Magazine.

Picture shown at 80%
GF-5   R   1.-3.
The stamp shown has a cancellation on it which is not part of the stamp design.

GF-6   RB   1.-3.
Individual imperforate.

GF-7   MC   1.-3.
From the book, *The 1990 Doonesbury Stamp
Album* by Gary Trudeau. The book contains
about 250 stamps, including two copies of GF-7.
*SEE ALSO RMN-51 WHICH
MENTIONS FORD.*

Nelson A. Rockefeller
Vice President

NAR-1   B   1.-3.
Individual imperforate.

Paul Cunningham,
1976 Constitutional Party

PCC-1   RB   2.-4.

Jimmy Carter, 1976, 1980

JC-1   Bk   1.-3.

JC-2   Bk (photo)   1.-3.

JC-3   Bk (photo)   1.-3.

JC-4   Bk/B   1.-3.

Picture shown at 90%

JC-5   Bk/B   2.-4.

Hopefuls, 1980

RWR-14	Bk (Ronald Reagan)	2.-4.
PC-1	Bk (Philip Crane)	1.-2.
JK-1	Bk (Jack Kemp)	2.-3.
RD-1	Bk (Bob Dole)	2.-3.
PL-1	Bk (Paul Laxalt)	1.-2.
JC-1	Bk (John Connally)	1.-2.
WS-1	Bk (William Simon)	1.-2.
GF-1	Bk (Gerald Ford)	2.-4.
GB-1	Bk (George Bush)	1.-3.
YAF-1	Bk (Entire sheet)	10.-20.

This sheet of nine different 1980 hopefuls was
issued by Young Americans for Freedom as part
of a mail-in poll.

RONALD REAGAN   PHILIP CRANE   JACK KEMP   BOB DOLE   PAUL LAXALT

JOHN CONNALLY   WILLIAM SIMON   GEORGE BUSH   GERALD FORD   OTHER

TO VOTE: DETACH PRESIDENTIAL CANDIDATE STAMP OF YOUR CHOOSING;
MOISTEN AND APPLY TO OFFICIAL BALLOT IN POSITION INDICATED.

Picture shown at 95%   Y.A.F. Hopefuls sheet 1980.

George H. Bush, 1980, 1988, 1992

GEORGE
BUSH

GHB-1   Bk   3.-5.

Sheet of nine different 1980 hopefuls issued by YAF as part of a mail-in poll.

GHB-2   MC (photo)   1.-2.
GHB-2a   MC (paper)   1.-2.

> Keep George Bush At
> 1600 Pennsylvania Ave.
> Washington, DC, In 1992

GHB-3   Bk/B   .25-.50
GHB-4   Bk/Y   .25-.50
GHB-5   Bk/Pk   .25-.50
GHB-6   Bk/Gr   .25-.50

GHB-7   MC   1.-2.

GHB-8   MC thin paper   1.-2.
GHB-8a   MC thick paper 1.-2.

GHB-8 was printed on dry-gum paper. GHB-8a was printed on regular paper, with glue added later, as a prototype.

GHB-9   MC thin paper   1.-2.
GHB-9a   MC thick paper 1.-2.

GHB-9 was printed on dry-gum paper. GHB-9a was printed on regular paper, with glue added later, as a prototype.

GHB-10   Multicolored   4.-8.
GHB-11   Multicolored   4.-8.
GHB-12   Multicolored   4.-8.

These were designed and produced by an artist in Holland. They are part of a sheet of at least twenty-eight different satirical stamps. The stamps do not have glue on the backs.

GHB-13   Bk   1.-3.

This stamp is included in a sheet of thirty-six different satirical political stamps. See the next page.

GHB-14   MC   1.-3.
GHB-15   MC   1.-3.
GHB-16   MC   1.-3.
GHB-17   MC   1.-3.
GHB-18   MC   1.-3.
GHB-19   MC   1.-3.
GHB-20   MC   1.-3.
GHB-21   MC   1.-3.
GHB-22   MC   1.-3.
GHB-23   MC   1.-3.
GHB-24   MC   1.-3.

Stamps GHB-15 through 24 have perforations down the middle. See page 60.

From the book, *The 1990 Doonesbury Stamp Album* by Gary Trudeau. The book contains about 250 stamps, including two sets of the above Bush stamps.

GHB-25   Bk/B   1.-3.

GHB-25 is known in pairs with both GHB-26 and GHB-27.

GHB-26   Bk/B   1.-3.

THANK GOD FOR DUMB SHITS LIKE YOU OR I WOULDN'T HAVE A JOB

 ASSISTANT ASSHOLE

 I DON'T TAKE DRUGS I SELL THEM

 DON'T WORRY BE HAPPY GIVE ME YOUR MONEY

 PLEASE BE BRIEF I'VE GOT DIARRHEA

 FUCK THIS JOB. TOMORROW I BECOME A TERRORIST

 HEY, I'M A LIBERAL FUCK YOU TOO

 CARD CARRYING CHICKEN CHOKER

 AIN'T IT ABOUT TIME FOR ANOTHER WAR

 SAVE AMERICA! GET OUT THERE & SHOP

 DON'T BELIEVE ANYTHING UNTIL IT'S OFFICIALLY DENIED

 I WAS IN THE CAR WHEN JFK GOT BLOWN AWAY

 I'LL DO ANYTHING FOR THE WORKER EXCEPT BECOME ONE

 JUST ANOTHER THUMB-SUCKING POLYESTER EX-NAZI

 NEVER ACTUALLY CONVICTED OF BEASTIALITY

 BY FRIDAY WE EXPECT TO CONTROL THE PLANET

 I GAVE UP SEX AND DRUGS FOR MONEY AND POWER

 GOD BLESS ALL THE PEOPLE I FUCKED OVER

 DON'T BOTHER. IT WAS SHOT OFF IN THE WAR

 CUT THE HYPE AND START THE BOMBING

 I PUT ON A SUIT & GO BLANK

 THERE'S ONLY A COUPLE OF PUNKS BETWEEN ME AND THE TOP SPOT

 IF YOU DON'T LIKE THE NEWS, TURN IT OFF

 SALUTE ME, YOU IMBECILES

 AMERICA IS FOR PERFECT PEOPLE WITH LAWYERS

 YOU'D BE SAFER IF I WERE IN JAIL

 PROUDLY SERVING MY CORPORATE MASTERS

 IF I OPEN MY MOUTH THE FLIES WILL ESCAPE

 I WASN'T THE VILLAGE IDIOT. I CAME IN SECOND.

 I WAS RAISED BY A PACK OF WILD CORNDOGS

 SMOKING IS OUT. CHEMICAL WARFARE IS IN.

 OF COURSE DEMOCRACY WORKS . . . NOW DO WHAT I SAY, ASSHOLE!

 DAZZLING PROOF OF LIFE AFTER DEATH

 I'VE GOT THE TIME IF YOU'VE GOT THE KNEEPADS

 100% FACT RESISTANT

 SMILE, YOU'RE ON SATELLITE SURVEILLANCE

Sheet of 36 different political satire stamps

Top row: GHB-13, JDQ-3, unlisted, L-109, RB-1, L-110

Second row: L-13, L-111, L-14, L-112, L-120, LB-1

Third row: EMK-1, L-16, L-15, JG-1, unknown, L-113

Fourth row: RD-2, L-114, L-115, unknown, AC-1, AG-1

Fifth row: unknown, unknown, unknown, L-116, unknown, PS-1

Sixth row: L-117, L-118, unknown, JK-1, L-119, unknown

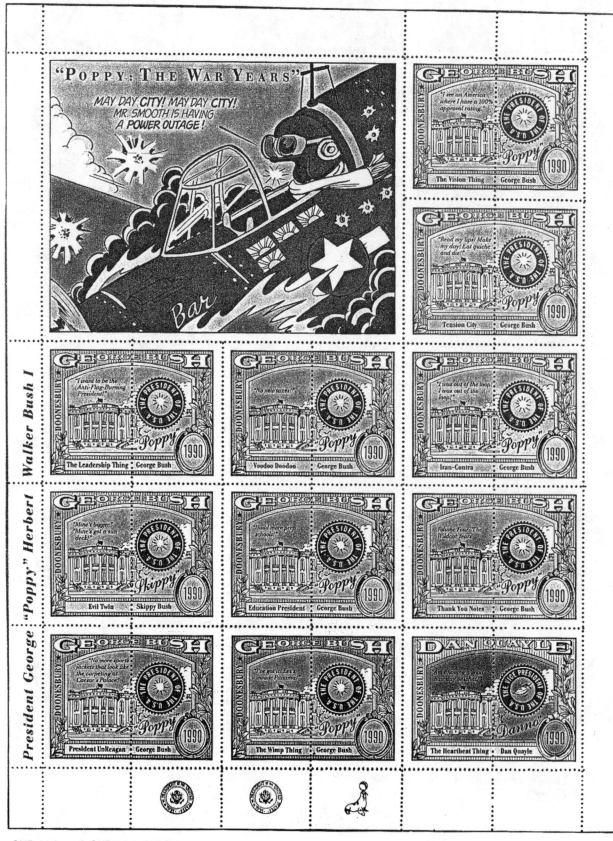

GHB-14 through GHB-24 and JDQ-2.

GHB-27   Bk/B   1.-3.

Mr. Bobby L. May
Star Route Box 261
Hurley VA 24620   Bush '88

GHB-28   RBBk   1.-3.

These preprinted address labels were sent to persons on a Republican mailing list as a fund raiser.

Jack Kemp, 1980, 1988, 1996 Hopeful

JACK KEMP

JK-1   Bk   2.-3.

From a sheet of nine different 1980 hopefuls issued by Young Americans for Freedom as part of a mail-in poll.

I'VE GOT THE TIME IF YOU'VE GOT THE KNEEPADS

JK-2   Bk   1.-2.

This stamp is included in a sheet of 36 different satirical political stamps. See page 59.

J. Danforth Quayle, 1988, 1992 Vice President

Picture shown at 70%
JDQ-1   Bk/B   1.-3.

Picture shown at 70%
JDQ-2   MC   1.-3.

From the book, *The 1990 Doonesbury Stamp Album* by Gary Trudeau. The book contains about 250 stamps, including two copies of this stamp. See page 60. Stamp is perforated down the center.

ASSISTANT ASSHOLE

JDQ-3   Bk   1.-3.

This stamp is included in a sheet of thirty-six different satirical political stamps. See page 59.

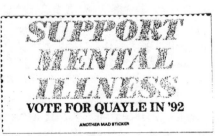

SUPPORT MENTAL ILLNESS
VOTE FOR QUAYLE IN '92
ANOTHER MAD STICKER

Picture shown at 77%
JDQ-4   1.-3.
From MAD Magazine.

Alan Cranston, 1984 Hopeful

AC-1   Bk   1.-2.

This stamp is included in a sheet of 36 different satirical political stamps.
See page 59.

John Glenn, 1984 Hopeful

JG-1   Bk   1.-2.

This stamp is included in a sheet of 36 different satirical political stamps.
See page 59.

Jesse Jackson, 1984, 1988

HOPE
Jesse Jackson for President

JJ-1   MC (text in blue)   1.-2.
JJ-2   MC (text in red)   1.-2.
JJ-3   MC (text in yellow)   1.-2.
JJ-4   MC (text in green)   1.-2.

Sheet of eight (4x2) containing two blocks of the four different.

Lloyd Bentson, 1988 Vice-presidential Candidate

I WAS IN THE CAR WHEN JFK GOT BLOWN AWAY

LB-1   Bk   1.-2.

This stamp is included in a sheet of thirty-six different satirical political stamps. See page 59.

Paul Simon, 1988 Hopeful

PS-1   Bk   1.-2.

This stamp is included in a sheet of 36 different satirical political stamps. See page 59.

If you have any items which are not pictured in this book but should be, please send photocopies to the author in care of Krause Publications, 700 E. State St., Iola, WI 54990-0001.

William J. Clinton, 1992, 1996

| WJC-1 | MC | 1.-3. |
| WJC-1a | MC | 1.-3. |

WJC-1 was printed on dry-gum paper. WJC-1a was printed on regular paper, with glue added later, as a prototype.

| WJC-2 | MC | 1.-3. |
| WJC-2a | MC | 1.-3. |

WJC-2 was printed on dry-gum paper. WJC-2a was printed on regular paper, with glue added later, as a prototype.

**Bring Back Prosperity
Clinton and Gore
In 1992**

WJC-3	Bk/B	.25- .50
WJC-4	Bk/Pk	.25- .50
WJC-5	Bk/Y	.25- .50
WJC-6	Bk/Gr	.25- .50

| WJC-7 | MC | 1.-3. |

| WJC-8 | MC | 1.-3. |

WJC-9	Bk/B (1993)	1.-3.
WJC-9a	Bk/B (1997) (larger)	1.-3.
WJC-10	Bk/Pk (1993)	1.-3.
WJC-10a	Bk/Pk (1997) (larger)	1.-3.
WJC-11	Bk/Gr (1997)	1.-3.

WJC-12	Bk/B (1993)	1.-3.
WJC-13	Bk/Pk (1993)	1.-3.
WJC-14	Bk/Gr (1997)	1.-3.

| WJC-15 | Bk/Gd | 1.-3. |

AMERICAN PATHETIC

© 1994 Slick Times
To order, call 1-800-669-8444

| WJC-16 | MC | 1.-3. |

©1994 Sphinx, POB 25, Clearwater, FL 34617

Remember when America had a real president?	Don't blame me. I voted for **Bush.**	Don't blame me. I voted for **Perot.**	First Hillary Then Gennifer Then Paula Now us!
Where is Oswald now that we need him?	Jack Kevorkian for White House Physician.	How many days left 'til 1996?	I want a $200 haircut too, Bubba.
Inhail to the Chief!	Mandate my ass. 57% of us voted against Slick Willie.	"Bill Clinton's got a small penis and Hillary's got fat ankles." -Gennifer Flowers Penthouse, Dec. 1992	Hope ain't in Arkansas... It's in 1996!
SMILE! If Clinton thinks you're rich	At least Gennifer got kissed.	Bill Clinton: Commander and Cheat	Clinton in Germany: "Ich bin ein Beginner"
From a chicken in every pot to a chicken who smoked pot	Clinton Gore: Gone in Four	Hillary: The broad who would be king.	Bill: Go see a play at Ford's Theatre.

Picture shown at 72% (WJC-17 through WJC-36)

Sheets of sixteen (4x4). SE:TBLR.

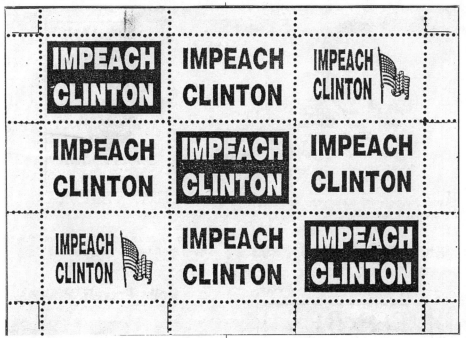

AG-5   MC   .50-1.

Sheet of four (2x2) containing two copies each of AG-4 and AG-5 alternating. MIT: "USE THESE STAMPS ON YOUR LETTERS TO HELP MAKE ALL GORE PRESIDENT IN 2000"

H. Ross Perot, 1992, 1996

HRP-1	MC	1.-3.
HRP-1a	MC	1.-3.

HRP-1 was printed on dry-gum paper. HRP-1a was printed on regular paper, with glue added later, as a prototype.

Picture shown at 92% (WJC-37 through WJC-40)

WJC-17	RRBk "remember "	.50-1.
WJC-18	RBBk "Don't...Bush."	.50-1.
WJC-19	RBBk "Don't...Perot."	.50-1.
WJC-20	RBBk "First..."	.50-1.
WJC-21	RB "Where is..."	.50-1.
WJC-22	RBBk "Jack..."	.50-1.
WJC-23	RBBk "How many..."	.50-1.
WJC-24	RBBk "I want..."	.50-1.
WJC-25	RB "Inhale..."	.50-1.
WJC-26	RBBk "Mandate..."	.50-1.
WJC-27	RBBk "'Bill..."	.50-1.
WJC-28	RB "Hope..."	.50-1.
WJC-29	RB "SMILE!..."	.50-1.
WJC-30	RBBk "At least..."	.50-1.
WJC-31	BBk "Bill..."	.50-1.
WJC-32	RBBk "Clinton in..."	.50-1.
WJC-33	RBBk "From..."	.50-1.
WJC-34	RB "Clinton..."	.50-1.
WJC-35	RB "Hillary..."	.50-1.
WJC-36	RBBk "Bill: Go..."	.50-1.
WJC-37	R	1.-2.
WJC-38	B	1.-2.
WJC-39	RB	1.-2.
WJC-40	RB	1.-2.

Sheet of nine (3x3) contains two of WJC-37, one of WJC-38, two of JWC-39, and four of WJC-40.

This stamp is included in a sheet of thirty-six different satirical political stamps. See page 59.

AG-2	Bk/Pk (1993)	1.-3.
AG-3	Bk/B (1997)	1.-3.

HRP-2	MC	1.-3.
HRP-2a	MC	1.-3.

HRP-2 was printed on dry-gum paper. HRP-2a was printed on regular paper, with glue added later, as a prototype.

Albert Gore, Jr., 1992, 1996, 2000 Vice President

AG-1   Bk   1.-3.

AG-4   MC   .50-1.

HRP-3	Bk/B	.25-.50
HRP-4	Bk/Pk	.25-.50
HRP-5	Bk/Y	.25-.50
HRP-6	Bk/Gr	.25-.50

Andre Marou, 1992 Libertarian Party

AM-1   Bk   1.-2.
AM-1a   Bk   1.-2.
AM-1 was printed on dry-gum paper. AM-1a was printed on regular paper, with glue added later, as a prototype.

Mario M. Cuomo, 1992 Hopeful

Vote For
Mario Cuomo
For President In 1992

MMC-1   Bk   .50

Vote For
Mario Cuomo
For President In 1992

Picture shown at 67%
MMC-2   Bk   .50
MMC-2 was a misprint of MC-1.

Robert Dole, 1980, 1988, 1996

BOB
DOLE

RD-1   Black   2.-4.
From a sheet of nine different 1980 hopefuls issued by Young Americans for Freedom as part of a mail-in poll.

DON'T BOTHER. IT WAS
SHOT OFF IN THE WAR

RD-2   Black   1.-2.
From a sheet of thirty-six different satirical political stamps. See page 59.

Steve Forbes, 1996, 2000

SF-1   MC   1.-2.

SF-2   MC   .50-1.
The above stamps are in a sheet containing one copy of SF-1 and two copies of SF-2.

Colin Powell, 2000

CP-1   MC   .50-1.
Sheet of six (3x2)

If you have any items which are not pictured in this book but should be, please send photocopies to the author in care of Krause Publications, 700 E. State St., Iola, WI 54990-0001.

Presidential Stamp Sets are relatively inexpensive and often overlooked by political collectors, yet each set includes one stamp which was issued during the term of a sitting president and which may have been used during his reelection campaign. We believe that most sets issued during the last 60 years have been included in this listing, but there were probably many more older sets. If you have one which has not been pictured, please send me a photocopy.

For most sets I have pictured the last stamp in the set because that is the one issued during the term of the sitting president. These theoretically could have been used to promote his reelection. In a couple of cases only one stamp is known to the author and it is not known who the last president in the set was. The values shown are for the full sets.

PSS-1
Colors: Multicolored
Format: Die cut on a sheet
Total number is set unknown.
Value: 50.-100.

PSS-2
Colors: Black, green, reddish-orange, and flesh colored.
Format: Sheet of twenty-eight (7x4) with the first stamp showing the White House.
This set was made during Wilson's first term by someone who apparently didn't expect him to have another. (Note dates.)
Value: 20.-40.

PSS-3
Colors: Black design with the background in color.
Format: Unknown
©1919 by Ohio War Savings Committee. The known denominations are:

$5	Washington
$10	Adams
$20	Jefferson
$25	Madison
$30	Monroe
$35	Adams
$40	Jackson
$50	Van Buren
$65	Harrison
$80	Tyler
$100	Polk
$150	Taylor
$200	Filmore
$5,000	Roosevelt
$10,000	Wilson

Value: 50.-100.

PSS-4
Colors: Black portrait with the rest is green, orange, pink, or blue.
Format: Sheet of thirty-two (8x4) with the last stamp showing the White House.
Issued by Colonial Press, Indianapolis, IN.
Value: 10.20.

PSS-5
Colors: Medals in yellow, signature in black, frame in pink, purple, green, or blue.
Format: Blocks of forty-eight stamps (8x6) of which seventeen are flags and the balance presidents which appear to have come from larger sheets.
Distributed by Helms Bakeries, Los Angeles, CA, beginning in 1941. A coupon good for one stamp was given with each loaf of bread delivered by the bakery.
At least two different albums were distributed, one from the bakery and one with no source noted.
Value: 15.-20.

FRANKLIN D. ROOSEVELT
Thirty-second President
ROOSEVELT

PSS-6
Colors: Vignette and text in brown, frame in red.
Format: Unknown.
Value: 10.-15.
PSS-7 (Same design)
Colors: Vignette and text in brown, frame in brown.
Format: Unknown.
Value: 10.-15.
PSS-8 (Same design)
Colors: Vignette and text in brown, frame in orange.
Format: Unknown.
Value: 10.-15.
PSS-9 (Same design)
Colors: Vignette and text in brown, frame in yellow.
Format: Unknown.
Value: 10.-15.
PSS-10 (Same design)
Colors: Vignette and text in brown, frame in green.
Format: Unknown.
Value: 10.-15.
PSS-11 (Same design)
Colors: Vignette and text in brown, frame in purple.
Format: Unknown.
Value: 10.-15.
PSS-12 (Same design)
Colors: Vignette and text in brown, frame in blue.
Format: Unknown.
Value: 10.-15.

FRANKLIN D. ROOSEVELT
1882- 32ª PRES. 1933-

PSS-13
Colors: Sepia
Format: Unknown. Known in blocks of 4.
Value: 10.-15.
PSS-14 (Same design)
Colors: Orange, blue, brown, or green.
Format: Unknown. Distributed in envelopes of

twenty-five strips of four, one stamp in each color. There is an album for these stamps issued by American Oil Co. in 1936. Other companies may have issued similar promotional albums. One strip of four stamps was distributed each week.
Value: 10.-15.

PSS-15
Colors: Sepia (photograph)
Format: Unknown
Value: 10.-20.

32ND PRESIDENT
1933-1945
FRANKLIN D. ROOSEVELT

PSS-16
Colors: Black and Gold
Format: Sheet of thirty-five (7x5).
Issued in 1941 with the presumption that Roosevelt would not have more than three terms. Published by Frederick H. Dietz, New York, N.Y.
Value: 10.-20.

HARRY S TRUMAN
1884- 33ª PRES. 1945-

PSS-17
Color: Orange
Format: Unknown. This stamp may have been a single issue to update set PSS-12. This stamp is roulette perforated unlike set PSS-12.
Value: 1.-3. (single stamp)

PSS-18
Colors: Natural
Format: Sheet of thirty-two (8x4)

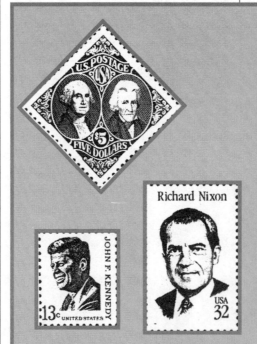

Collectors seeking an extensive collection based upon a U.S. president can add many U.S. postage stamps to their collections. Since the second U.S. postage stamp in 1847, the government has issued hundreds of stamps picturing our presidents. Unlike many countries, no living presidents can be pictured on stamps. At present the policy is to honor a deceased president on his next birthday following his death.

Distributed along with a 36-page booklet by New York Central Railroad in 1946.
Value: 10.-15.

PSS-19 (Same design)
Colors: Natural
Format: Sheet of sixteen (4x4) with sixteen issued as singles. Printed on light card stock without glue.
Distributed along with a 36-page booklet by Kellogg Company in 1948.
Value: 10.-15.

DWIGHT D. EISENHOWER

Picture shown at 87%
PSS-20
Colors: Natural
Format: Four pages of twelve stamps each, bound into the book *The Golden Stamp Book of Presidents of the United States.*
Published by Simon and Schuster, Inc. ©1954.
Value: 5.-10.

PSS-21
Colors: Vignettes in black, borders and text in red, blue, or green.
Format: Sheet of thirty-six (9x4).
Published by H. E. Harris & Co. ©1957.
Note error in date for end of Eisenhower's term.
Value: 5.-10.

PSS-22
Colors: Vignettes in black and yellow, borders and text in red, blue, purple, or green.
Format: Sheet of thirty-six (9x4).
Published by H. E. Harris & Co. ©1961.
Value: 5.-10.

JOHN F. KENNEDY

Picture shown at 85%
PSS-23
Colors: Natural
Format: Four pages of twelve stamps each, bound into the book *The Golden Learn-About Book: Presidents of the United States.*
Published by Simon and Schuster, Inc. ©1954.
Value: 5.-10.

PSS-24

Colors: Vignettes in black and yellow, borders and text in red, blue, purple, or green.
Format: Sheet of thirty-six (9x4).
Published by H. E. Harris & Co. ©1964.
Value: 4.-8.

LYNDON B. JOHNSON

Picture shown at 90%
PSS-25
Colors: Natural
Format: Four pages of twelve stamps each, bound into the book *The Golden Stamp Book of Presidents of the United States.* Published by Golden Press, Inc. ©1966, 1954, Revised Edition 1966.
Value: 5.-10.

Unlike the U.S., many foreign governments have no restrictions on picturing living persons on postage stamps. Therefore, many U.S. presidents have been pictured on foreign stamps during their term in office. Anyone collecting items made during a president's term should look into these.

PSS-26
Colors: Vignettes in black and yellow, borders and text in red, blue, purple, or green.
Format: Sheet of thirty-eight with the presidential seal as the last stamp.
Published by H. E. Harris & Co. ©1970.
Value: 4.-8.

PSS-27
Colors: Vignettes in black and yellow, borders and text in red, blue, purple, or green.
Format: Sheet of thirty-eight
Published by H. E. Harris & Co. ©1974.
Value: 4.-8.

PSS-28
Colors: Natural
Format: Sheets of forty (5x8).
Published by H. E. Harris & Co., Inc., Boston, MA ©1976
Value: 5.-10.

PSS-29

Colors: Vignettes, names and dates in black, borders in green, blue, or red.
Format: Sheet of eighty-four including forty-five famous Americans. Published by Grossman Stamp Co, New York City.
Value: 5.-10.

PSS-30
Colors: Natural
Format: Sheets of forty (5x8).
Published by H. E. Harris & Co., Inc., Boston, MA ©1980
Note: Presidents Washington through Nixon in this set are the same as in set PSS-20, but the Ford stamp is a different pose.
Value: 4.-8.

PSS-31
Colors: Natural
Format: Sheets of forty-five (5x9).
Published by H. E. Harris & Co., Inc., Boston, MA ©1993
Value: 3.-6.

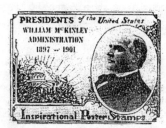

PSS-32
Colors: Blue
Format: Unknown.
This is the only stamp known from this set.

PSS-33
Colors: Black
Format: Unknown.

PSS-34
Colors: Vignettes in black, borders in blue, green, red, yellow, or black.
Format: Unknown.

Chapter 2

Party, Local, Vote, and Fantasy Candidates

This chapter includes items which were issued for local candidates, political parties which cannot be attributed to a specific candidate, generic "get out the vote" stamps, and fantasy political candidates.

Any of the party stamps which can be attributed to a presidential election year (such as being found on a postmarked envelope) can be moved to the presidential candidate for that election.

Communist and Socialist party items are included in Chapter 4 rather than this chapter because so many which mention communism, socialism, or the Soviet Union are in that chapter and it is easier to keep them together. Fantasy candidate stamps are political satire items issued to make a statement about actual candidates or issues.

Political Party Stamps

Republican

PPR-1   B (1954)   .50-1.

PPR-2   .50-1.

PPR-3   (1962)   .50-1.

Picture shown at 85%
PPR-4   RBBk   .50-1.

Vote Republican
For A Better Virginia.

PPR-5   Bk (1980s)   .50-1.

PPR-6   B/Go foil   .50-1.

★ REGISTER & VOTE ★
REPUBLICAN!

PPR-7   RB   .50-1.

PPR-8   RB   1.-2.
Found on a 1950 envelope from Alaska. Origin of stamp may be earlier.

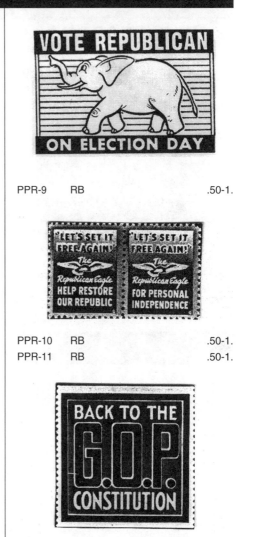

PPR-9   RB   .50-1.

PPR-10   RB   .50-1.
PPR-11   RB   .50-1.

PPR-12   RB   .50-1.

PPR-13   Br   .50-1.

PPR-14   RB   .50-1.

PPR-15   .50-1.

Picture shown at 80%

PPR-16   .50-1.

Picture shown at 75%

PPR-17   B/Go foil   .50-1.

PPD-1   .50-1.

PPD-2   RB   .50-1.

PPD-3   TuGy   1.-3.

PPD-4   Br   .50-1.

PPD-5   Bk   .50-1.

PPD-6   .50-1.

Other Parties

PPO-1   RB   3.-6.
Issued my Marcia Matthews, McAllen, TX, who
also created DMA-3 and ACS-9.

State and Local Candidate Stamps

U.S. Senate

Picture shown at 85%

L-1   Bk   5.-10.

Picture shown at 65%

L-2   RB (ME)   .50-2.

Picture shown at 75%

L-3   YBk (TX)   .50-2.

L-4   B (WA)   .50-2.

L-5   RBBk (OR)   .50-2.

L-6   R (IL, 1960)   .50-2.

L-7   (IN, 1958)   .50-2.

REELECT

FRANCIS CASE

as our

UNITED STATES SENATOR

L-8   (SD)   .50-2.

L-9   RB (NY, 1964)   .50-2.

L-10   RB (NY, 1964)   .50-2.

L-11   (Montana 1964)   .50-2.
Part of a sheet of thirteen different.

```
┌─────────────────────────────────────┐
│  ┌──┐   United States Senator        │
│  │  │  GERALD L. K. SMITH            │
│  └──┘                                 │
└─────────────────────────────────────┘
```

L-12   Bk (1942-Michigan)   1.-3.
Sheets of twenty-eight (4x7). Smith was also the
America First Party candidate for President in
1944 and the Christian Nationalist Party candidate for president in 1948.

The following stamps are shown on page 59.
L-13   Bk (Schroeder)   .50-1.
L-14   Bk (Helms)   .50-1.
L-15   Bk (Heflin)   .50-1.
L-16   Bk (Thurmond)   .50-1.

U.S. House of Representatives

L-101   Bk   3.-6.

L-102   RB   .50-2.

L-103   R   .50-2.

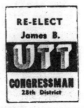

L-104   RB (CA)   .50-2.

L-105   RBk   .50-2.

L-106   (Montana 1964)   .50-2.
Part of a sheet of thirteen different.

L-107   (Montana 1964)   .50-2.
Part of a sheet of thirteen different.

L-108   R   .50-2.
The following stamps are shown on page 59.
L-109   Bk (Wilson)   .50-1.
L-110   Bk (Bliley)   .50-1.
L-111   Bk (Lipinski)   .50-1.
L-112   Bk (Roukema)   .50-1.
L-113   Bk (Gonzalez)   .50-1.
L-114   Bk (Pepper)   .50-1.
L-115   Bk (Johnson)   .50-1.
L-116   Bk (Vucanovich)   .50-1.

L-117	Bk (Wright)	.50-1.
L-118	Bk (Bentley)	.50-1.
L-119	Bk (Young)	.50-1.
L-120	Bk (Early)	.50-1.

State Governors

L-201   Bk (OH, 1908)   2.-4.

L-202   (IL, 1928)   2.-4.

L-203   RB (GA, 1966)   2.-4.

L-204   1.-3.

Picture shown at 65%

L-205   Bk (NY, 1916)   1.-3.

L-206   RBk (NJ, 1925)   .50-2.

L-207   RB (NJ)   .50-2.

L-208   RBBk (IN)   .50-2.

L-209   RBBk (IN)   .50-2.

L-210   RBBk (IN)   .50-2.

L-211   RBBk (IN)   .50-2.

L-212   RBk (WV, 1956)   .50-2.

L-213   PuBk   .50-2.

L-214   RB (CO, 1938)   .50-2.

L-215   BBkY (KS)   .50-2.

L-216   RB (PA)   .50-2.

72 • Party, Local, Vote, and Fantasy Candidates

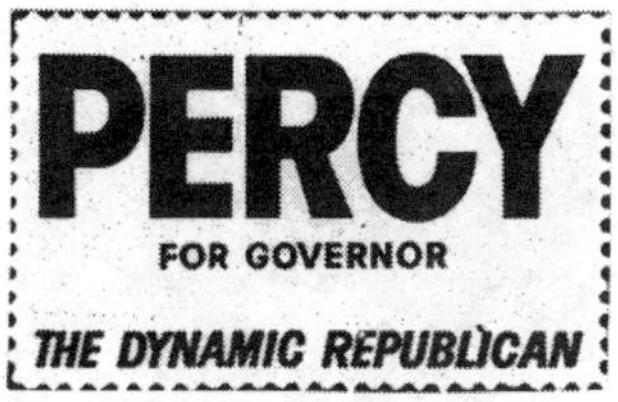

L-217 RB (IL, 1964) .50-2.

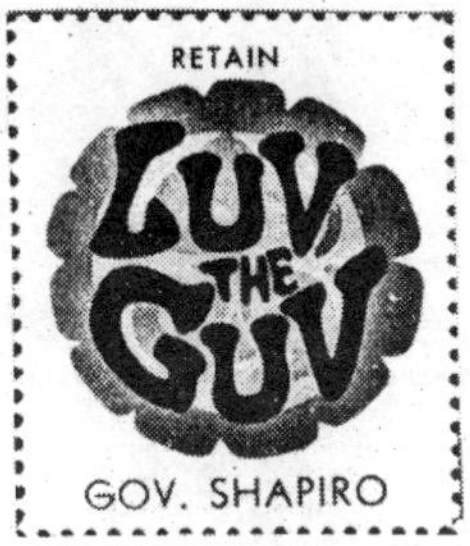

L-218 BkPkY (IL, 1968) .50-2.

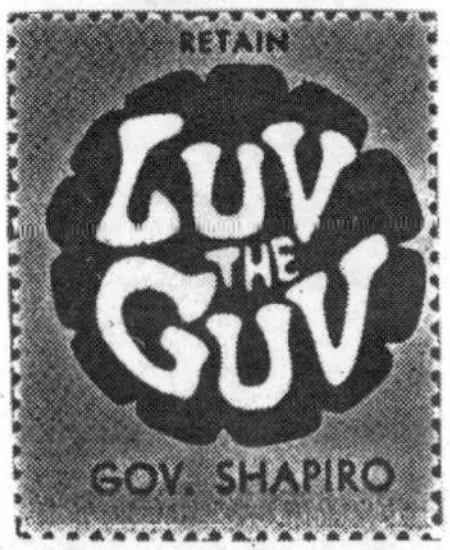

L-219 B (IL, 1968) .50-2.

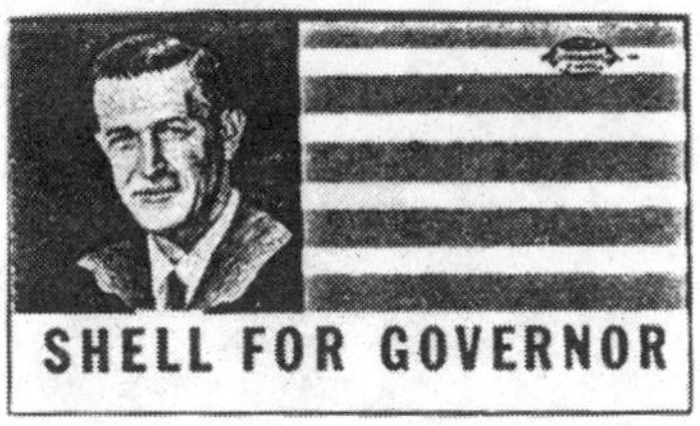

L-220 RBBk (CA, 1962) .50-2.

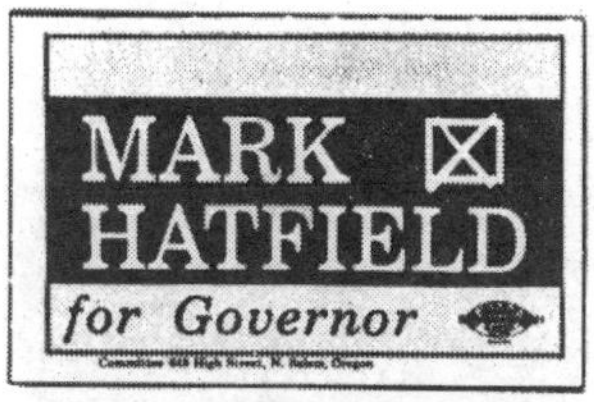

L-221 BkY (OR) .50-2.

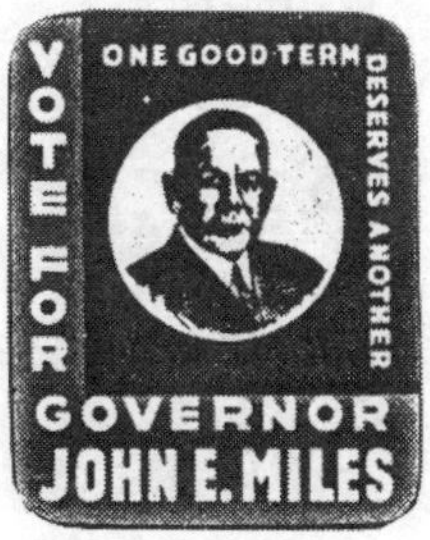

L-222 RB (NM) .50-2.

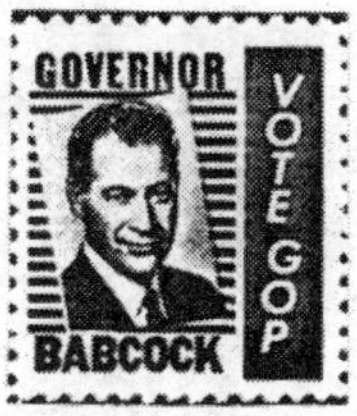

L-223 (Montana 1964) .50-2.
Part of a sheet of thirteen different.

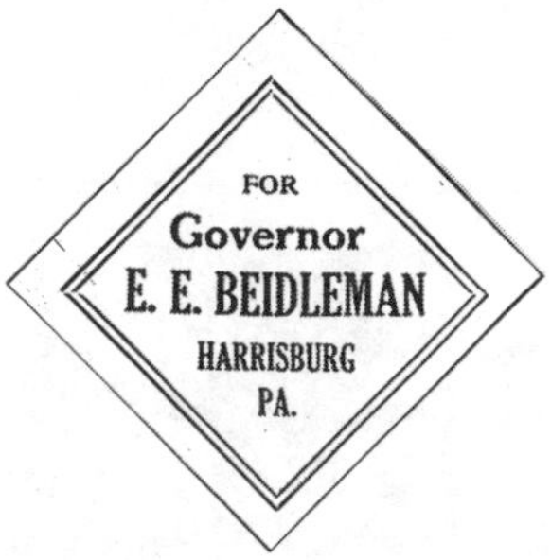

Picture shown at 65%

L-224 Bk/Pk .50-2.
L-225 Bk/Gr .50-2.

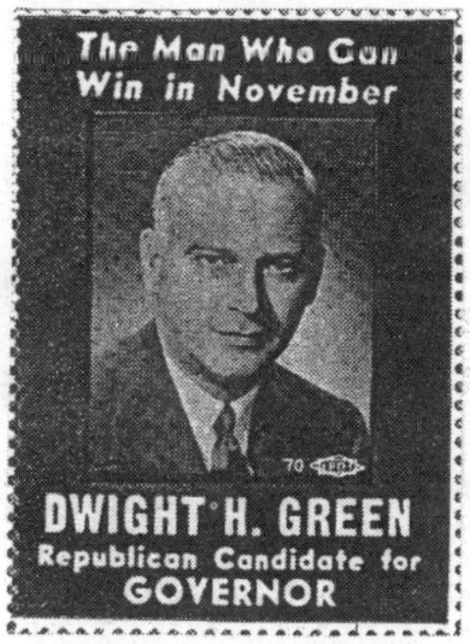

L-226 BkGr (IL) .50-2.
Sheets of six (3x2). SE:LBR, MIT: Vote for the Man Who Can Win in November/DWIGHT H. GREEN/REPUBLICAN CANDIDATE FOR GOVERNOR/Place these gummed stickers on all letters which you mail to your friends in Illinois. For additional stamps call Central 4315. COPYRIGHT REGISTERED 1940—GEO. B. DIETRICH—SIMPLEX PRINTING CO. MONROE 7048.

Local Offices, Minor State Offices, and Unknown Office

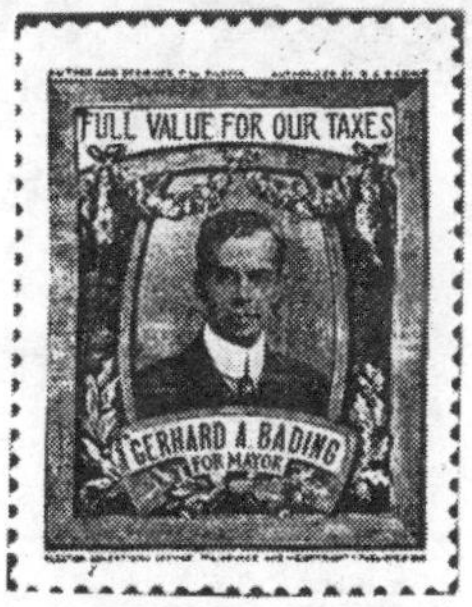

L-301 R 1.-3.
L-301a Br 1.-3.
L-301b Tn 1.-3.

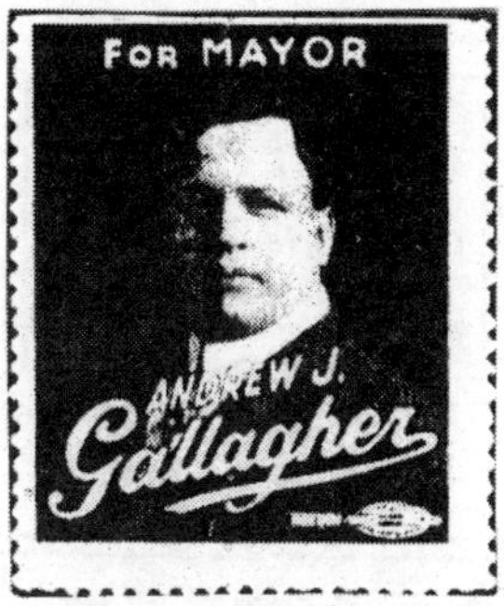

L-302 Br 1.-3.

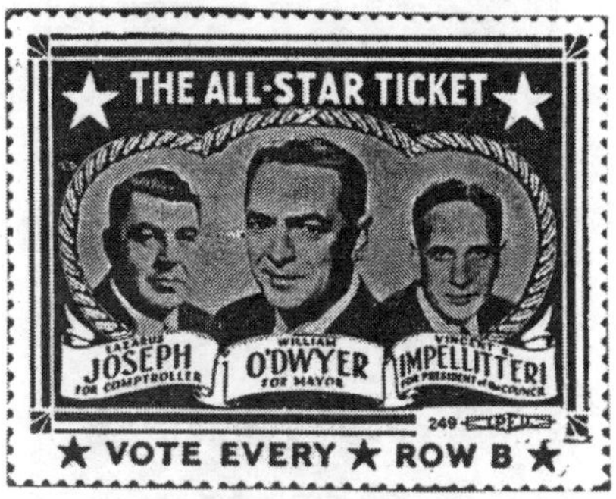

L-303 Gr (NYC) .50-2.

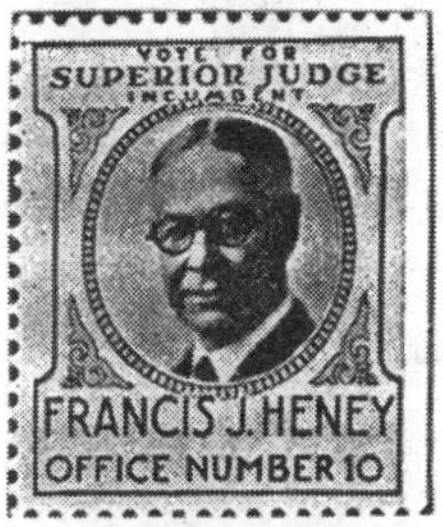

L-304 B .50-2.

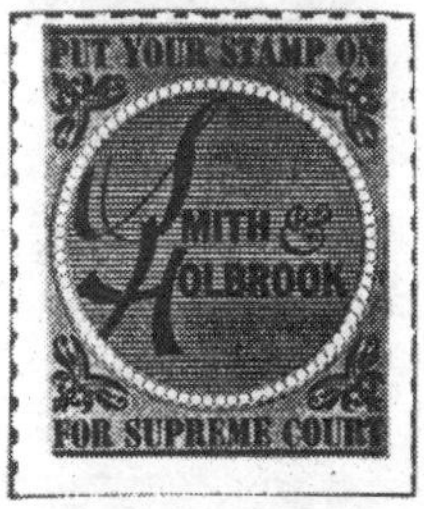

L-305 BkGr .50-2.

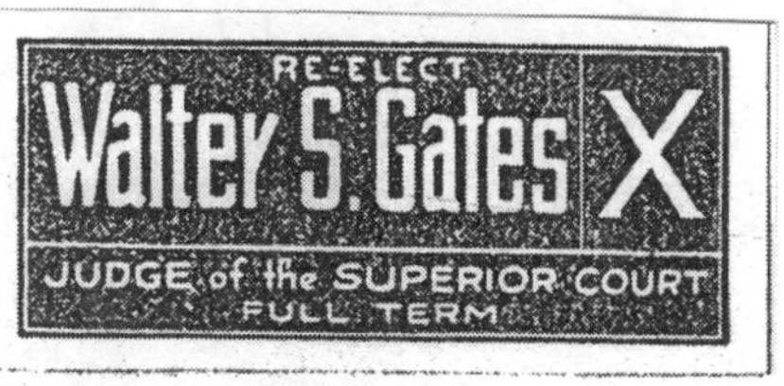

Picture shown at 85%

L-306 .50-2.

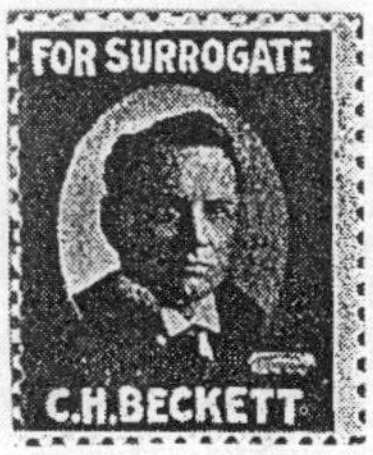

L-307 B .50-2.

L-308   B   .50-2.

L-309   .50-2.

Picture shown at 85%

L-310   .50-2.

L-311   .50-2.

Picture shown at 75%

L-312   .50-2.

L-313   .50-2.

L-314   .50-2.

L-315   .50-2.

Picture shown at 85%

L-316   .50-2.

L-317   RB   .50-2.

Picture shown at 75%

L-318   Gr   .50-2.

L-319   BBkGy   .50-2.

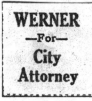

L-320   R   .50-2.

Picture shown at 85%

L-321   .50-2.

L-322   .50-2.

Picture shown at 85%

L-323   .50-2.

L-324   .50-2.

L-325   .50-2.

Picture shown at 85%

L-326   .50-2.

Picture shown at 90%

L-327   .50-2.

L-328   .50-2.

Picture shown at 80%

L-329   2.-4.

Picture shown at 85%

L-330   (PA, 1914)   2.-4.

L-331   (Montana 1964)   .50-2.
L-332   (Montana 1964)   .50-2.
Part of a sheet of thirteen different.

L-333   (Montana 1964)   .50-2.
L-334   (Montana 1964)   .50-2.
Part of a sheet of thirteen different.

L-335   (Montana 1964)   .50-2.
L-336   (Montana 1964)   .50-2.
Part of a sheet of thirteen different.

L-337   (Montana 1964)   .50-2.
L-338   (Montana 1964)   .50-2.
Part of a sheet of thirteen different.

L-339   R (NYC, 1969)   .50-2.

L-340   RBk   .50-2.

L-341   .50-2.

L-342   .50-2.

L-343 Bk/Gd   .50-1.

Picture shown at 80%

L-344 Bk   .50-2.

Picture shown at 80%

L-345 B   .50-2.

L-346   .50-2.

For State Engineer and Surveyor,
HORATIO SEYMOUR, Jr.

L-347 Bk/Or   1.-3.
L-348 Bk/Y   1.-3.

Get Out the Vote Stamps

Picture shown at 85%

V-1 RB (1924)   2.-4.

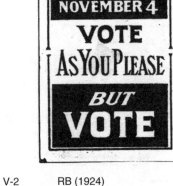

V-2 RB (1924)   2.-4.

V-3 RB (1932)   .50-2.

V-4 RB (1940)   .50-2.

V-5 RB (1944)   .50-2.

V-6 RB (1948)   .50-2.

VOTE NOV. 6
BE A *good* CITIZEN!

Picture shown at 70%

V-7 (1952)   .50-2.

V-8   .50-2.

V-9   MC (1960)   .50-2.
Issued by Amvets.

V-10   MC (1976)   .50-2.
Issued by Amvets.

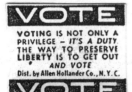

V-11   .50-2.

V-12   .50-2.

V-13   RGr   .50-2.

V-14   RB   .50-2.

V-15   RB   .50-2.

V-16   RB   .50-2.

V-17   .50-2.

V-18   .50-2.

V-19   .50-2.

Picture shown at 120%

V-20   BkGr   .50-2.
Printed on S&H green stamp.

V-21   RB   .50-2.

V-22   RB   .50-2.

Picture shown at 90%

V-23   MC   .50-2.

Picture shown at 60%

V-24　　　R　　　　　　　　　　　　.50-2.

From MAD Magazine.

Picture shown at 85%

V-25　　　　　　　　　　　　　　　.50-2.

If you have any items which are not pictured in this book but should be, please send photocopies to the author in care of Krause Publications, 700 E. State St., Iola, WI 54990-0001.

Fantasy Candidates

F-1　　　MC　　　　　　　　　　　1.-2.

From MAD Magazine, 1964.

F-2　　　MC　　　　　　　　　　　1.-2.

From a Swedish version of MAD Magazine.

F-3

F-13

Picture shown at 85%

F-3	MC "Vote MAD"	.50-1.
F-4	MC "Not just another..."	.50-1.
F-5	MC "YECCH"	.50-1.
F-6	MC "Amid the uncertainty..."	.50-1.
F-7	MC "Bring back..."	.50-1.
F-8	MC "He understands..."	.50-1.
F-9	MC "America is on..."	.50-1.
F-10	MC "W.I.N...."	.50-1.
F-11	MC "E. Pluribus..."	.50-1.
F-12	MC "Don't Waste..."	.50-1.
F-13	MC "The one..."	.50-1.
F-14	MC "Put some..."	.50-1.
F-15	MC "It's the least..."	.50-1.
F-16	MC "We don't have..."	.50-1.
F-17	MC "We've always..."	.50-1.
F-18	MC "Voting for..."	.50-1.
F-19	MC "Sure he's..."	.50-1.
F-20	MC "He'll keep..."	.50-1.

F-21	MC "A car in..."	.50-1.
F-22	MC "You could..."	.50-1.
F-23	MC "Put Alfred..."	.50-1.
F-24	MC "Foreign powers..."	.50-1.

From MAD Magazine, 1980. Issue contains twenty-four copies of F-3 and twenty-four different larger stamps similar to F-4.

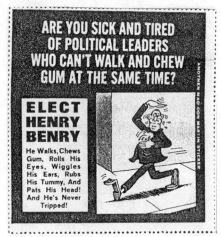

F-28

Picture shown at 75%

F-25	MC "It's the least..."	.50-1.
F-26	MC "We don't have..."	.50-1.
F-27	MC "Let's end..."	.50-1.
F-28	MC "Are you sick..."	.50-1.
F-29	MC "Help the..."	.50-1.
F-30	MC "Let's get rid..."	.50-1.
F-31	MC "Let's get back..."	.50-1.
F-32	MC "What can..."	.50-1.
F-33	MC "Let's bring..."	.50-1.
F-34	MC "Vote "who cares..."	.50-1.
F-35	MC "Want decent..."	.50-1.
F-36	MC "Vote smut..."	.50-1.
F-37	MC "This year..."	.50-1.
F-38	MC "It's time..."	.50-1.

From MAD Magazine, 1976.

Chapter 3
Civil Rights

It may be hard to believe today, but when our nation was founded only white males could vote. Since then both women and minorities have won the right to vote, and other groups have fought for expanded political rights. Campaign stamps have played a part in the campaigns of many of these groups, and their stories are told in this chapter.

Labels issued by the Ku Klux Klan were hard to categorize in this book. While their cause may be considered political, their interest was negative rather than positive because they were against rights for certain groups. Because their position was in opposition to groups in this chapter, they are included here.

Women

Votes for Women

The campaign for woman suffrage began in the nineteenth century and ended in the ratification of the nineteenth amendment to the U. S. Constitution effective August 26, 1920, just in time for the 1920 election of Warren G. Harding over James Cox.

W-1   BkYGy   20.-50.

W-2   GrPu   20.-50.

W-3   GrPu   20.-50.

W-4   Bk/Y   5.-10

W-5   15.-30.

VOTES FOR WOMEN

Picture shown at 50%

W-6   BGr   15.-30.

W-7   Gr Y Bk Tu   20.-50.

VOTES FOR WOMEN

W-8   Gr Pu   15.-30.

W-9   Bk Y R   15.-30.

VOTES For WOMEN

W-10   Bk/Y   10.-20.

VOTES FOR WOMEN

Picture shown at 90%
W-11   GrPu   25.-50.

VOTES FOR WOMEN

Picture shown at 67%
W-12   GrPu   25.-50.

Picture shown at 90%
W-13   BTuTn (English)   15.-30.
W-14   BrYTn (English)   15.-30.
W-15   BTuTn (Hungarian)   10.-20.
W-16   BrYTn (Hungarian)   10.-20.
W-17   BTuTn (German)   10.-20.
W-18   BrYTn (German)   10.-20.
W-19   BTuTn (French)   10.-20.
W-20   BrYTn (French)   10.-20.

Picture shown at 80%
W-21   RBBk   20.-30.

Picture shown at 85%
W-22   GrPu   20.-50.

Picture shown at 85%
W-23   BkYB   10.-20.

Picture shown at 85%
W-24   RBY   15.-30.

Picture shown at 85%
W-25   RB   20.-40.

Picture shown at 85%
W-26   BK   20.-40.

Picture shown at 90%
W-27   BYRGy   20.-50.

WOMEN VOTE IN HALF THE TERRITORY
OF THE UNITED STATES
WHY NOT IN NEW YORK?
JOIN THE MAJORITY
VOTE YES ON THE
WOMAN SUFFRAGE AMENDMENT
NOVEMBER 2, 1915

Picture shown at 62%
W-28   B   20.-50.

Picture shown at 80%
W-29   BKOr   20.-50.

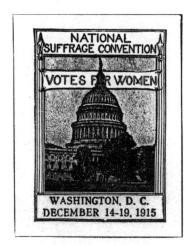

W-30   BK YTu   15.-30.

W-31   20.-50.
Date has been handwritten on this copy of stamp.

W-32   20.-50.
Date has been handwritten on this copy of stamp.

W-33   20.-40.

W-34   BK Y   15.-30.

W-35   Gr Pu   20.-50.

W-36   20.-50.

W-37   BkB   10.-20.
Booklets of 100.

W-38   BY   10.-20.

W-39   B   10.-20.

W-40   B   10.-20.

W-41   15.-30.

W-42   15.-30.

W-43   BKR   15.-30.

W-44   15.-30.

W-45   GrR   15.-30.

W-46   GrPu   15.-30.

W-47   Gr Pu   10.-20.

W-48   B   15.-30.

W-49   B/Y   20.-50.

Picture shown at 85%
W-50   MC   20.-50.

Picture shown at 90%
W-51   20.-50.

W-52   15.-30.

W-53   10.-20.

W-54   15.-30.

W-55   20.-40.

W-56   15.-30.

W-57   15.-30.

W-58   20.-50.

W-59   15.-30.

W-60   15.-30.

Picture shown at 90%
W-61   15.-30.

W-62   15.-30.

W-63   10.-20.

W-64   10.-20.

VOTES for Women

W-65   10.-20.

W-66   15.-30.

Picture shown at 75%
W-67   15.-30.

W-68   20.-50.

1919   1934

ANNIVERSARY
OF THE
RATIFICATION
OF THE
19th AMENDMENT

For centuries Women had
nothing to say!

Picture shown at 80%
W-69   10.-20.

W-70   B   10.-20.

W-71   OrBk   10.-20.

W-72   B   10.-20.

W-73   Pu   10.-20.

W-74   B   10.-20.
W-75   R   10.-20.
W-76   Tn   10.-20.
W-77   Pu   10.-20.
W-78   Or   10.-20.

Women's Rights (General)

W-101   5.-10.

W-102   3.-6.

W-103   .50-2.

W-104   3.-6.

W-105   1.-3.

Picture shown at 75%
W-201   BKR Pk   10.-30.

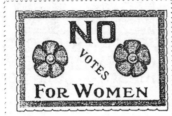

Picture shown at 75%
W-202   1.-3.

THIS IS
Women's Lib Week
TAKE A BROAD TO LUNCH
AND MAKE HER PAY!

ANOTHER MAD STICKER

Picture shown at 75%
W-203   1.-3.
From MAD Magazine.

WOMEN'S LIB IS Ms.GUIDED
ANOTHER MAD STICKER

Picture shown at 70%
W-204   1.-3.
From MAD Magazine.

THIS URINAL RESERVED FOR WOMEN'S LIB
ANOTHER MAD STICKER

Picture shown at 70%
W-205   1.-3.
From MAD Magazine.

FOR OTHER WOMEN'S ISSUES STAMPS, SEE PPD-3 IN CHAPTER 2 AND AW-10 THROUGH 18 IN CHAPTER 6.

Blacks

B-1   Bk (1932)   3.-6.
Sheet of 100 (10x10) SE:LBR MIT; "THEY SHALL NOT DIE SAVE THE NINE INNOCENT NEGRO SCOTTSBURO BOYS!..." (four more lines)

B-2   B/B (1934)   5.-10.
Sheet of 100 (10x10).

FOR IMMEDIATE RELEASE OF SCOTTSBORO BOYS
— ALL OUT —
Union Sq. **MAY 1** at 2 p.m.
United Front May Day Committee

B-3   R   10.-20.

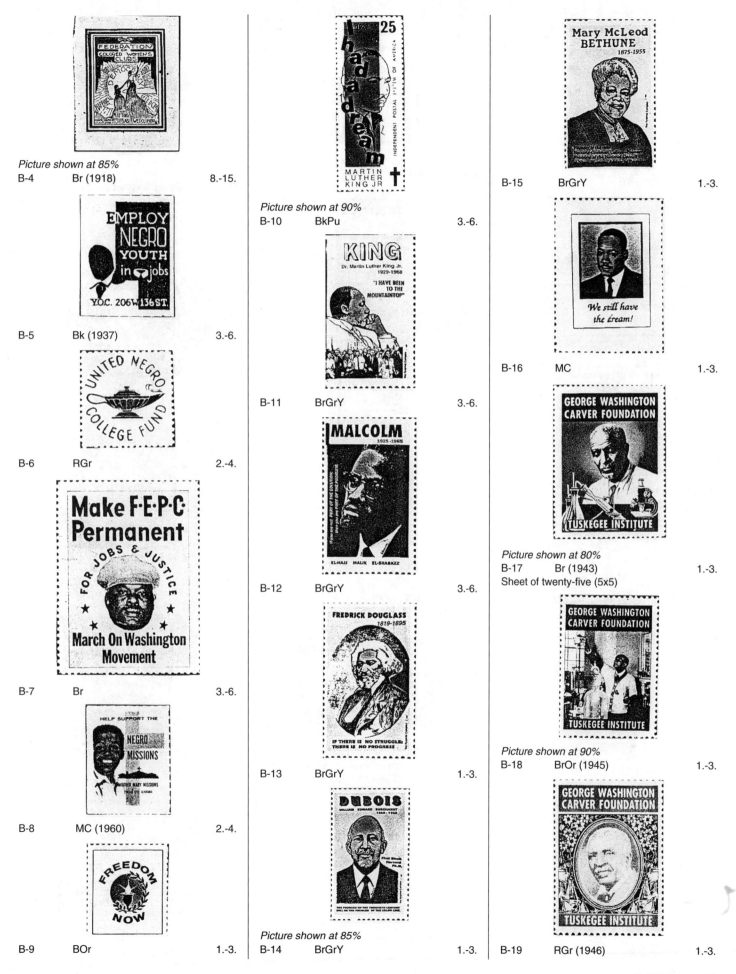

Picture shown at 85%
B-4   Br (1918)   8.-15.

B-5   Bk (1937)   3.-6.

B-6   RGr   2.-4.

B-7   Br   3.-6.

B-8   MC (1960)   2.-4.

B-9   BOr   1.-3.

Picture shown at 90%
B-10   BkPu   3.-6.

B-11   BrGrY   3.-6.

B-12   BrGrY   3.-6.

B-13   BrGrY   1.-3.

Picture shown at 85%
B-14   BrGrY   1.-3.

B-15   BrGrY   1.-3.

B-16   MC   1.-3.

Picture shown at 80%
B-17   Br (1943)   1.-3.
Sheet of twenty-five (5x5)

Picture shown at 90%
B-18   BrOr (1945)   1.-3.

B-19   RGr (1946)   1.-3.

Picture shown at 85%
B-20   BY (1947)   .50-2.

Picture shown at 85%
B-21   BR (1948)   .50-2.

Picture shown at 90%
B-22   BrY (1949)   .50-2.

Picture shown at 80%
B-23   RB (1950)   .50-2.

Picture shown at 75%
B-24   RB (1951)   .50-2.

Picture shown at 85%

B-25	MaB (1952)	2.-4.
B-25a	MaB (1952)	3.-6.
B-25b	Imperf. pair (proof)	8.-15.

B-26   BSi (1949)   1.-3.

B-27   OrB (1950)   1.-3.

B-28   RBr (1952)   1.-3.

B-29   GrR (1956)   4.-8.
Sheet of 100 (10x10).

B-30   MC (1956) (full sheet)   5.-10
Sheet of fifty (5x10) different license plates (forty-eight states, DC and AK). See page 87.

B-31   Br Gr (1958)   1.-2.
Piney Woods School was a school for black children.

B-32	Gr/Go foil (1959)	1.-2.
B-33	Br/Go foil(1959)	1.-2.
B-34	R/ Go foil (1959)	1.-2.

B-35   Bl/Si foil (1959)   1.-2.

B-36   BkBr (1936)   2.-4.

B-37   BkR   2.-4.

B-38   BkB   2.-4.

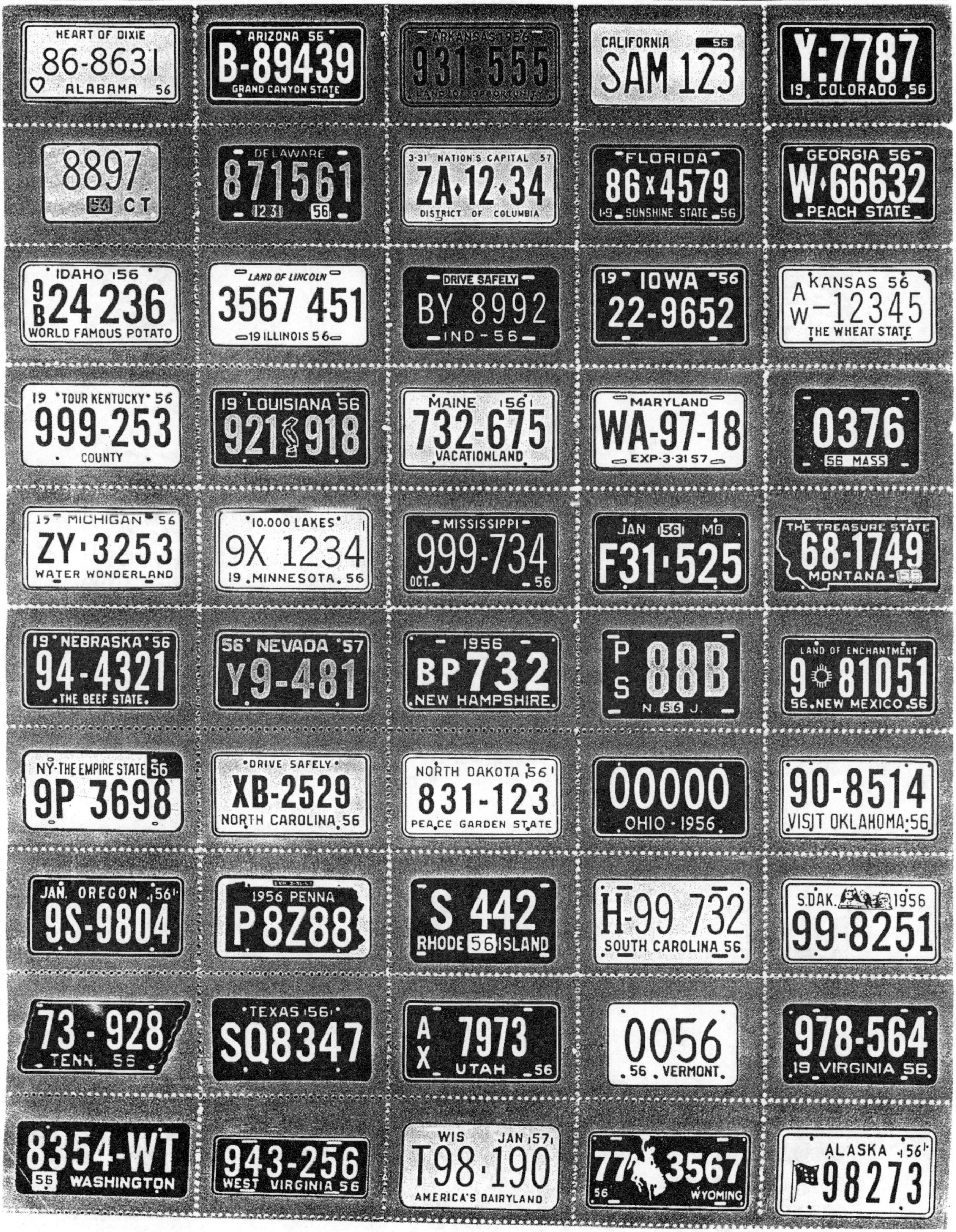

Individual stamps would be numbered from B-30A to B-30XX

B-101   GrR (1927-8)   8.-15.
Pane of twenty (5x4).

B-102   GrR (1929)   8.-15.
Pane of twenty (5x4).

B-103   GrR (1930)   8.-15.
Pane of twenty (5x4).

B-104   GrR (1931)   10.-20.
Differs from 1930 in that the bottom nub has
been removed from the scale.
Pane of twenty (5x4).

B-105   BkTu (1932)   3.-6.
Pane of twenty (5x4).

B-106   GrR (1933)   2.-4.

B-107   GrR (1934) (perf.14)   2.-4.
Pane of twenty (5x4).

B-108   GrR (1935-6) (perf.12.5)   1.-3.
Pane of twenty (5x4).

B-109   GrR (1937-8)   1.-2.
Pane of twenty-five (5x5).

B-110   Bk/Si (1939)   1.-2.
Pane of twenty-five (5x5).

B-111   RSi (1940)   1.-2.
Pane of twenty-five (5x5).

B-112   BSi (1941)   1.-2.
Pane of twenty (5x4).

B-113   GrSi (1942)   .50-1.
Pane of 100 (10x10).

B-114   R (1943)   .50-1.
Pane of twenty-five (5x5).

B-115   BkR (1944)   1.-2.
Pane of twenty-five (5x5).

B-116   GrR (1945)   .50-1.
Pane of twenty-five (5x5).

B-117   B (1946)   .50-1.
Pane of twenty-five (5x5).

B-118   GrR (1947)   .50-1.
Pane of twenty-five (5x5).

B-119   BrGr (1948)   .50-1.
Pane of twenty-five (5x5).

B-120   GrR (1949)   .50-1.
Sheet of 100 (10x10).

B-121   R (1950)   .50-1.
Sheet of 100 (10x10).

B-122   R (1951)   .50-1.
Sheet of 100 (10x10).

B-123   GrR (1952)   .50-1.
Sheet of 100 (10x10).

B-124   R (1953)   .50-1.
Sheet of 100 (10x10).

B-125   GrR (1954)   .50-1.
Sheet of 100 (10x10).

B-126   GrR (1955)   .50-1.
Sheet of 100 (10x10).

B-127   GrR (1956)   .50-1.
Sheet of 100 (10x10).

B-128A   Gr (1957)   .50-1.
B-128B   R (1957)   .50-1.
Sheet of 100 (10x10) contains alternating designs.

B-129A   Gr (1958)   .50-1.
B-129B   R (1958)   .50-1.
Sheet of 100 (10x10) contains alternating designs.

B-130A   BGo (1959)   .50-1.
B-130B   BGo (1959)   .50-1.
Sheet of seventy-two (9x8) contains alternating designs.

B-131A   DkBLtBGo (1960)   .50-1.
B-131B   DkBGo (1960)   1.-2.
Sheet of 100 (10x10) contains eighty of B-131A and twenty of B-131B.

B-132   BGo (1960)   .50-1.
Sheet of 100 (10x10).

B-133A   RBGo (1961)   .50-1.
B-133B   BGo (1961)   1.-2.
Sheet of 100 (10x10) contains eighty of B-133A and twenty of B-133B.

B-134A   RGrGo (1962)   .50-1.
B-134B   GrGo (1962)   1.-2.
Sheet of 100 (10x10) contains eighty-eight of B-134A and twelve of B-134B.

B-135A   BkBGo (1963)   .50-1.
B-135B   BGo (1963)   1.-2.
Sheet of 100 (10x10) contains eighty of B-135A and twenty of B-135B.

B-136A   BGo (1964)   .50-1.

B-136B   BGo (1964)   1.-2.
Sheet of 100 (10x10) contains eighty of B-136A
and twenty of B-136B.

B-137A   DkBLtBGo (1965)   .50-1.
B-137B   DkBGo (1965)   1.-2.
Sheet of 100 (10x10) contains eighty of B-137A
and twenty of B-137B.

B-138A   MC (1966)   .50-1.
B-138B   BRGo (1966)   1.-2.
Sheet of 100 (10x10) contains eighty of B-138A
and twenty of B-138B.

B-139A   RGrGo (1967)   .50-1.
B-139B   GrGo (1967)   1.-2.
Sheet of 100 (10x10) contains eighty of B-139A
and twenty of B-139B.

B-140A   RGrGo (1968)   .50-1.
B-140B   GrGo (1968)   1.-2.
Sheet of 100 (10x10) contains eighty of B-140A
and twenty of B-140B.

B-141A   DkBrRGrGo (1969)   .50-1.
B-141B   RGo (1969)   1.-2.
Sheet of 100 (10x10) contains eighty of B-141A
and twenty of B-141B.

B-142A   BkRGr (1970)   .50-1.
B-142B   R (1970)   1.-2.
Sheet of 100 (10x10) contains eighty of B-142A
and twenty of B-142B.

B-143A   DkBLtBGo (1971)   .50-1.
B-143B   DkBGo (1971)   1.-2.
Sheet of 100 (10x10) contains eighty of B-143A
and twenty of B-143B.

B-144A   LtGrDkGrGo (1972)   .50-1.
B-144B   RGo (1972)   1.-2.
Sheet of 100 (10x10) contains eighty of B-140A
and twenty of B-140B.

B-145A   MC (1973)   .50-1.
B-145B   B (1973)   1.-2.
Sheet of 100 (10x10) contains eighty of B-145A
and twenty of B-145B.

B-146A   MC (1974)   .50-1.
B-146B   R (1974)   1.-2.
Sheet of 100 (10x10) contains eighty of B-146A
and twenty of B-146B.

B-147A   RGr (1975)   .50-1.
B-147B   R (1975)   1.-2.
Sheet of 100 (10x10) contains eighty of B-147A
and twenty of B-147B.

B-148A   RB (1976)   .50-1.
B-148B   R (1976)   1.-2.
Sheet of 100 (10x10) contains eighty of B-148A
and twenty of B-148B.

B-149A   MC (1977)   .50-1.
B-149B   R (1977)   1.-2.
Sheet of 100 (10x10) contains eighty of B-149A
and twenty of B-149B.

Political Prisoners and Defense Funds

The following stamps were issued to raise funds or support for political prisoners or those alleged to be political prisoners. The author is aware that some people alleged to be political prisoners were actually common criminals, but rather than make that judgment the section includes any stamps issued for someone claimed to be a political prisoner.

PP-1   B (1911)   10.-20.

PP-2   RB (1911)   5.-10.

PP-3   Bk/Y (1937)   8.-15.

PP-4   Bk   5.-10.

Angelo Herndon was believed to be a member of the Communist party charged with insurrection in Atlanta, Georgia, for protesting inhumane treatment of the unemployed.

PP-5   B/B   2.-4.
PP-6   B/Or   5.-10.
PP-7   B/Gr   8.-15.

Panes of twenty (10x2).

PP-8   RB   4.-8.

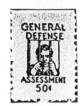

PP-9   Gr   4.-8.

Booklets of two panes of ten (5x2). Issued by IWW.

PP-10   B (1922)   5.-10.
PP-11   B (1923)   5.-10.
PP-12   R (1924)   5.-10.

Picture shown at 80%

PP-13   Bk   5.-10.

PP-14   Bk (1935)   3.-6.

PP-15   GrR (1937)   3.-6.

Sheets of 100 (10x10).

PP-16   Gr   4.-8.

PP-17 $1 Y   3.-6.

PP-18 $2 Br   3.-6.

PP-19 $3 B   3.-6.

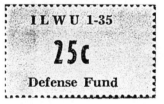

PP-20   25¢ Gr/B   1.-3.
PP-21   50¢ Gr/Y   2.-4.
PP-22 $1 Gr   3.-6.

International Longshoremen's and Warehousemen's Union.

PP-23   3.-6.

PP-24   DkBLtBOrBr (1938)   2.-4.

PP-25   DkBLtB (1939)   3.-6.
Same as PP-24, but two ink colors have been
omitted.

PP-26   Bk   3.-6.

PP-27   Bk   2.-4.

PP-29   MC   .50-2.

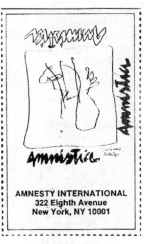

PP-30   MC   .50-2.

PP-31   Bk   .50-2.

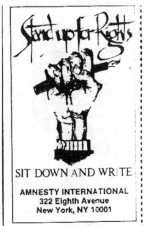

PP-32   MC   .50-2.

PP-33   MC   .50-2.

Issued by Amnesty International, New York, NY,
in sheets containing one each of PP-29, 30, 32,
33, and two of PP-31.

Picture shown at 110%
PP-34   .50-2.
From MAD Magazine.

Picture shown at 125%
PP-35   .50-2.
From MAD Magazine. This was a parody of the
"Free Huey Newton" campaign.

The right to read and view material that others deem offensive is one that has been fought over in the courts time and again. Judging by the stamps, those against such rights are more active in their campaign.

| CEN-1 | RB | 1.-3. |

| CEN-2 | RBBk | .50-2. |

RESTORE DECENCY
CLEAN UP AMERICA

| CEN-3 | Bk | .50-1. |

| CEN-4 | BkPk | .50-2. |

| CEN-5 | BkPk | .50-2. |

| CEN-6 | BkPk | .50-2. |

| CEN-7 | R | 1.-2. |

DO NOT BUY OR READ
INDECENT LITERATURE
Tell your friends to do likewise

| CEN-8 | | .50-2. |

WHAT DO THEY READ?

STAMP **O**UT **S**MUT!

Citizens For Decent Literature, Inc.

| CEN-9 | RBk | .50-2. |

᛭ uu. 3096 ᛭
von **DENIED**

No! Our letters are not yet opened by Nazi censors, and they won't be if we

FIGHT FOR FREEDOM

Fight For Freedom Committee
111 W. Washington St.,
Chicago, Ill.

Picture shown at 120%
| CEN-101 | Bk | 1.-3. |

CENSORSHIP IN A FREE SOCIETY.
IT'S A BAD MATCH.
People For The American Way

| CEN-102 | MC | 1.-3. |
Note: "AGE" on the illustration is part of a postal marking.

Miscellaneous Rights

District of Columbia voting rights

MR-1   Bk   2.-4.

General Rights

MR-2   B   2.-4.

MR-3   GrR   1.-3.
MR-4   BR   1.-3.

Anti-Civil Rights

Ku Klux Klan

ACR-1   R   10.-20.

Picture shown at 85%
ACR-2   R   10.-20.

ACR-3   RB   8.-15.

Picture shown at 85%
ACR-4   R   8.-15.

ACR-5   R   8.-15.

ACR-6   10.-20.

ONE BRICK

K. K. K.

ACR-7   R   5.-10.

ACR-8   10.-20.

ACR-9   8.-15.

KNIGHTS of the KU KLUX KLAN

Wanted 100 percent Americans
No others need apply.
For information write
P. O. Lock Box 1548, Phila., Pa.

The old State of Pennsylvania is not what it used to be
Since the Ku Klux Klan came to town.

ACR-10   10.-20.

Wake Up America!

1918·
    we fought to make the world Safe for Democracy! - -   and now:

1941:
    are we going to make the world safe

for de mockies?

כשר

19??:   Jewnited States of America

Picture shown at 90%
ACR-101   Bk   4.-8.

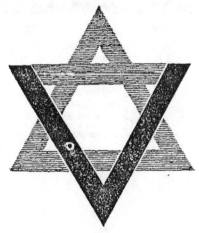

ACR-102   Bk (1934)   4.-8.

Break His Stranglehold!

BUY GENTILE!

Picture shown at 85%
ACR-103   Bk/Gd   5.-10.

Don't Let It Happen Here!

BUY GENTILE!

Picture shown at 60%
ACR-104   Bk/Gd   8.-15

Some commentators have predicted that animals will be the next group to be granted rights in society. Whether or not this is true is yet to be seen. In the meantime several groups have issued stamps to promote the rights of animals. While the author has not considered these to be political enough to include a complete listing, here are a few to show you a sample of what is available.

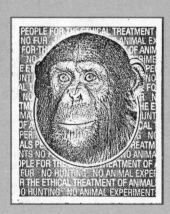

Chapter 4

Economic Causes

This chapter covers stamps which were issued for all types of economic causes, including labor unions and strikes, communism, pensions, Medicare, taxes, the Great Depression, the National Recovery Administration, Buy American campaigns, and a few others.

While some may argue that labor union items go in the previous chapter under civil rights, the underlying issues are usually economic, so they are included here.

Labor Unions and Strikes

LU-1	3.-6.	
LU-2	4.-8.	
LU-3	2.-4.	
LU-4 Bk	2.-4.	
LU-5	2.-4.	
LU-6	2.-4.	
LU-7 B/Si	3.-6.	
LU-8	2.-4.	
LU-9 Bk/Or	1.-3.	
LU-10 R	3.-6.	
LU-11 Bk (1939)	2.-4.	

LU-12   R   2.-4.

Picture shown at 70%
LU-13   R   4.-8.

LU-14   BkR   2.-4.

LU-15   BkOr   2.-4.

Picture shown at 75%
LU-20   MC   4.-8.

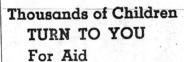

Picture shown at 65%
Attached pair of LU-21 and 22
LU-21   B/Pk   2.-4.
LU-22   BkB/Pk 10¢   2.-4.
LU-23   25¢   2.-4.
LU-24   50¢   2.-4.

LU-25   Bk   2.-4.

LU-26   2.-4.

LU-27   2.-4.

LU-28   Bk   2.-4.

LU-29   R   2.-4.

LU-30   (1931)   2.-4.

LU-31   2.-4.

LU-16 $1 Br (1947)   2.-4.
LU-17 $2 Gr (1946)   2.-4.
LU-18 $3 Gr/Pk (1946)   3.-6.
LU-19 $5 Gr/Gr (1946)   3.-6.

LU-32   Gr   2.-4.

LU-33   4.-8.

Picture shown at 80%
LU-34   4.-8.

DON'T READ The
TRIBUNE
The Voice of
REACTION
and FASCISM

Picture shown at 85%
LU-35   RB   4.-8.

Picture shown at 70%
LU-36   4.-8.

S. S.
KRESGE
STORES
ARE
UNFAIR
TO
ORGANIZED
LABOR

LU-37   Bk   3.-6.

LU-38   B (1937)   2.-4.

Picture shown at 90%
LU-39   B (1937)   2.-4.

LU-40   B (1937)   2.-4.
LU-40a   B   2.-4.
LU-40a has a larger "28" next to the union bug.

LU-41   BR   2.-4.

LU-42   Gr (1939)   3.-6.
LU-43   B (1939)   2.-4.
Sheets of 100 (10x10).

LU-44   Gr (1939)   3.-6.
LU-45   Or (1939)   4.-8.

BOYCOTT HEARST

Hearst's "Pay-triotism"
Has Made Him a
Millionaire!

*DON'T READ—DON'T ADVERTISE
IN HERALD-EXAMINER AND
CHICAGO AMERICAN*

Picture shown at 75%
LU-46   Bk   5.-10.

NEWSPAPER GUILD
ON STRIKE!
Don't Read
AMERICAN
and
EXAMINER
YOUR PENNIES PAY HEARST THUGS TO SLUG UNION MEN

Picture shown at 90%

LU-47	Bk/Gd (1939)	10.-20.
LU-48	Bk/Gr (1939)	10.-20.

DON'T BUY
HEARST'S
AMERICAN
and
EXAMINER
Don't Fight Union NEWSPAPERMEN ON STRIKE

LU-49	Bk/Y (1939)	10.-20.

Picture shown at 70%

LU-50	Bk/Gr (1939)	10.-20.

HEARST
IS A
FASCIST
●
BOYCOTT
HEARST NEWSPAPERS

Picture shown at 85%

LU-51	Gr	10.-20.

Picture shown at 90%

LU-52	B (1939)	10.-20.

HELP
ORGANIZE
THOMPSON PRODUCTS EMPLOYEES
●
U.A.W.A. — C.I.O.
LOCAL 300
See Your Local Secretary

Picture shown at 70%

LU-53		10.-20.

LU-54	R	2.-4.

LU-55		2.-4.

Picture shown at 75%

LU-56		3.-6.

Picture shown at 95%

LU-57		.50-1.

Another type of stamp issued by labor unions is the dues stamp, which is usually issued monthly. There are thousands of these, but because they do not promote a political cause we have not included them in this catalog. However, if you collect labor union material, you may wish to include them in your collection. Although they are not common, they are not in great demand, so when you come across them you can expect to pay anywhere from 10¢ to $1 for most of them.

Pictures shown at 50%

LU-58	MC (1971)	.50-1.
LU-59	MC (1971)	.50-1.
LU-60	MC (1971)	.50-1.
LU-61	MC (1971)	.50-1.
LU-62	MC (1971)	.50-1.
LU-63	MC (1971)	.50-1.
LU-64	MC (1971)	.50-1.
LU-65	MC (1971)	.50-1.
LU-66	MC (1971)	.50-1.
LU-67	MC (1971)	.50-1.
LU-68	MC (1971)	.50-1.
LU-69	MC (1971)	.50-1.

Sheets of forty-eight (8x6).

| LU-70 | Bk/B | 2.-4. |

Picture shown at 80%

| LU-71 | RB | 2.-4. |

| LU-72 | Bk/B | .50-2. |

| LU-73 | RB | .50-2. |

Picture shown at 90%

| LU-74 | RBkY | .50-2. |

International Workers of the World

Picture shown at 70%

| LU-101 | | 8.-15. |

Picture shown at 70%

| LU-102 | | 8.-15. |

Picture shown at 80%

| LU-103 | | 8.-15. |

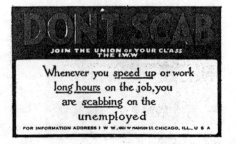

Picture shown at 90%

| LU-104 | | 8.-15. |

Picture shown at 70%
LU-105   8.-15.

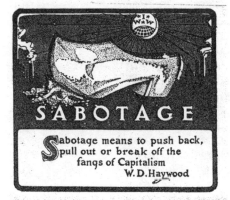

Picture shown at 95%
LU-106   8.-15.

LU-107   5.-10.

LU-108   8.-15.

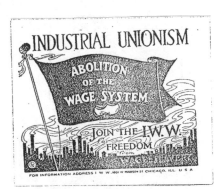

Picture shown at 70%
LU-109   8.-15.

Picture shown at 85%
LU-110   8.-15.

Picture shown at 85%
LU-111   8.-15.

Picture shown at 70%
LU-112   8.-15.

Picture shown at 75%
LU-113   5.-10.

Picture shown at 75%
LU-114   8.-15.

Picture shown at 85%
LU-115   Bk   5.-10

LU-116   Bk/Pk   3.-6.

LU-117   R   2.-4.

| LU-118 | R | | 2.-4. |

| LU-119 | Gr | | 2.-4. |

Overprint "I.U. 120" in red is hard to see.

| LU-120 | R | | 2.-4. |

Picture shown at 120%

| LU-121 | Gr | | 2.-4. |

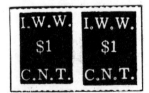

| LU-122 | R | | 2.-4. |
| LU-123 | Bk | | 2.-4. |

Picture shown at 120%

| LU-124 | R | | 1.-3. |

| LU-125 | R | | 2.-4. |

| LU-126 | R | | 8.-15. |

See also PP-9

Women's International Auxiliary to International Typographical Union

LU-201

LU-243

LU-248

Stamps are various designs.

LU-201	RGr (1935)		1.-3.
LU-201	RGr (1938)		4.-8.
LU-202	RGr (1939)		1.-3.
LU-203	RGr (1940)		1.-2.
LU-204	SiGr (1941)		.50-1.
LU-205	SiB (1941)		.50-1.
LU-206	SiR (1941)		.50-1.
LU-207	SiB (1942)		.50-1.
LU-208	SiR (1942)		.50-1.
LU-209	SiGr (1943)		.50-1.
LU-210	SiR (1943)		.50-1.
LU-211	SiB (1944)		.50-1.
LU-212	PuPk (1944)		.50-1.
LU-213	SiMa (1945)		.50-1.
LU-214	SiR (1945)		.50-1.
LU-215	SiGr (1945)		.50-1.
LU-216	RGr (1945)		.50-1.
LU-217	SRB (1945)		.50-1.
LU-218	DkRGr (1946)		.50-1.
LU-219	RGr (1946)		.50-1.
LU-220	Gr (1947)		.50-1.
LU-221	R (1947)		.50-1.
LU-222	Gr (1948)		.50-1.
LU-223	R (1948)		.50-1.
LU-224	RGrSi (1948)		1.-2.
LU-225	Gr (1949)		.50-1.
LU-226	R (1949)		.50-1.
LU-227	B (1950)		.50-1.
LU-228	R (1951)		.50-1.
LU-229	BY (1952)		.50-1.
LU-230	R (1953)		.50-1.
LU-231	Gr (1954)		.50-1.
LU-232	B (1955)		.50-1.
LU-233	B (1956)		.50-1.
LU-234	Br (1956)		.50-1.
LU-235	R (1957)		.50-1.
LU-236	R/Gr (1958)		.50-1.
LU-237	R/Gr (1958)		.50-1.
LU-238	B (1959)		.50-1.
LU-239	BY (1960)		.50-1.
LU-240	SiR (1961)		.50-1.
LU-241	SiGr (1961)		.50-1.
LU-242	B (1962)		.50-1.
LU-243	B (1963)		.50-1.
LU-244	SiR (1964)		.50-1.
LU-245	R (1965)		.50-1.
LU-246	Pu (1966)		.50-1.
LU-247	SR (1967)		.50-1.
LU-248	RY (1968)		.50-1.
LU-249	Gr (1969)		.50-1.

International Typographical Union

| LU-251 | GoBk (1950) | | .50-1. |
| LU-252 | BrB (1952) | | .50-1. |

Communist Party

Picture shown at 80%
CS-1   10.-20.

CS-2   R   8.-15.

MAY FIRST
LABOR'S INTERNATIONAL HOLIDAY
CELEBRATE
(Communist Labor Party)

Picture shown at 80%
CS-3   R   5.-10.

INTERNATIONAL
LABOR DAY
MAY FIRST
DON'T WORK
(Communist Labor Party)

Picture shown at 85%
CS-4   R   5.-10.

OUT OF THE WORKSHOPS
MAY FIRST
Rest Up and Think
(Communist Labor Party)

Picture shown at 85%
CS-5   R   5.-10.

May Day
IS
Supreme
in Soviet
Russia
FOLLOW SUIT
(C. L. P.)

CS-6   R   5.-10.

MAY FIRST
YOUR DAY
STOP
WORK
INTERNATIONAL
LABOR DAY
1920
(C. L. P.)

CS-7   R   5.-10.

DOWN TOOLS
ONE DAY
MAY FIRST
1920
INTERNATIONAL
LABOR DAY
(C. L. P.)

CS-8   5.-10.

SHUT
UP
SHOPS
MAY FIRST
INTERNATIONAL
LABOR DAY
(C. L. P.)

CS-9   5.-10.

Picture shown at 90%
CS-10   R   8.-15.

UNITY
CONVENTION
1921
50c
Asses'nt Stamp

CS-11   5.-10.

10c Demonstrate April 30th 10c
Reyburn Plaza, 1 P. M.
Build the Democratic Front
For Social Security
Issued by The Communist Party
250 S. Broad Street
10c   10c

CS-12   R   5.-10.

CS-13   4.-8.

CS-14   50¢   2.-4.
CS-15 $1   2.-4.

Pictures shown at 85%
CS-16   RBk   5.-10.
Single stamps in booklets of twenty-five with
plain brown covers.

CS-17   RBk   4.-8.
Booklets of twenty-five panes of six (2x3) with
plain brown covers. SE:LBR

CS-18   3.-6.

CS-19   10¢ RBk   5.-10.
CS-20   50¢ RBk/B   5.-10.

CS-21 $1 RBk/Y   10.-20.
CS-22 $2 RBk/Gr   10.-20.
CS-23 $5 GrBk   10.-20.
Sheets of ten (2x5). SE:TRBL

CS-24   10.-20.

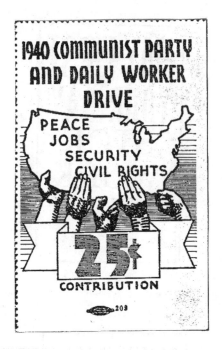

CS-25   R   10.-20.

CS-26   DkBLtB   8.-15.
The denomination appears to have been printed
separately, so there may be other denominations.

In 1944 the Communist Part endorsed
Roosevelt for president so this can be considered a Roosevelt item.

Pictures shown at 90%
CS-27   RB   5.-10.
CS-28   RB   5.-10.
Believed to be from 1944.

Picture shown at 90%
CS-29   B   5.-10.
Believed to be from 1944.

Socialist Party

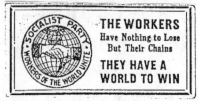

CS-101   B   2.-4.

The Masters Fear Slaves That
THINK
IF YOU THINK RIGHT YOU
WILL ACT RIGHT
STUDY SOCIALISM

CS-102   B   2.-4.

SOCIALISM
Means a chance for every body and abundance for all who toil. . . . . .

CS-103   B   2.-4.

CS-104   Bk/R   3.-6.

CS-105   2.-4.
This may be a paper for making a button rather than a stamp or sticker.

1934
STATE CAMPAIGN
NEW YORK
SOCIALIST PARTY
10c
CONTRIBUTION
201

CS-106   BkR   3.-6.

CS-107   R/Y   3.-6.

CS-108   1.-3.

CS-109   1.-3.

CS-110   1.-3.

Pro-Soviet Russia

CS-201   B   3.-5.

CS-202   B   3.-5.

CS-203   B   3.-5.

CS-204   B   3.-5.

CS-205   B   3.-5.

CS-206   B   3.-5.
CS-201 through CS-206 were isued in booklet panes of 8. One pane of each design was included in a booklet sold to raise money for the Red Army in the 1940s.

CS-207   Bk/B (1933)   4.-8.

CS-208   Bk (1933)   10.-20.

CS-209   Bk/Pk (1933)   10.-20.

CS-210   Br   3.-6.

If you have any items which are not pictured in this book but should be, please send photocopies to the author in care of Krause Publications, 700 E. State St., Iola, WI 54990-0001.

CS-211   R   3.-6.

Anti-Communism/Socialism

ACS-1   MC   1.-3.

Pictures shown at 95%
ACS-3   RB (1948)   1.-2.
Issued by the Anti-Communist Society of California.

Pictures shown at 90%
ACS-5   RB   .50-2.

ACS-6   RBBk (1962)   .50-2.
Issued by VFW Post 3639, Mt. Morris, Illinois.

ACS-7   RBBk   .50-2.
Mosbaugh claims this stamp was issued by "Fight Communism" of Los Angeles, CA. However, it appears to have been produced by the same source as ACS-6.

ACS-2   RBBk   1.-2.

ACS-4   BkYR (1965)   .50-2.

ACS-8   RBBk   .50-2.

ACS-9   RB   .50-2.
Issued by Marcia Matthews, MacAllen, TX, who also issued DMA-3 and PPO-1.

ACS-10   RBk (1968) (roulette)   .50-1.
ACS-11   RBk (1968) (perf.)   .50-1.

ACS-12   BkR   .50-1.
ACS-12A   BkR (no shading on edge)   .50-1.

ACS-13   GrR   .50-2.

ACS-14   B   .50-2.

ACS-15   .50-2.

ACS-16   DkRY (1954)   .50-2.
ACS-16   BPk (1955)   .50-2.
Issued by the Army & Navy Union, Lakemore, OH. Sheets of ninety (9x10)

Front

Back

ACS-17   RB (1940)   .50-2.

ACS-18   BR/Gr   .50-2.

ACS-19   RB   .50-2.

ACS-20   RB   .50-2.

ACS-21   RB (1951)   .50-2.

ACS-22   DkBLtBR   .50-2.

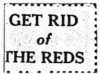

ACS-23   R   .50-2.
Sheets of eighty-eight (8x11). Issued by Jasperite Co., Omaha.

ACS-24   Bk   .50-1.

ACS-25   Bk   .50-2.
Sheets of eight (2x4) imperforate.
ACS-26   Bk/Gr   .50-2.
Single stamps distributed in pads.

ACS-27   R   1.-3.

ACS-28   RBk   1.-3.

ACS-29   BR   .50-2.

ACS-30   BR   .50-2.

ACS-31   B   .50-2.

OPPOSE
Socialism
Communism
SUPPORT
Catholic Action
Americanism
Catholic War
Veterans of
the U.S.A.

ACS-32   RB   .50-2.

REGISTER COMMIES
...NOT GUNS!

ACS-33   Bk   .50-1.

REGISTER COMMUNISTS
NOT FIREARMS

Pictures shown at 80%
ACS-34   RB   .50-2.

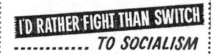

Pictures shown at 75%
ACS-35   RB   .50-2.

ACS-36   MC   .50-2.

ACS-37   (1923)   .50-2.
Issued by the Committee of Russian Anti-Communist Artists, New York, NY in sheets of 100
(10x10).

Pictures shown at 80%
ACS-38   RB   .50-2.

For God, for People, for Freedom!
JOIN THE
HOLY WAR
Against
Godless Communism!
The Free Press - V. Grundmanis, U.S.A.

ACS-39   .50-2.

FREEDOM FOR RUSSIA!
DOWN WITH COMMUNISM!
DON'T BELIEVE THE
COMMUNIST PROPAGANDA!
NEW YORK, JULY, 1959

Pictures shown at 70%
ACS-40   .50-2.

ACS-41   .50-2.

Help Fight Communism
Join Now
Veterans of World War I
201 So. MISSION DRIVE
SAN GABRIEL, CALIFORNIA

ACS-42   .50-2.

Biggest blow to block Communist
aims:
Sever All Relations With
Soviet Russia and Satellites!

ACS-43   .50-2.

ACS-44   .50-2.

Townsend Plan

The Townsend Plan was put forth in the 1930s by Dr. Francis E. Townsend as a system to allow the elderly to retire on a government pension paid out of the wages of workers. Clubs sprang up around the country to support it but it was never passed by Congress.

| SS-1 | RBk | 8.-15. |

| SS-2 | MC (1948) | 2.-4. |

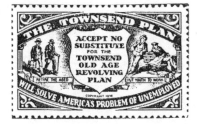

| SS-3 | B (1936) | 3.-5. |
| SS-4 | B (die cuts around curves) | 3.-5. |

| SS-5 | RBGr | 3.-5. |

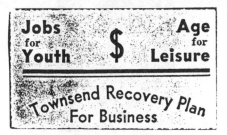

| SS-6 | BkY/B | 2.-4. |

| SS-7 | RB (1944) | 2.-4. |

| SS-8 | OrBk (1934) | 2.-4. |

| SS-9 | RB (1940) | 2.-4. |

| SS-10 | OrBk (1941) | 2.-4. |

> There is no
> Substitute
> for the
> Townsend
> Plan

| SS-11 | | 2.-4. |

This may be from the margin of a sheet of stamps of another design.

| SS-12 | BrOr (1943) | 2.-4. |

| SS-13 | RB (perf.) | 2.-4. |
| SS-14 | RB (roulette) | 2.-4. |

| SS-15 | BrTu | 2.-4 |

| SS-16 | | 2.-4. |

```
★  JOIN    THE  ★
★ TOWNSEND PARTY ★
```

Pictures shown at 90%

| SS-17 | Pu | 1.-3. |
| SS-18 | B | 1.-3. |

```
T JOIN  THE  P
  OWNSEND    ARTY
```

Pictures shown at 75%

| SS-19 | Pu | 1.-3. |
| SS-20 | B | 1.-3. |

```
T JOIN  THE  P
  OWNSEND    ARTY
```

Pictures shown at 85%

| SS-21 | Pu | 1.-3. |
| SS-22 | B | 1.-3. |

| SS-23 | Pu | 1.-3. |
| SS-24 | B | 1.-3. |

SS-25	RB "Attend... your"	2.-4.
SS-26	RB "Attend... TOWNSEND"	2.-4.
SS-27	RB "Boost the..."	2.-4.
SS-28	RB "Both (Democratic..."	2.-4.
SS-29	RB "...committee..."	2.-4.
SS-30	RB "Do Not..."	2.-4.
SS-31	RB "Everyone is..."	2.-4.
SS-32	RB "Have you looked..."	2.-4.
SS-33	RB "Have you read..."	2.-4.
SS-34	RB "HIRED..."	2.-4.
SS-35	RB "Hypothetical..."	2.-4.
SS-36	RB "If you wish..."	2.-4.
SS-37	RB "Inadequate..."	2.-4.
SS-38	RB "Insist that..."	2.-4.
SS-39	RB "Isn't it..."	2.-4.
SS-40	RB "It is an..."	2.-4.
SS-41	RB "It would..."	2.-4.
SS-42	RB "No just..."	2.-4.
SS-43	RB "Political..."	2.-4.
SS-44	RB "Read the TOWNSEND..."	2.-4.
SS-45	RB "Read... TOWNSEND..."	2.-4.
SS-46	RB "Remember this..."	2.-4.
SS-47	RB "Retirement..."	2.-4.
SS-48	RB "Study and..."	2.-4.
SS-49	RB "Supporters..."	2.-4.
SS-50	RB "The MORE..."	2.-4.
SS-51	RB "The PATHFINDER..."	2.-4.
SS-52	RB "The President...	2.-4.
SS-53	RB "The Townsend..."	2.-4.
SS-54	RB "The Townsend...system"	2.-4.
SS-55	RB "The TOWNSEND..."	2.-4.
SS-56	RB "The TOWNSEND...for all"	2.-4.
SS-57	RB "The TOWNSEND...Plan!"	2.-4.
SS-58	RB "The T...factory."	2.-4.
SS-59	RB "The T...citizens."	2.-4.
SS-60	RB "THE T... balanced PROSPERITY."	2.-4.
SS-61	RB "THE T... is PROSPERITY."	2.-4.
SS-62	RB "The...for all."	2.-4.
SS-63	RB "Those who..."	2.-4.
SS-64	RB "TOWNSEND..."	2.-4.
SS-65	RB "TOWNSEND CLUBS..."	2.-4.
SS-66	RB "TOWNSEND PLAN..."	2.-4.
SS-67	RB "TOWNSEND Old..."	2.-4.
SS-68	RB "VOTE for..."	2.-4.
SS-69	RB "What IS..."	2.-4.
SS-70	RB "Why pay $200..."	2.-4.
SS-71	RB "Wise persons..."	2.-4.
SS-72	RB "WORK for the..."	2.-4.

See PAT-623 through PAT-630 and AW-119 through AW-123 which appear to be from the same manufacturer.

| SS-81 | | 1.-3. |

| SS-82 | | 1.-3. |

| SS-83 | | 1.-3. |

| SS-84 | | 1.-3. |

| SS-85 | | 1.-3. |

| SS-86 | | 1.-3. |

| SS-87 | | 1.-3. |

| SS-88 | | 1.-3. |

| SS-89 | | 1.-3. |

| SS-90 | | 1.-3. |

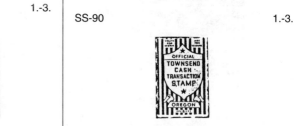

| SS-91 | | 1.-3. |

| SS-92 | (1942) | 1.-3. |

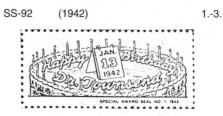

| SS-93 | (1942) | 1.-3. |

| SS-94 | (1942) | 1.-3. |

| SS-95 | (1942) | 1.-3. |

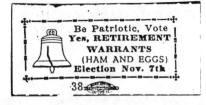

SS-101   1.-3.

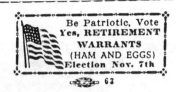

SS-102 RB   1.-3.

I AM 100%
for a National Old Age
Compensation which
will create Employment
and help restore
Prosperity

SS-103 R   1.-3,

SS-104   1.-3.

Social Security

SS-201 RB   .50-2.

SS-202 RB   .50-2.

Social Security
and Medicare
SUPPORT INDEPENDENT
FUNDING
NATIONAL COMMITTEE TO PRESERVE
SOCIAL SECURITY AND MEDICARE

SS-203 RB   .50-2.

SS-204 RB   .50-2.

SS-205 RB   .50-2.

Social Security
& Medicare
INSURANCE
NOT WELFARE

SS-206 RB   .50-2.

American Association of Retired Persons

SS-301 RB   1.-3.

SS-302 MC   .50-2.

Medical Care

Over the years there have been many proposals to nationalize the health care system in the U.S. As this book goes to press the debate is still going on.

MC-1 BkY   .50-2.

Picture shown at 65%
MC-2 B/Y   .50-2.

Picture shown at 65%
MC-3 B/Y   .50-2.

Picture shown at 65%
MC-4 B/Y   .50-2.

Picture shown at 65%
MC-5 B/Y   .50-2.

Under the Proposed Socialized Medicine Plan private consultation with Your Doctor might become a Thing of the Past

Picture shown at 65%
MC-6   B/Y   .50-2.

The Best Medical Care is available to all through The American System of Voluntary-Pre-payment Plans

Picture shown at 65%
MC-7   B/Y   .50-2.

Waiting in a Doctor's Office is sometimes unavoidable but Socialized Medicine will mean YOUR Standing in Line Repeatedly

Picture shown at 65%
MC-8   B/Y   .50-2.

The Government Can Give You Nothing it doesn't Take From YOU First— Free Medicine Is No Exception

Picture shown at 65%
MC-9   B/Y   .50-2.

The proposed Socialized Medical Plan would mean another Compulsory Tax deducted from Every Paycheck

Picture shown at 65%
MC-10   B/Y   .50-2.

Picture shown at 75%
MC-11   YBk   .50-2.

Picture shown at 75%
MC-12   BBk   .50-2.

AS YOUR PERSONAL PHYSICIAN
I OPPOSE COMPULSORY HEALTH INSURANCE BECAUSE—
It would bring you inferior medical care at high cost—Invade your medical privacy—Put both of us under political control!
If you agree, please write your U. S. Senators and Representatives. For more information, ask me.

MC-13   Gr   .50-2.

Taxes

TX-1   B   .50-2.

TX-2   Gy   .50-2.

TX-3   Gr   .50-2.

How much of Your TAX $ will be wasted?

TX-4   DkR   .50-2.

AMERICA'S CHOICE SAVE TAXES OR....

TX-5   R   .50-2.

TX-6   R   .50-2.

If you have any items which are not pictured in this book but should be, please send photocopies to the author in care of Krause Publications, 700 E. State St., Iola, WI 54990-0001.

TX-7   MC   .50-2.

TX-8   MC   .50-2.

TX-9   MC   .50-2.

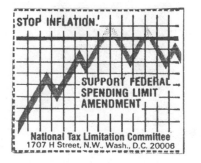

TX-10   RBBk   .50-2.

TX-11   RBBk   .50-2.

TX-12   R   .50-2.

TX-13   RB   .50-2.

TX-14   RB   .50-2.

TX-15   RB   .50-2.

TX-16   RB   .50-2.

TX-17   RB   .50-2.

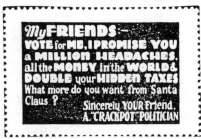

TX-18   RB   .50-2.

TX-19   RB   .50-2.

TX-20   .50-2.

TX-21   BkR   .50-2.

Picture shown at 80%
TX-22   RB   .50-2.

TAXES MUST BE REDUCED!
Approximately **25%** of your room rent is paid for taxes.

Picture shown at 75%
TX-23   R/Y   .50-2.

TX-24   B   .50-2.

TX-25   RBBk   .50-2.

TX-26   BkGr   .50-2.

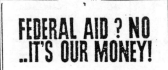

TX-27   BkGr   .50-2.

HELP PROTECT PROP. 13!
Howard Jarvis Taxpayers Association

TX-28   GrBk   .50-2.

TX-29	Bk (Light)	.50-1.
TX-30	Bk (Powder)	.50-1.
TX-31	Bk (Candy bar)	.50-1.
TX-32	Bk (Rent)	.50-1.
TX-33	Bk (Meat)	.50-1.
TX-34	Bk (Tissue)	.50-1.
TX-35	Bk (Mower)	.50-1.
TX-36	Bk (Movie ticket)	.50-1.
TX-37	Bk (Refrigerator)	.50-1.
TX-38	Bk (Gasoline)	.50-1.
TX-39	Bk (Purse)	.50-1.
TX-40	Bk (House)	.50-1.
TX-41	Bk (Hosiery)	.50-1.
TX-42	Bk (Shovel)	.50-1.
TX-43	Bk (Baby shoes)	.50-1.
TX-44	Bk (Soap)	.50-1.
TX-45	Bk (Clock)	.50-1.
TX-46	Bk (Phone service)	.50-1.
TX-47	Bk (Air in tires)	.50-1.
TX-48	Bk (Milk)	.50-1.

TX-49   .50-1.
There may be others, similar to the above set.

FEDERAL AID ? NO ..IT'S OUR MONEY!

TX-50   Bk   .50-1.

TX-51   Bk   .50-1.

TX-52   Bk   .50-1.

TX-53   Bk   .50-1.

TX-54   Gr (1938)   .50-1.
TX-55   Gr (1938)   .50-1.
Issued by Tax Facts, Inc., New York, NY. There may be more in this set.

TX-101   BRBk   .50-2.

TX-102   RGr   .50-2.

PAY TAXES PROMPTLY
I NEED MY WELFARE!

TX-103   Bk   .50-2.

Keep the Sales Tax
Protect Our Schools!

TX-104   R   .50-1.

Great Depression

DEP-1   Bk/R   .50-2.

WASN'T THE
DEPRESSION
TERRIBLE!

DEP-2	Gr/Gr	.50-2.
DEP-3	BkOr	.50-2.
DEP-4	BkOr	.50-2.
DEP-5	BkOr	.50-2.
DEP-6	BkOr	.50-2.
DEP-7	BkOr	.50-2.

Pioturo ohown at 90%

DEP-8	BkOr	.50-2.

DEP-9	Gr 1¢ (1932)	.50-1.
DEP-10	Gr 2¢ (1932)	.50-1.
DEP-11	Gr 5¢ (1932)	.50-1.
DEP-12	Gr 10¢ (1932)	.50-1.

Full booklet of sixteen panes   25.-35.
Booklets include six panes of 1¢, eight panes of
2¢, one pane of 5¢ and one pane of 10¢, in
panes of twenty-five (5x5). SE:LBR

DEP-13	10¢ R (1932)	.50-2.
DEP-14	25¢ B (1932)	.50-2.
DEP-15	50¢ Gr (1932)	.50-2.
DEP-16	$1 Or (1932)	.50-2.

Picture shown at 80%

DEP-17	R	.50-2.

DEP-18   Ma   .50-2.

DEP-19   BBkR   .50-2.

DEP-20   BR   .50-2.

DEP-21   BR   1.-3.

DEP-22   BR   1.-3.

DEP-23   1.-3.

DEP-24   BR   1.-3.

The stamp has a copyright date of 1937 suggesting that it may relate to President Roosevelt's attempt to "pack" the U. S. Supreme Court by adding more than the usual nine justices. This was proposed because the conservative court held many of Roosevelt's economic recovery programs unconstitutional.

DEP-25   Bk/Gd   .50-2.

Fix-up Campaign

Encouraging people to fix up their property was one way to help the economy.

DEP-51   Rtu   .50-2.

DEP-52   GrOr   .50-2.

DEP-53   Bk/Gd   .50-2.

DEP-54   RBBk   .50-2.

Picture shown at 65%

DEP-55   RB   .50-2.

DEP-56   RB   .50-2.

DEP-57   MC   .50-2.

Soldiers' Bonus

There was much talk after World War I of paying a bonus to those who served. The issue lingered for years and when the depression struck the need for the bonus was much greater. At one point thousands of veterans came to Washington to set up camps known as Hoovervilles. Eventually the U.S. army demolished the encampments.

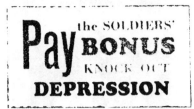

DEP-101   RB   .50-2.
DEP-101a RB   .50-2.
DEP-101a has the words "KNOCK OUT" in a
slightly thinner font.

DEP-102   B   .50-2.

DEP-103 RB.50-2.

Picture shown at 57%
DEP-104   RB   .50-2.

National Recovery Administration (N.R.A.)

The N.R.A. was established under the National Industrial Recovery Act, enacted within two months after President Roosevelt took office. It was one of the important components of the New Deal and established industrial codes regulating wages, hours, and prices for nearly all of American industry. However, in 1935 much of the Act was declared by the Supreme Court to be unconstitutional and the N.RA. was soon liquidated.

Note: While some of the following stamps look similar, there are slight differences in the lettering, design, or ink shade.

Stamps on foil

Picture shown at 50%
NRA-1   B/Si   2.-4.

NRA-2   BR/Go   2.-4.

NRA-3   B/Go   2.-4.

NRA-4   BR/Si   1.-3.

NRA-5   BR/Si   1.-3.

NRA-6   BR/Si   1.-3.

NRA-7   BR/Si   .50-2.

NRA-8   BR/Si   .50-2.

NRA-9   BR/Si   .50-2.

Round and oval

NRA-101   RB   .50-2.

NRA-102   RB   .50-2.

NRA-103   RB   .50-2.

NRA-104   RB   .50-2.

NRA-105   RB   .50-2.

NRA-106   RB   .50-2.

NRA-107   RB   .50-2.

NRA-108   RB   .50-2.

NRA-109   RB   .50-2.

NRA-110   RB   .50-2.

NRA-111   RB   .50-2.

NRA-112   RB   .50-2.

NRA-113   B/R   1.-3.

NRA-114   .50-2.

NRA-115   3.-6.

Rectangular

NRA-201   RB   2.-4.

NRA-202   RB   1.-3.

NRA-203   B   1.-3.

NRA-204   RB   1.-3.

NRA-205   RB   1.-3.

NRA-206   RBY   2.-4.

NRA-207   RB   2.-4.

NRA-208   RB   1.-3.

NRA-209   RB   1.-3.

NRA-210   RB   1.-3.

NRA-211   RB   1.-3.

NRA-212   B   1.-3.

NRA-213   RB   1.-3.

NRA-214   RB   1.-3.

Picture shown at 65%
NRA-215   RB   1.-3.

Picture shown at 65%
NRA-216   RB   1.-3.

Picture shown at 70%
NRA-217   RB   1.-3.

Picture shown at 70%
NRA-218   B   1.-3.

Picture shown at 70%
NRA-219   RB   1.-3.

Picture shown at 70%
NRA-220   RB   1.-3.

Picture shown at 80%
NRA-221   RB   1.-3.

Picture shown at 80%
NRA-222   RB   1.-3.

NRA-223   RB   2.-4.

Picture shown at 80%
NRA-224   RB   1.-3.

NRA-225   RB   1.-3.

NRA-226   RB   1.-3.

Picture shown at 70%
NRA-227   B   1.-3.

Picture shown at 75%
NRA-228   RB   1.-3.

Picture shown at 80%
NRA-229   RB   1.-3.

NRA-230   RB   1.-3.

NRA-231   RB   .50-2.

NRA-232   RB   .50-2.

NRA-233   RB   .50-2.

NRA-234   RB   .50-2.

NRA-235   RB   .50-2.

NRA-236   RB   .50-2.

NRA-237   RB   .50-2.

NRA-238   RB   .50-2.

NRA-239   RB   .50-2.

NRA-240   RB   .50-2.

NRA-241   RB   .50-2.

NRA-242   RB   .50-2.

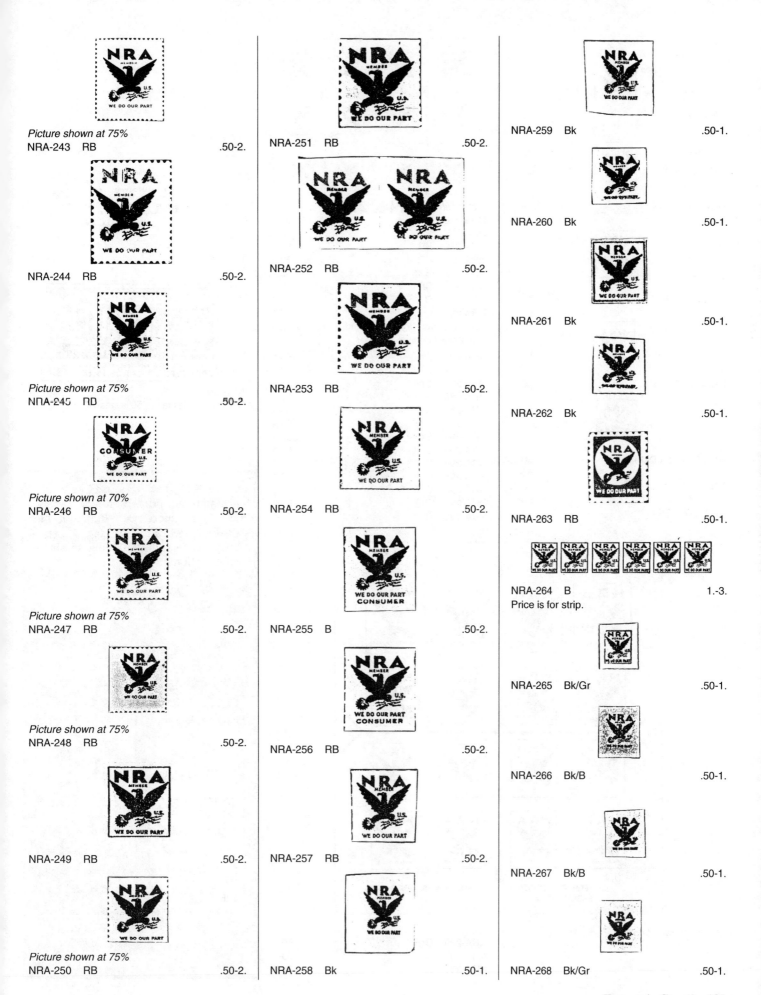

Picture shown at 75%
NRA-243   RB   .50-2.

NRA-244   RB   .50-2.

Picture shown at 75%
NRA-245   RB   .50-2.

Picture shown at 70%
NRA-246   RB   .50-2.

Picture shown at 75%
NRA-247   RB   .50-2.

Picture shown at 75%
NRA-248   RB   .50-2.

NRA-249   RB   .50-2.

Picture shown at 75%
NRA-250   RB   .50-2.

NRA-251   RB   .50-2.

NRA-252   RB   .50-2.

NRA-253   RB   .50-2.

NRA-254   RB   .50-2.

NRA-255   B   .50-2.

NRA-256   RB   .50-2.

NRA-257   RB   .50-2.

NRA-258   Bk   .50-1.

NRA-259   Bk   .50-1.

NRA-260   Bk   .50-1.

NRA-261   Bk   .50-1.

NRA-262   Bk   .50-1.

NRA-263   RB   .50-1.

NRA-264   B   1.-3.
Price is for strip.

NRA-265   Bk/Gr   .50-1.

NRA-266   Bk/B   .50-1.

NRA-267   Bk/B   .50-1.

NRA-268   Bk/Gr   .50-1.

NRA-269   Bk/Gr   .50-1.

NRA-270   Bk/Y   .50-1.

NRA-271   Bk/Cr   .50-1.

NRA-272   Bk/Pk   .50-1.

NRA-273   Bk/DkPk   .50-1.
NRA-274   B   .50-1.
NRA-275   R   .50-1.
NRA-276   BR   .50-1.
NRA-277   BR   .50-1.

Picture shown at 55%

NRA-278	B	.50-1.
NRA-279	R	.50-1.
NRA-280	BR	.50-1.
NRA-281	BR	.50-1.
NRA-282	B	.50-1.
NRA-283	BR	.50-1.
NRA-284	R	.50-1.
NRA-285	R	.50-1.

Vertical perforations are inked in red and horizontal ones in blue.

NRA-286	Gr	.50-1.
NRA-287	Gr	.50-1.
NRA-288	GrR	.50-1.
NRA-289	GrR	.50-1.
NRA-290	Gr	.50-1.
NRA-291	R	.50-1.
NRA-292	GrR	.50-1.
NRA-293	GrR	.50-1.
NRA-294	Gr	.50-1.
NRA-295	GrR	.50-1.
NRA-296	GrR	.50-1.
NRA-297	GrR	.50-1.
NRA-298	Gr	.50-1.

NRA-302   .50-2.

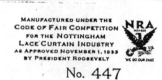

NRA-303   .50-2.

NRA-304   1.-3.
NRA-305   Same but 50% smaller   1.-2.

The N.R.A. symbol was used as a rubber stamp and printed on tags, labels, and other paperwork. While not the subject matter of this catalog, the specialist may wish to add these to his or her collection.

Embossed into paper

Dress tag

Picture shown at 50%
Stamped on package

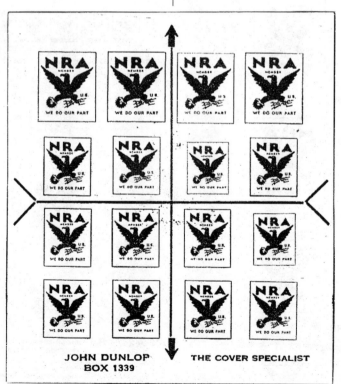

JOHN DUNLOP   THE COVER SPECIALIST
BOX 1339

Picture shown at 65%

NRA-299	GrR	.50-1.
NRA-300	Gr	.50-1.
NRA-301	R	.50-1.

BA-1   RB   1.-2.

Picture shown at 85%
BA-2   RB   1.-2.

BA-3   RB   .50-2.
Issued by Made in America Club, New York, NY.

BA-4   RB   .50-2.

BA-5   RB (1933)   .50-2.

BA-6   RB   .50-2.

BA-7   RB   .50-2.
Issued by Buy American Association, Inc., New York, NY. See also BA-101.

BA-8   RB   .50-2.
Issued by Made in America Club, New York, NY.

BA-9   R   .50-2.
BA-10   B/Pk   .50-2.

BA-11   RB   .50-2.

BA-12   RB   .50-2.
Issued by Buy American Institute, Inc.

BA-13   RB   1.-2.

BA-14   RB (1932)   .50-2.

BA-15   RB   .50-2.
Issued by Made in America League, Washington, DC. See also BA-27.

BA-16   RB   .50-2.

BA-17   RB   .50-2.
Issued by Puritan Memorial Assn., Boston, MA.

BA-18   RB   .50-2.
Issued by National Buy American Association, Washington, DC.

Picture shown at 80%
BA-19   RB   .50-2.

Picture shown at 80%
BA-20   RB   .50-2.

BA-21   RB   .50-1.

BA-22   RB   .50-1.

BA-23   RB   .50-2.

Picture shown at 90%
BA-24   RB   .50-1.

BA-25   RB   .50-1.

BA-26   Bk/Y   .50-2.

Picture shown at 80%
BA-27   B (1938) (roulette)   .50-2.
Issued by Buy American League.

BA-28   RB   .50-2.
Issued by Buy American League.

BA-29   BR   .50-2.

BA-30   R   .50-2.

BA-31   B   .50-2.

BA-32   RB   .50-2.

BA-33   RB   .50-1.

BA-34   RB   1.-2.

BA-35   B   .50-2.

BA-36   RB   .50-2.
Issued by Buy American League.

BA-37   RB   1.-3.
Issued by United Spanish War Veterans.

BA-38   (1933)   2.-4.
BA-39   (1934)   2.-4.
BA-40   2.-4.
BA-39 is similar to BA-38 but has initials omitted and the font is different. BA-40 has "Buy Now" in place of "VFW."
Panes of ten (5x2).

BA-41   RB   1.-2.

BA-42   RB   .50-2.

BA-43   RB   .50-2.

BA-44   RB (1938)   .50-1.
Issued by Citizens Association for America First, Inc., Los Angeles, CA.

BA-45   RB   .50-1.
Issued by Made in America League, Washington, DC. See also BA-15.

BA-46   RB   .50-1.

BA-47   RB   .50-1.

Picture shown at 57%

BA-48   RBBk   .50-1.
From MAD Magazine.

BA-49   Gr   1.-3.

Round and Die Cut

BA-101   RB (1933)   .50-2.
Issued by Buy American Association, Inc. N.Y.C.

BA-102   RB   .50-2.

BA-103   RB   .50-2.

BA-104   RB   .50-2.

BA-105   .50-2.
Issued by Made in America Club, New York, NY.

BA-106   RB   .50-2.
Issued by Made in America Club, New York, NY.

BA-107   RB   .50-1.
Issued by Made in America Club, New York, NY.

BA-108   RB   .50-1.

BA-109   RB   .50-1.

BA-110   RB   .50-2.

BA-111   1.-2.
Issued by Made in America Club, New York, NY.

BA-112   1.-2.
Issued by Made in America Club, New York, NY.

Buy Now/Build Now

Picture shown at 90%
BA-201   Gr/Cr (1938)   .50-2.
Issued by Business Recovery Assn.

BA-202   BOr   .50-2.

BA-203   B   .50-2.
BA-204   BR   .50-2.

BA-205   Gr/Y   .50-2.

BA-206   Or   .50-2.
BA-207   Bk/Y   .50-2.

BA-208   OrBk   .50-2.

BA-209   RB "BUY NOW"   .50-2.
Issued by VFW Post 814.

Sell American/More Sales

BA-301   RB (1933)   1.-2.

BA-302   RB   .50-1.

BA-303   RB   .50-1.

BA-304   RB   .50-1.

BA-305   RB   .50-1.

BA-306   RB   .50-1.

BA-307   RB   .50-1.

Made in U.S.A.

70 BA-401 RBBk   .50-1.

BA-402   RB   .50-1.

BA-403   RB   .25-.50

BA-404   RB   .25-.50

BA-405   RBGdGy   .50-2.
BA-406   RBGdGy (double size)   .50-2.

BA-407   RBGdGy   .50-2.
BA-408   RBGdGy (double size)   .50-2.

BA-409   RBBkGd   .50-2.
BA-410   RBBkGd (double size)   .50-2.

Picture shown at 85%
BA-411   RBGdGy   .50-2.
There is probably a smaller version similar to the
above.

BA-412   MC   .50-2.

BA-413   MC   .50-2.

Buy Local

BA-501   RB   .50-2.

BA-502   B/Or   .50-2.

BA-503   RB   .50-2.

BA-504   B   .50-2.

BUY NOW!
IN TOPEKA
Sons of Union
Veterans of the
Civil War, Old
Abe Camp No. 16

BA-505   Bk   2.-4.
Issued by Sons of Union Veterans of the Civil
War, Old Abe Camp No. 16.

BUY NOW!
BOOST
SALT LAKE CITY
T. H. Gordon
Circle No. 4
Ladies of the G.A.R.

BA-506   B   2.-4.

BA-507   BkGr   1.-3.

BA-508   BR   1.-3.
Issued by VFW Post 814.

BUY
BOOST
AT HOME

BA-509   BR   1.-3.
Issued by VFW Post 814.

Miscellaneous Economic Causes

Pro-Business

SEND BUSINESS MEN TO CONGRESS. WHY SHOULD
BUSINESS BE THE FOOTBALL OF POLITICIANS?

Picture shown at 80%
BU-1   Ma   .50-2.

POLITICAL MACHINERY CANNOT IMPROVE INDUSTRY
GIVE THE BUSINESS MAN A CHANCE AT THE BAT
THE POLITICIAN HAS STRUCK OUT

Picture shown at 80%
BU-2   Ma   .50-2.

POLITICAL TURMOIL MEANS INDUSTRIAL DEPRESSION

Picture shown at 80%
BU-3   Ma   .50-2.

BU-4   RB   .50-2.

BU-5   R   .50-2.

Postal Rates & Service

PO-1   R   .50-2.

HALF YOUR LETTER
POSTAGE IS A TAX.
ONE
CENT
LETTER
POSTAGE
ADDRESS NATIONAL ONE
CENT LETTER POSTAGE
ASSOCIATION
CLEVELAND, O.

PO-2   R   .50-2.

PO-3   R   .50-2.

PO-4   R   .50-2.

Picture shown at 80%
PO-5   R   .50-2.

PO-6   RBBk   .50-2.
From MAD Magazine.

PO-7   BkPk   .50-2.
Sheets contain seventy-five of PO-7 and three of PO-8.

PROTEST POSTAL RATE INCREASE!
USE THESE LABELS ON ALL OF YOUR MAIL
MAKE YOUR FEELINGS KNOWN
PLACE LABEL BELOW RETURN ADDRESS

150 LABELS $3.20   ORDER   THE 1871 SHOP
POSTPAID   FROM   DRAWER 'E'
                            SOUTH LYON, MICH. 48178

Picture shown at 85%
PO-8   BkPk   .50-2.
Sheets contain seventy-five of PO-7 and three of PO-8.

Other Economic Causes

"If the American people ever allow private banks to control the issue of their money, first by inflation and then by deflation, the banks and the corporations that will grow up around them will deprive the people of their property until their children will wake up homeless on the continent their fathers conquered." - *Thomas Jefferson.*

Picture shown at 80%
ME-1   B   .50-2.

ME-2   Bk   .50-2.

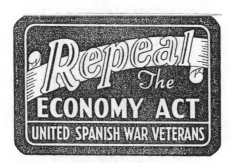

Picture shown at 72%
ME-3   3.-6.

ME-4   B   .50-2.

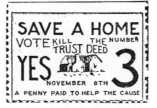

ME-5   RGr   .50-2.

Picture shown at 90%
ME-6   4.-8.
Believed to be issued by Production For Use, a Montana Farmer-Labor group.

ME-7   B/Y   .50-2.

I'M FIGHTING POVERTY
I WORK FOR A LIVING

ME-8   Bk   .50-1.

ME-9   RB   .50-1.
Large, die cut map shaped window stickers were also issued.

Chapter 5

Social Causes

Social issues have inspired Americans to action for more than a hundred years. From the anti-alcohol crusaders who destroyed saloons, to the abortion protesters who block clinics, activists have fought for their causes. Many of these activists, and those who opposed them, used campaign stamps to spread their messages.

This chapter includes stamps issued for campaigns involving alcohol, tobacco, narcotics, abortion, birth control, and social diseases. While in some countries these might not be considered political issues, Americans have made them so by campaigning for laws in these areas.

Prohibition/Anti-Alcohol

The prohibition movement was a strong political movement at the beginning of the twentieth century and was successful in amending the U. S. Constitution to prohibit the sale of alcohol. This lasted from 1919 until 1933 when the great experiment was deemed a failure by most Americans and the amendment was repealed.

Picture shown at 80%
P-1   RB   5.-10.

Picture shown at 85%
P-2   RB   5.-10.

P-3   RB   5.-10.

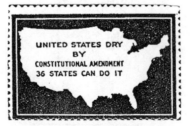

P-4   B   3.-6.

P-5   Bk/Pk   2.-4.

Picture shown at 92%
P-6   B/Y   1.-3.

P-7   RB   3.-6.
Die cut and embossed.

P-8   RB   2.-4.
Die cut and embossed.

P-9   Tu   2.-4.

P-10   Ma   3.-6.

P-11   B (1914)   3.-6.

P-12   B   3.-6.

P-13   4.-8.

P-14   10.-20.

P-15   BkRBPk   3.-6.

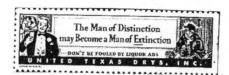

Picture shown at 90%
P-16   MC (Wash.)   4.-6.

The Man of Distinction may Become a Man of Extinction — DON'T BE FOULED BY LIQUOR ADS — UNITED TEXAS DRYS, INC.

Picture shown at 90%
P-17   MC (Texas)   4.-6.

Between the nations NO WAR *Within the nations* NO DRINK. *Duncan Miller*

P-18   B   2.-4.

Save Me BY VOTING DRY

P-19   3.-6.

500,000 BOYS
Sacrificed to the Liquor Traffic Every Year
GIVE a BOY, or VOTE DRY

P-20   2.-4.

KILL the SERPENT
SAVE THE BOYS
CALIFORNIA MUST GO DRY IN 1914
Register before Oct. 3

P-21   R frame B text   2.-4.
P-22   B frame R text   2.-4.

P-23   RGr   5.-10.
Text: "United Dry League"

VOTE DRY
WITH A DRY PARTY!

Picture shown at 80%
P-24   1.-3..

Feed Starving Children!
Grain For Food — Not Liquor!
CALIFORNIA TEMPERANCE FEDERATION, INC.

Picture shown at 75%
P-25   R/Y   1.-3.
Panes of eight (1x8) in pads.

STOP
THIS WASTE!
Millions are starving all over the world and yet the BEER and LIQUOR Interests continue to use scarce food grains to make their slop and fill their coffers with blood money.

Thse stickers obtained from THE CONTENDER Hunter town, Indiana.

P-26   R   1.-3.
P-27   R/Y   1.-3.
P-28   R/Or   1.-3.
P-29   R/Gr   1.-3.
Sheets of three (1x3).

P-30   RB   4.-8.

P-31   RB (No date)   2.-4.

P-32   RB Dated 1933   2.-4.
Sheets of 100 (10x10).

Picture shown at 80%

P-33   MC (1939)   1.-3.
P-34   MC (1939)   1.-3.
P-35   MC (1939)   1.-3.
P-36   MC (1939)   1.-3.
P-37   MC (1939)   1.-3.
P-38   MC (1939)   1.-3.
P-39   MC (1939)   1.-3.
P-40   MC (1939)   1.-3.

P-41   MC (1939)   1.-3.
P-42   MC (1939)   1.-3.
Bottom line reads "Copyright 1939 KANSAS UNITED DRY FORCES."

Picture shown at 80%

P-43   MC   1.-3.
P-44   MC   1.-3.
P-45   MC   1.-3.
P-46   MC   1.-3.
P-47   MC   1.-3.
P-48   MC   1.-3.
P-49   MC   1.-3.
P-50   MC   1.-3.
P-51   MC   1.-3.
P-52   MC   1.-3.
Bottom line is blacked out with no text.

Picture shown at 80%

P-53   B large   .50-2.

P-54   B small   .50-2.
Large size shown printed three (dif.) on a sheet (1x3), small size printed six (dif.) on a sheet (2x3).

Picture shown at 80%

P-55   B large   1.-3.
P-56   B small   1.-3.
Large size shown printed three (dif.) on a sheet (1x3), small size printed six (dif.) on a sheet (2x3).

Picture shown at 80%

P-57   B large   .50-2.
P-58   B small   .50-2.
Large size shown printed three (dif.) on a sheet (1x3), small size printed six (dif.) on a sheet (2x3).

P-59   B large   .50-2.
P-60   B small   .50-2.
Large size shown printed three (dif.) on a sheet (1x3), small size printed six (dif.) on a sheet (2x3).

Picture shown at 65%
Full set of P-33 to P-42.

P-61   B large   .50-2.
P-62   B small   .50-2.
Large size shown printed three (dif.) on a sheet (1x3), small size printed six (dif.) on a sheet (2x3).

Picture shown at 80%
P-63   B large   .50-2.
P-64   B small   .50-2.
Large size shown printed three (dif.) on a sheet (1x3), small size printed six (dif.) on a sheet (2x3).

Picture shown at 90%
P-65   B large   .50-2.
P-66   B small   .50-2.
Large size shown printed three (dif.) on a sheet (1x3), small size printed six (dif.) on a sheet (2x3).

Picture shown at 70%
P-67   B large   .50-2.
P-68   B small   .50-2.
Large size shown printed three (dif.) on a sheet (1x3), small size printed six (dif.) on a sheet (2x3).

Picture shown at 70%
P-69   B large   .50-2.
P-70   B small   .50-2.
Large size shown printed three (dif.) on a sheet (1x3), small size printed six (dif.) on a sheet (2x3).

Picture shown at 70%
P-71   B large   .50-2.
P-72   B small   .50-2.
Large size shown printed three (dif.) on a sheet (1x3), small size printed six (dif.) on a sheet (2x3).

Picture shown at 80%

P-73   B large   .50-2.
P-74   B small   .50-2.
Large size shown printed three (dif.) on a sheet (1x3), small size printed six (dif.) on a sheet (2x3).

Picture shown at 70%
P-75   B large   .50-2.
P-76   B small   .50-2.
Large size shown printed three (dif.) on a sheet (1x3), small size printed six (dif.) on a sheet (2x3).

Picture shown at 75%
Sample sheet of P-98 to P-120 small size.

If you have any items which are not pictured in this book but should be, please send photocopies to the author in care of Krause Publications, 700 E. State St., Iola, WI 54990-0001.

Temperance stickers cards etc. to educate against use of harmful habit-forming products, Walter Baker, Wawona, Y. N. P., Calif.

BE SOBER AND
TEMPERATE,
AND YOU WILL
BE HAPPY.
—B. FRANKLIN.

WINE IS A MOCKER,
STRONG DRINK IS
RAGING: WHOSO-
EVER IS DECEIVED
THEREBY IS NOT
WISE.   Prov. 20:1.

LIQUOR is a weapon in
the hands of the under-
world, by which parents
are robbed of means for
their children's support.
WALTER BAKER.

WOE unto him that
giveth his neighbor
drink, · · · and maketh
him drunken.·Hab.2:15.

There is way that seemeth right unto a man, but the end thereof are the
ways of death.   Prov. 14:12.

Picture shown at 70%

P-77	RB	.50-2.
P-78	RB	.50-2.
P-79	RB	.50-2.
P-80	RB	.50-2.
P-81	R	.50-2.

Full sheet of five stamps is shown.

Sheet No. 3-26-48 .1¢ each, from,
Walter Baker, Wawona, Calif.

A good character and a substantial backbone are improved by say-
ing "NO" to evil temptations.

A good character is formed around
a substantial backbone by a person,
who has courage to say "NO" to
the tempter.

Anyone who can't say "NO"
is worse than a sissie.

Cursed is he who makes food into
poison to sell to his neighbor.

There are three stages to all vices:
Learning, habit and disease.

As long as drinking is a habit it
can be broken but when it becomes
a disease it must be cured.

Drunkenness is produced by willing victims consuming the poisonous
secretion of the yeast germ.

Alcohol is an excremental waste
from the yeast germs that kills the
germs which produce it when the
concentration is about ten percent.

Picture shown at 75%

Several religious groups issued stamps which denounce alcohol as well as promote their religious theme. These are not considered political, but collectors of prohibition and alcohol-related material may be interested in adding them to their collection.

P-82	R	.50-2.
P-83	R	.50-2.
P-84	R	.50-2.
P-85	R	.50-2.
P-86	R	.50-2.
P-87	R	.50-2.
P-88	R	.50-2.
P-89	R	.50-2.

Full sheet of eight stamps is shown.

P-90		.50-2.

P-91	RB	1.-3.

P-92	Ma	1.-3.

I do hereby promise not to drink alcoholic beverages including beer and wine.

Picture shown at 72%

P-93	B	1.-3.

P-94	B	.50-2.

ARRIVE ALIVE!
DON'T DRINK
and DRIVE!

P-95		.50-2.

Picture shown at 80%

P-96	B/Y	1.-3.

Picture shown at 70%

P-97		2.-4.

A PENNY A DAY TO
KEEP LIQUOR AWAY

Picture shown at 50%

P-99	B	1.-3.

P-100   2.-4.

Picture shown at 75%
P-101   B   15.-25.

Keep Prohibition

P-201   2.-4.

P-202   B   2.-4.

P-203   B (1932)   2.-4.

P-204   BR   2.-4.

P-205   DkB   2.-4.
P-205a   LtB   2.-4.

P-206   RB   2.-4.

P-207   R   3.-6.

P-208   R   2.-4.

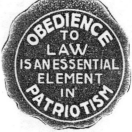

P-209   R   2.-4.

P-210   RB   2.-4.

P-211   RB   2.-4.

P-212   RB   2.-4.

P-213   2.-4.

P-214   2.-4.
P-215   2.-4.

P-216   2.-4.
P-217   2.-4.

P-218   2.-4.

P-219   B   3.-6.

P-220   RB   3.-6.
Bottom line reads: "SAVE the 18th Amendment."

P-221   RB (perforated)   2.-4.
P-221a   RB (roulette)   2.-4.

LET EVERY MAN REMEMBER

*T*HAT to *violate the law* is to *trample* on the blood of his father and *tear* the charter of his own and his children's liberty.

—*Abraham Lincoln.*

PROHIBITION IS A LAW

FAMILY WELFARE SOCIETY
404 TREMONT BLDG.
BOSTON, MASS.

P-222   Bk/Y   2.-4.

HELP THE PRESIDENT WITH LAW ENFORCEMENT

P-223   RB   1.-3.

Keep For OKLAHOMA Dry Youth

P-224   RB   2.-4.

Woman's Christian Temperance Union

WORLD'S WOMAN'S CHRISTIAN TEMPERANCE UNION — Academy of Music — NOV. 11-16 1922 — PHILADELPHIA PA. U.S.A.

P-301   LtBY   5.-10.

P-302   RBY   2.-4.

P-303   BSi   2.-4.

P-304   Bk   5.-10.

FRANCES E. WILLARD
BORN SEPT. 28, 1839
DIED FEB. 17, 1898

Picture shown at 75%

P-305   Bk   6.-12.

P-306   BGo   2.-4.

P-307	GrPk	2.-4.
P-308	GrPkS	2.-4.

P-309		2.-4.

P-310	B	1.-3.

Die cut and embossed.

P-311	B	1.-3.

Die cut and embossed.

P-312	RB	1.-3.

P-313	Br	1.-3.

P-314	BY	2.-4.

P-315	B	1.-3.

P-316	B	1.-3.

Picture shown at 80%

P-317		5.-10.

Picture shown at 85%

P-318		5.-10.

P-319	RB	2.-4.

LIQUOR ADS MUST GO!

Picture shown at 80%

P-401	R/Y	1.-3.

Panes of eight (1x8) in pads.

I DIDN'T LIKE THIS AD IN MY PAPER!

Picture shown at 80%

P-402	B/Gr	1.-3.

Panes of eight (1x8) in pads.

> *I most heartily commend your policy of not accepting alcoholic beverage ads in your publication.*
>
> Name ....
> Address ....

Picture shown at 60%

P-403		1.-3.

> *I am opposed to this ad from your publication and to all other forms of liquor advertising.*
>
> Name ....
> Address ....

Picture shown at 60%

P-404		1.-3.

P-405	Bk	1.-3.

Vote for California Prosperity by voting against Prohibition.

AP-1   MC   5.-10.

Protect the Barley Industry of California by voting against Prohibition.

Picture shown at 90%

AP-2   MC   5.-10.
AP-2a   MC ("229" is smaller)   5.-10.

REGISTER NOW and VOTE NO On Amendments 1 and 2

ALLIED INTERESTS OF SAN FRANCISCO

Picture shown at 90%

AP-3   MC   5.-10.

SAVE THE VINEYARDS WINE, RAISIN & TABLE GRAPES

VOTE "NO" ON BOTH PROHIBITION AMENDMENTS

AP-4   MC   5.-10.

WHO SAID THE DRYS WERE LICKED?

AP-5   MC   5.-10.

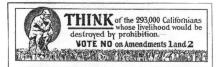

THINK of the 293,000 Californians whose livelihood would be destroyed by prohibition. VOTE NO on Amendments 1 and 2

Picture shown at 60%

AP-6   BkOrGr   5.-10.

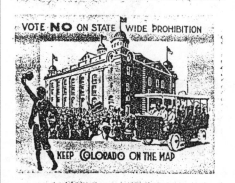

VOTE NO ON STATE WIDE PROHIBITION

KEEP COLORADO ON THE MAP

Picture shown at 95%

AP-7   5.-10.

COLUMBIA Accepts the Brewers' Contribution

BEER TAX $99,158,166

DRINK MODERATELY

AP-8   RB   5.-10.

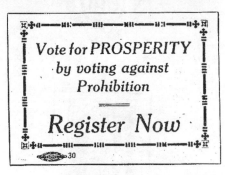

Vote for PROSPERITY by voting against Prohibition

Register Now

AP-9   BkBr/Y   3.-6.

PROHIBITION WOULD REDUCE OUR PURCHASING POWER

AP-10   RB   3.-6.

The full text reads "Prohibition would reduce our purchasing power that's where it affects you."

DO IT NOW! IF PROHIBITION GETS INTO THE CONSTITUTION, 13 STATES WITH ONLY 5,000,000 INHABITANTS CAN PREVENT YOU FROM TAKING IT OUT. BETTER STOP PROHIBITION ON THE WAY IN. TELL YOUR LEGISLATORS!

Picture shown at 70%

AP-11   BOrBk   3.-6.

OUR ALLIES ARE SOME FIGHTERS THEIR FIGHTERS AND WORKERS INSIST ON BEER. WHY TAKE IT AWAY FROM THE LABORING MEN WHO MUST WIN THE WAR FOR AMERICA? ASK YOUR LEGISLATORS!

Picture shown at 70%

AP-12   BOrBk   3.-6.

PROHIBITION BARS BEER THEY ARE TRYING TO PUT PROHIBITION INTO THE UNITED STATES CONSTITUTION. THAT MEANS NO MORE BEER. PROTEST TO YOUR LEGISLATORS!

Picture shown at 70%

AP-13   BOrGr   3.-6.

WHY PROHIBITION? WHY SHOULD YOU AND I AND MILLIONS OF OTHER LAW ABIDING CITIZENS BE DEPRIVED OF OUR GLASS OF BEER? ASK YOUR LEGISLATORS!

Picture shown at 70%

AP-14   BOrGr   3.-6.

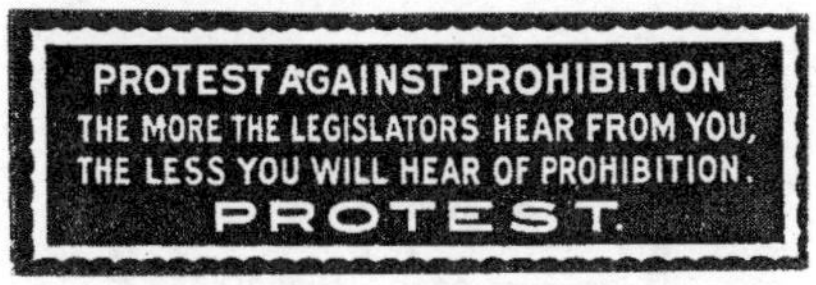

Picture shown at 70%

AP-15	BOrGr	3.-6.

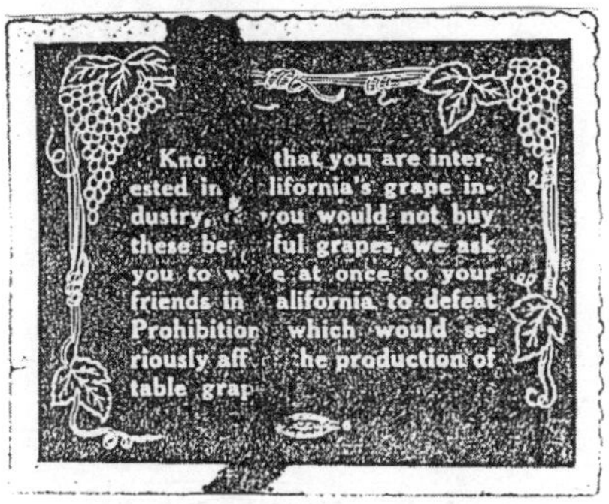

Picture shown at 80%

AP-16		3.-6.

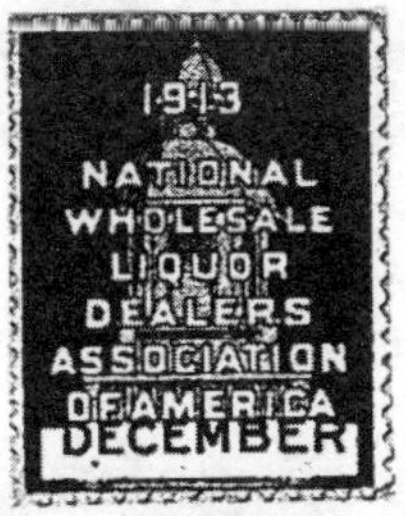

AP-104

AP-101	Br Sep. 1913	4.-8.
AP-102	Br Oct. 1913	4.-8.
AP-103	Br Nov. 1913	4.-8.
AP-104	Br Dec. 1913	4.-8.
AP-105	Br Jan. 1914	4.-8.
AP-106	Br Feb. 1914	4.-8.

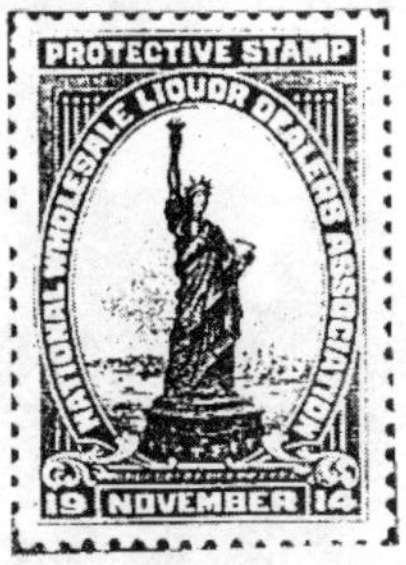

AP-107	DkPk Mar. 1914	2.-5.
AP-108	DkPk Apr. 1914	2.-5.
AP-109	DkPk May 1914	2.-5.
AP-110	DkPk Jun. 1914	2.-5.
AP-111	DkPk Jul. 1914	2.-5.
AP-112	DkPk Aug 1914	2.-5.
AP-113	DkPk Sep. 1914	2.-5.
AP-114	DkPk Oct. 1914	2.-5.
AP-115	DkPk Nov. 1914	2.-5.
AP-116	DkPk Dec. 1914	2.-5.
AP-117	DkPk Jan. 1915	2.-5.
AP-118	DkPk Feb. 1915	2.-5.
AP-119	DkPk Mar. 1915	2.-5.
AP-120	DkPk Apr. 1915	2.-5.
AP-121	DkPk May 1915	2.-5.
AP-122	DkPk Jun. 1915	2.-5.
AP-123	DkPk Jul. 1915	2.-5.
AP-124	DkPk Aug 1915	2.-5.
AP-125	DkPk Sep. 1915	2.-5.
AP-126	DkPk Oct. 1915	2.-5.
AP-127	DkPk Nov. 1915	2.-5.
AP-128	DkPk Dec. 1915	2.-5.
AP-129	DkPk Jan. 1916	2.-5.
AP-130	DkPk Feb. 1916	2.-5.
AP-131	DkPk Mar. 1916	2.-5.
AP-132	DkPk Apr. 1916	2.-5.
AP-133	DkPk May 1916	2.-5.

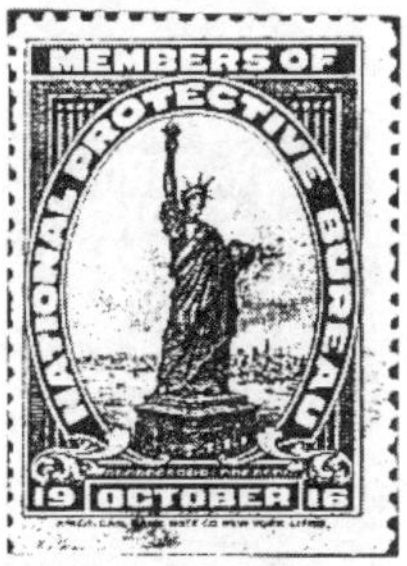

AP-134	DkPk Jun. 1916	2.-5.
AP-135	DkPk Jul. 1916	2.-5.
AP-136	DkPk Aug 1916	2.-5.
AP-137	DkPk Sep. 1916	2.-5.
AP-138	DkPk Oct. 1916	2.-5.
AP-139	DkPk Nov. 1916	2.-5.
AP-140	DkPk Dec. 1916	2.-5.
AP-141	DkPk Jan. 1917	2.-5.
AP-142	DkPk Feb. 1917	2.-5.
AP-143	DkPk Mar. 1917	2.-5.
AP-144	DkPk Apr. 1917	2.-5.
AP-145	DkPk May 1917	2.-5.
AP-146	DkPk Jun. 1917	2.-5.
AP-147	DkPk Jul. 1917	2.-5.
AP-148	DkPk Aug 1917	2.-5.
AP-149	DkPk Sep. 1917	2.-5.
AP-150	DkPk Oct. 1917	2.-5.
AP-151	DkPk Nov. 1917	2.-5.
AP-152	DkPk Dec. 1917	2.-5.

These were issued by the National Wholesale Liquor Dealers Assn.

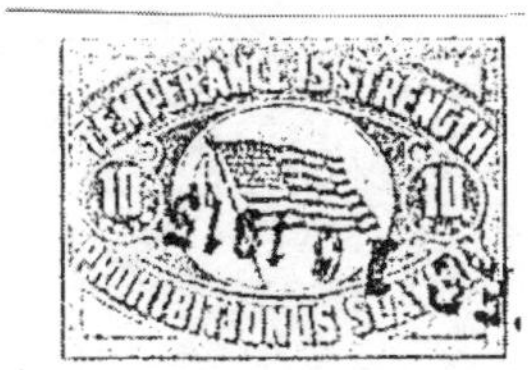

AP-161	2¢	3.-6.
AP-162	10¢	3.-6.

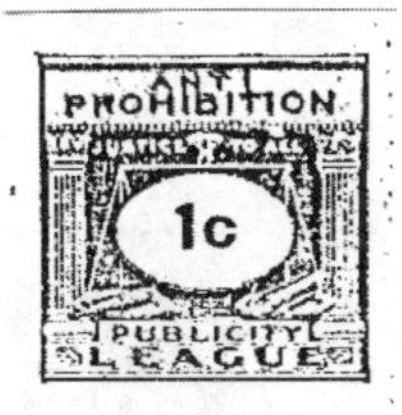

AP-171	1¢	3.-6.
AP-172	2¢	3.-6.
AP-173	3¢	3.-6.
AP-174	5¢	3.-6.
AP-175	10¢	3.-6.
AP-176	25¢	3.-6.
AP-177	$2	3.-6.

Other denominations might exist.

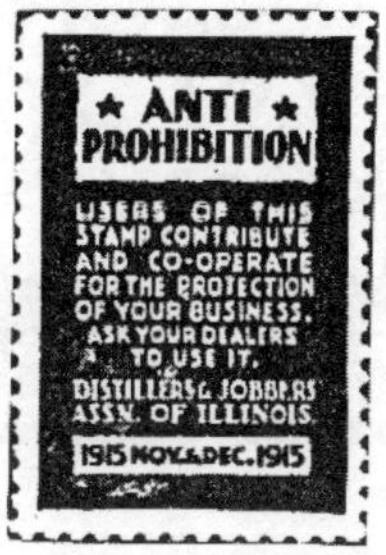

AP-211	Nov.-Dec. 1915 Gr	3.-6.

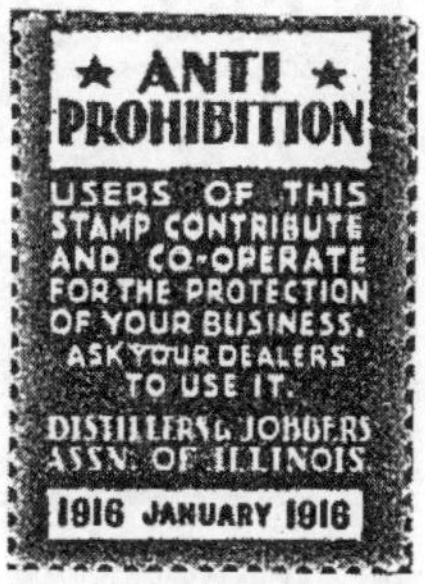

AP-212	Jan. 1916 R	3.-6.
AP-213	Feb. 1916	3.-6.
AP-225	Mar.-Apr. 1917	3.-6.

Above four issues were produced by Distillers & Jobbers Assn. of Illinois. They may have been produced for other months but no others are known to the author.

Repeal of Prohibition

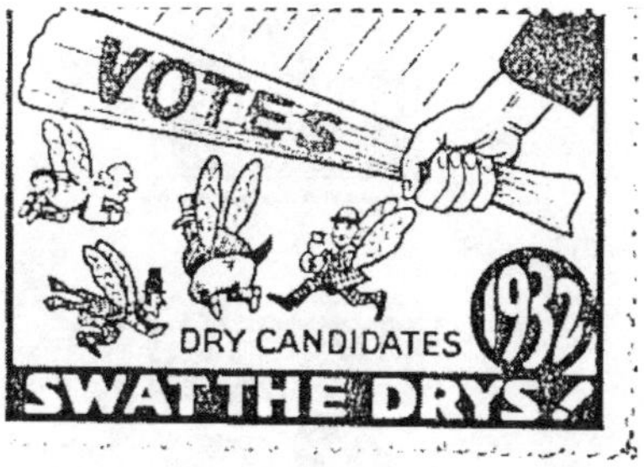

AP-501	B	3.-6.

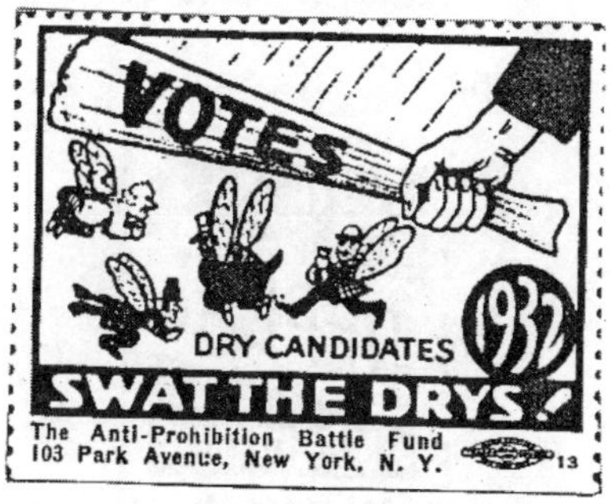

AP-502	B	3.-6.

AP-503   B   3.-6.

AP-504   RB   4.-8.

AP-505   RB   3.-6.

AP-506   R   3.-6.

AP-507   RB   3.-6.

AP-508   RBBk   3.-6.

AP-509   3.-6.

AP-510   BrBl   3.-6.

AP-511   RB   3.-6.

AP-512   3.-6.

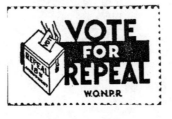

AP-513   B   3.-6.

AP-514   B   3.-6.

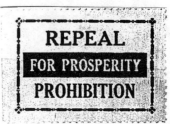

AP-515   3.-6.

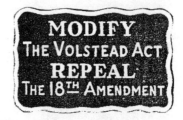

AP-516   Gr   3.-6.
Die cut and embossed.

AP-517   3.-6.

AP-518   3.-6.

AP-519   3.-6.

While some people still claim that tobacco is harmless, and that surely no one knew it was harmful decades ago, there were people much earlier warning against its dangers. Most of the stamps listed are about 50 years old.

ALARMING!!

DOCTERS say,

THREE out of every FIVE BABIES born of habitual CIGARETTE SMOKING MOTHERS

D I E

before the age of TWO YEARS"

TOBACCO KILLS

Send for this Anti-Vise Stamp to Mrs. Katherine Wenger, Jamesburg, N. J. Supported by free-will offerings

T-1   R   .50-2.

ALARMING!

DOCTORS say Three out of every FIVE BABIES born of habitual CIGARETTE SMOK-ING MOTHERS die before the AGE OF TWO YEARS.

TOBACCO KILLS!

Send for this Anti-Vice stamp to Mrs. Katherine E. Wenger, Jamesburg, New Jersey. Supported by Free Will Offerings.

T-2   R   .50-2.

ALARMING

DOCTORS SAY

THREE out of every FIVE BABIES born of HABITUAL CIGARETTE SMOKING MOTHERS DIE before the age of 2 YEARS

TOBACCO KILLS

Supported by free-will offerings. Send for this Ant-Vice Stamp to MRS. W. WENGER, R. R 1 Old Bridge, N. J.

Picture shown at 90%
T-3   Ma   .50-2.
Sheets of three (1x3).

A New Arithmetic

"I am not much of a mathe-matician," said the Cigaret, "but I can add to a man's nervous troubles. I can subtract from his physical energy. I can multi-ply his aches and pains. I can divide his mental powers. I take interest from his work and dis-count his chances for suc-ess."

T-4   R   1.-3.

THOSE WHO HAVE SHRIVELED THEIR RESPECT FOR OTHERS by *Absorbing* 19 POISONS from Cigarette Smoke FOG UP THE AIR WITHOUT THEIR HOST'S PERMISSION

Large Assortment, 25c   STICKERS, WAWONA, CALIF.

T-5   Bk large   .50-2.
T-6   Bk small   .50-2.
Large size shown printed three (dif.) on a sheet (1x3), small size printed six (dif.) on a sheet (2x3). Mixed with anti-liquor stamps.

With SPECIAL GAS MASKS STRAWS and OTHER GADGETS, those allergic to second-hand TOBACCO SMOKE can ENJOY EATING at RESTAUR-ANTS ONCE MORE

Large Assortment, 25c   STICKERS, WAWONA, CALIF.

T-7   Bk large   .50-2.
T-8   Bk small   .50-2.
Large size shown printed three (dif.) on a sheet (1x3), small size printed six (dif.) on a sheet (2x3). Mixed with anti-liquor stamps.

Have A Heart — PLEASE

It LOOKS LIKE THE FOLKS WHO ARE ALLERGIC TO TOBACCO SMOKE WILL NEED GAS MASKS, SINCE SO MANY PEOPLE HAVE LOST THEIR SELF RESTRAINT

Large Assortment, 25c   STICKERS, WAWONA, CALIF.

Picture shown at 80%
T-9   Bk large   .50-2.
T-10   Bk small   .50-2.
Large size shown printed three (dif.) on a sheet (1x3), small size printed six (dif.) on a sheet (2x3). Mixed with anti-liquor stamps.

GIVE HER A REEFER SHELL DO ANYTHING FOR YOU

AH, COME ON BE A SPORT

"YIELD NOT TO TEMPTATION"

PLAY SAFE! PART COMPANY WITH THOSE WHO TEMPT YOU WITH BAD HABITS

Large Assortment, 25c   STICKERS, WAWONA, CALIF.

Picture shown at 80%
T-11   Bk large   .50-2.
T-12   Bk small   .50-2.
Large size shown printed three (dif.) on a sheet (1x3), small size printed six (dif.) on a sheet (2x3). Mixed with anti-liquor stamps.

If you have any items which are not pictured in this book but should be, please send photocopies to the author in care of Krause Publications, 700 E. State St., Iola, WI 54990-0001.

Picture shown at 75%

D-1	B (perf.)	8.-15.
D-2	B (roulette)	8.-15.
D-3	LtB (roulette)	8.-15.
D-4	Pu (perf.)	8.-15.

Issued by the California Narcotic and Crime Prevention League.

Picture shown at 85%

| D-5 | B (1932) | 2.-4. |

Issued by the White Cross Anti-Narcotic Society, San Francisco, CA. Sheets of 100 (10x10).

Picture shown at 85%

| D-6 | B | 2.-4. |

Issued by the White Cross Anti-Narcotic Society, San Francisco, CA.

Picture shown at 85%

| D-7 | B | 2.-4. |

Issued by the White Cross Anti-Narcotic Society, San Francisco, CA.

Picture shown at 85%

| D-8 | B | 2.-4. |

Issued by the White Cross Anti-Narcotic Society, San Francisco, CA.

| D-9 | BkGr (1938) | 3.-6. |

| D-10 | B (1939) | 8.-15. |

| D-11 | PkBk (1975) | .50-2. |

Issued by Large Families of America, Fairfield, CT, in sheets of forty (4x10) mixed stamps of five different designs. See CEN-4 through CEN-6 and M-162.

Picture shown at 67%

| D-12 | Bk | 8.-15. |

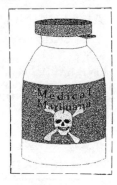

Picture shown at 80%

| D-13 | BkY | .50-1. |

Pro-Drugs

| D-101 | GrR | .50-2. |

Picture shown at 75%

| D-102 | | 1.-2. |

Pro-Life

Picture shown at 70%

| AB-1 | MC | .50-2. |

Issued by Human Life International, MO.

| AB-2 | R (1977) | .50-2. |

| AB-3 | BBk | .50-2. |

AB-4   Bk   .50-2.

AB-5   Bk   .50-2.

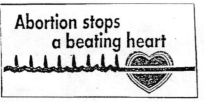

Picture shown at 85%
AB-6   Bk   .50-2.

ABORTION DOESN'T MAKE YOU UNPREGNANT
IT MAKES YOU THE MOTHER OF A DEAD BABY

Picture shown at 60%
AB-7   Bk   .50-2.

Picture shown at 80%
AB-8   Bk   .50-2.

What Right Does a Mother and Her Abortionist Have
to Impose Their Morality
Upon Her Unborn Child ... Fatally?

Picture shown at 65%
AB-9   Bk   .50-2.

Picture shown at 70%
AB-10   Bk   .50-2.

RU 486? RU CRAZY?

Picture shown at 85%
AB-11   Bk   .50-2.

Abortion strikes at:
the baby's *BODY*
the mother's *HEART*
the nation's *SOUL*

Picture shown at 75%
AB-12   Bk   .50-2.

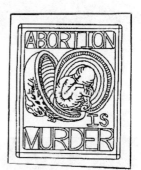

Picture shown at 80%
AB-13   PkMaBk   .50-2.
From MAD Magazine.

AB-14   Bk/B   .50-1.

Pro-Choice

AB-101   RBk   .50-2.

Birth Control

BC-1   BkOrGo   .50-2.
Panes of four (2x2). SE:TRB

If you have any items which are not pictured in this book but should be, please send photocopies to the author in care of Krause Publications, 700 E. State St., Iola, WI 54990-0001.

Picture shown at 45%
BC-2 through BC-17.

BC-2	R Washington	.50-1.
BC-3	R Adams	.50-1.
BC-4	R Madison	.50-1.
BC-5	R Adams	.50-1.
BC-6	Gr Van Buren	.50-1.
BC-7	Gr Lincoln	.50-1.
BC-8	Gr Grant	.50-1.
BC-9	Gr Garfield	.50-1.
BC-10	Or Cleveland	.50-1.
BC-11	Or McKinley	.50-1.
BC-12	Or Taft	.50-1.
BC-13	Or Wilson	.50-1.
BC-14	B Harding	.50-1.
BC-15	B Coolidge	.50-1.
BC-16	B Hoover	.50-1.
BC-17	B Roosevelt	.50-1.

Issued by Planned Parenthood
Federation of America in 1952.

Anti-Birth Control

BC-101   Bk   .50-2.

Social Diseases

Picture shown at 80%
SD-1   MC (1918)   10.-20.
Issued by American Social Hygiene Assn., New
York, NY.

Picture shown at 75%
SD-2   B/Si (1939)   4.-8.
Issued by American Social Hygiene Assn., New
York, NY.

Picture shown at 75%
SD-3   Bk/B   3.-6.
Issued by American Social Hygiene Assn., New
York, NY.

SD-4   Tu (1936)   1.-3.
Issued by California Medico-Legal Civic
League, Inc.

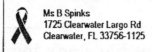

SD-5   RBk.50-1.
Issued by Gay Men's Health Crisis, New York,
NY. Address labels were sent to persons on a
gay mailing list.

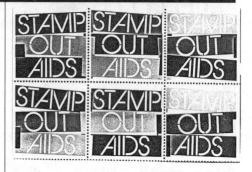

Picture shown at 50%
Set of SD-6 to SD-11.

SD-6	RBY	.50-1.
SD-7	RBY	.50-1.
SD-8	RBY	.50-1.
SD-9	RBY	.50-1.
SD-10	RBY	.50-1.
SD-11	RBY	.50-1.

Sheet of six dif. color arrangements.

SD-12   1.-2.

PRESIDENTIAL CAMPAIGN STAMPS, 1856-1928

JCF-1

AL-4

AL-7

JAG-1

WSH-1

WMK-7

WJB-1

TR-1

ABP-1

GC-2

TWW-2

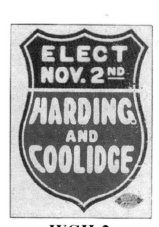

WGH-2

EVD-2

JMC-1

JWD-1

HCH-1

WILLKIE FOR PRESIDENT SET, 1940

From Left to Right: Row 1 WLW-47 to PLW-51   Row 3 WLW-52 to WLW-56

                        Row 2 WLW-57 to WLW-61   Row 4 WLW-62 to WLW-66

WILLKIE FOR PRESIDENT SET, 1940

From Left to Right: Row 1 WLW-22 to WLW-26   Row 2 WLW-27 to WLW-31
Row 3 WLW-32 to WLW-36   Row 4 WLW-37 to WLW-41
Row 5 WLW-42 to WLW-46

PRESIDENTIAL CAMPAIGN STAMPS, 1932-2000

FDR-5

FDR-18

AML-31

WLW-5

TED-1

DDE-2

HK-1

AES-2

DDE-1

JFK-1

RMN-3

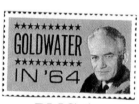

BMG-1

WJC-16

RMN-9

RWR-1

AG-4

GHB-9

WJC-8

WOMAN SUFFRAGE

W-34

W-2

W-46

W-27

W-201

W-38

W-47

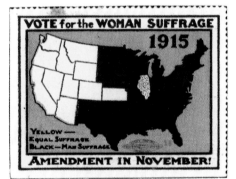

W-23

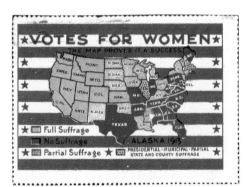

W-24

W-7

W-35

W-1

W-30

W-13

PROHIBITION

VOTE DRY 1916

P-2

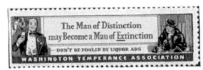

The Man of Distinction may Become a Man of Extinction

DON'T BE FOOLED BY LIQUOR ADS

WASHINGTON TEMPERANCE ASSOCIATION

P-16

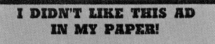

I DIDN'T LIKE THIS AD IN MY PAPER!

P-402

AMERICAN TEMPERANCE SOCIETY OF SEVENTH-DAY ADVENTISTS

RETAIN 18TH AMENDMENT

WE DON'T WANT LIQUOR

TAKOMA PARK, D.C.

P-27

ON YE DRYS ADVANCE Not Retreat

P-12

NATIONAL WOMAN'S CHRISTIAN TEMPERANCE UNION FRANCES E. WILLARD CENTENARY FUND

EDUCATION

1839 1939

CONTRIBUTE TO CENTENARY FUND THRU LOCAL STATE OR NATIONAL W.C.T.U.

P-302

THE NATION

AMEND-MENT MUST REMAIN

P-204

Protect the Barley Industry of California by voting against Prohibition.

AP-2

WHO SAID THE DRYS WERE LICKED?

AP-5

HELP END PROHIBITION

The Crusaders

AP-504

Vote for California Prosperity by voting against Prohibition.

AP-1

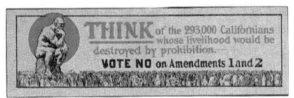

THINK of the 293,000 Californians whose livelihood would be destroyed by prohibition.

VOTE NO on Amendments 1 and 2

AP-6

PROHIBITION BARS BEER
THEY ARE TRYING TO PUT PROHIBITION INTO THE UNITED STATES CONSTITUTION. THAT MEANS NO MORE BEER.
PROTEST TO YOUR LEGISLATORS!

AP-13

WAR AND PEACE

WW-3

WW-2001

AW-1

WW-2

WW-4

AW-3

WW-901

AW-2

WW-104

WW-302

WW-401

AW-54

AW-8

WW-209

VARIOUS CAUSES

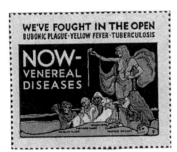

SD-1

ACS-2

ACS-1

B-2

B-1

PP-15

PAT-29

PP-2

LU-44

LU-43

PP-5

SS-9

CS-201

NRA-107

NRA-236

ACS-36

V-3

Chapter 6

Patriotic, War, and Peace

The issue of war and peace may be the most emotional of all political causes. While the Vietnam war protests have been well publicized, little is remembered of the anti-war activists prior to World Wars I and II. The stamps in this chapter tell their story as well as the story of those who supported the wars.

The cause of war and peace has inspired numerous issues of campaign stamps. Some have advised the author to avoid this area because there are too many to catalog. One dealer estimated that 10,000 different items may exist. Admittedly, only a small fraction of the stamps printed for or against our war efforts can be included, but a complete listing has to start somewhere. This listing includes all items of which the author could obtain pictures from his and others' collections. Collectors with unlisted items are asked to send photocopies to the author to be included in a future edition or update of this catalog.

Civil War

Civil War material has now been studied for well over 100 years and there have been several books on patriotic postal material. Included here are the items shown in these books—it is therefore believed that this listing is fairly complete. The only others known to the author are items picturing presidential candidates which are included in Chapter 1.

CW-1   RB   10.-20.

CW-2   RB   10.-20.
CW-3   RB   10.-20.

CW-4   RBBk   10.-20.

CW-5   RBBk   10.-20.

CW-6   RBBk   10.-20.

CW-7   RBBk   10.-20.

CW-8   RB   10.-20.

CW-9   RB   10.-20.

CW-10   RB   10.-20.

CW-11   RB   10.-20.

CW-12   RB   10.-20.

Picture shown at 70%
CW-13   RB   10.-20.

Picture shown at 70%
CW-14   RB   10.-20.

Picture shown at 70%
CW-15   RB   10.-20.

CW-16   RB   8.-15.

Picture shown at 70%
CW-17   RB   8.-15.

Picture shown at 70%
CW-18   RB   8.-15.

CW-19   RB   8.-15.

CW-20   RB   8.-15.

Picture shown at 70%
CW-21   RB   8.-15.

WWI and WWII

While some "win the war" stamps are obviously from one war or the other, it is sometimes hard to tell for which war a stamp was issued—World War I and World War II were only separated by 21 years. Rather than have some separated and the others unknown, they are all shown in this section. For easier reference some of them are broken down by subject matter. Where a stamp contains subjects that fit into two or more categories, it has been included in the subject which is most obvious on the face of the stamp.

War Bonds and Loans

Picture shown at 70%
WW-1   MC   10.-20.

Picture shown at 85%
WW-2   MC   10.-20.

Picture shown at 85%
WW-3   MC   10.-20.

Picture shown at 77%
WW-4   MC   10.-20.

Picture shown at 80%
WW-5   RBBk   5.-10.

Picture shown at 80%
WW-6   RBBk   4.-8.

Picture shown at 90%
WW-7   RBGy   2.-4.

Picture shown at 80%
WW-8   RB   2.-4.

Picture shown at 80%
WW-9   RBGy   2.-4.

Picture shown at 80%
WW-10   RBGy   2.-4.

Picture shown at 75%
WW-11   RBGd   2.-4.

Picture shown at 80%
WW-12   R   2.-4.

WW-13   RB   .50-2.

WW-14   RB   .50-2.

WW-15   B   .50-2.
This stamp is from the margin of a sheet of WW-14.

WW-16   RB   .50-2.

WW-17   RB   .50-2.

Picture shown at 72%
WW-18   R   .50-2.

Picture shown at 95%
WW-19   RB   .50-2.

WW-20   RB   .50-2.

WW-21   RB   .50-2.

WW-22   RB   .50-2.

WW-23   RB   .50-2.

WW-24   RB   1.-3.

WW-25   B   .50-2.

Picture shown at 90%
WW-26   RB   .50-2.

WW-27   RB   .50-2.

WW-28   RB   .50-2.

WW-29   B/B   .50-2.

WW-30   Bk/Pk   .50-2.

WW-31   Br   .50-2.

WW-32   Gr   .50-2.

WW-33   RBk   .50-2.

WW-34   Bk/Gr   .50-2.

WW-35   RB   .50-2.

Picture shown at 67%
WW-36   RB   .50-2.

WW-37   GrR/Gr (roulette)   .50-2.
WW-38   RB (roulette)   .50-2.
WW-39   GrR/Gr (perf.)   .50-2.

WW-40   OrBk   .50-2.

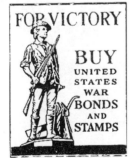

WW-41   RB   .50-2.

WW-42   RB   .50-2.

WW-43   B   .50-2.

WW-44   RB   .50-2.
Apparently from the margin of a sheet of similar
stamps.

WW-45   MC   .50-2.
WW-46   MC   .50-2.
WW-47   MC   .50-2.
Sheets of six (3x2).

Picture shown at 70%
WW-48   Bk   .50-2.
WW-49   B   .50-2.
WW-50   B/Gd   .50-2.
WW-51   Br/Gd   .50-2.
Individual imperforate. There are probably other
color combinations.

Picture shown at 80%
WW-52   RB   .50-2.

WW-53   RB   .50-2.

WW-54   RB   .50-2.
From MAD Magazine.
See also WW-104, 105, 107, 108, 110, 111,
112, 115, 116, 117, 134.

Picture shown at 110%
WW-101   RBY   2.-4

WW-104   RB   .50-2.

WW-105   RB   .50-2.

WW-106   RB   .50-2.

WW-102   R   .50-2.

WW-103   RB   .50-2.

Picture shown at 75%
WW-107   RB   .50-2.

Invest In Victory

Buy War Stamps & Bonds

Picture shown at 75%
WW-108   RB   .50-2.

Let's Go! U.S.A.

Keep 'em Rolling

Picture shown at 75%
WW-109   RB   .50-2.

Keep 'em Flying

Buy War Stamps & Bonds

Picture shown at 75%
WW-110   RB   .50-2.

Share Freedom!

Get War Stamps Today!

Picture shown at 75%
WW-111   RB   .50-2.

Give Him Wings!

Buy Those Bonds Now!

WW-112   RB   .50-2.

Our Flag

Long May It Wave

Picture shown at 70%
WW-113   RB   .50-2.

Our Flag

Long May It Wave

Picture shown at 70%
WW-114   RB   .50-2.

Invest In Victory

Buy War Stamps and Bonds

Picture shown at 85%
WW-115   RB   .50-2.

Invest In Victory

Buy War Stamps and Bonds

WW-116   RB   .50-2.

Keep 'em Flying

Buy War Stamps and Bonds

WW-117   RB   .50-2.

Picture shown at 75%
WW-118   RB   .50-2.

Picture shown at 75%
WW-119   RB   .50-2.

Picture shown at 85%
WW-120   RB   .50-2.

Picture shown at 75%
WW-121   RB   .50-2.

Picture shown at 85%
WW-122   Gr   .50-2.

WW-123   RB   .50-2.

WW-124   RB   .50-2.

WW-125   Bk   .50-2.

WW-126   RB   1.-3.

WW-127   RB   .50-2.

WW-128   RB   .50-2.

Picture shown at 75%
WW-129   RB   1.-3.

WW-130   RBGo   .50-2.

Picture shown at 80%
WW-131   RB   .50-2.

WW-132   GrRSi   .50-2.

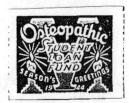

WW-133   GrRSi   .50-2.

WW-134   RBk   .50-2.

WW-135   RB   .50-2.

WW-136   RB   .50-2.

WW-137   RB   .50-2.

WW-138   RGr   .50-2.

WW-139   B/Gr   .50-2.

WW-140   RB   .50-2.

WW-141   RB/Si foil   .50-2.
WW-142   R/Si foil   .50-2.

Picture shown at 80%
WW-143   RB/Si foil   .50-2.

WW-144   RB   1.-3.

BUDDY BURNSIDE WRITES 3 OPEN LETTERS:

1: ★★ TO THE DAILY NEWS:
90% Unity is not sufficient.

2: ★★ TO BILL KNUDSEN:
A year ago I asked you to use the REUTHER PLAN...A year from now I'd like the American People to thank you for using it.

3: ★★ TO ALL AMERICANS:
Remember Captain Kelly—Buy Bonds and Beat the Bandits.

We need your help. Will you join us in our work. Send a 10¢ Defense Stamp for 50 of these stickers.

Write **BUDDY BURNSIDE**
P. O. BOX 7, TIMES SQUARE, N. Y. C.

WW-145   RB   1.-3.

Picture shown at 70%
WW-146   RB   .50-2.

WW-147   RB   .50-2.

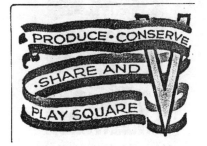

WW-148   RB   .50-2.

WW-149   .50-2.

WW-150   RB   .50-2.

WW-151   R   .50-2.

Remember Pearl Harbor

Picture shown at 50%
WW-201   RB   .50-2.

Picture shown at 50%
WW-202   RB   .50-2.

Picture shown at 50%
WW-203   RB   .50-2.

Picture shown at 60%
WW-204   RB   .50-2.

Picture shown at 60%
WW-205　　R　　　　　　　　　　　.50-2.

Picture shown at 60%
WW-206　　RB　　　　　　　　　　.50-2.

WW-207　　R　　　　　　　　　　　.50-2.

WW-208　　RB　　　　　　　　　　.50-2.

WW-209　　RB　　　　　　　　　　.50-2.

Picture shown at 80%
WW-210　　RB　　　　　　　　　　1.-3.

Picture shown at 80%
WW-211　　MC　　　　　　　　　　1.-2.

Loose Lips Sink Ships

WW-301　　RBBkY　　　　　　　　.50-2.

WW-302　　RBBkY　　　　　　　　1.-3.

WW-303　　RBBkY　　　　　　　　.50-2.

WW-304　　RBBkY　　　　　　　　.50-2.
Issued by House of Seagram.

WW-305　　RB　　　　　　　　　　1.-3.

WW-306　　RB　　　　　　　　　　1.-3.

WW-307　　RB　　　　　　　　　　1.-3.

WW-308   RB   1.-3.

WW-309   RB   1.-3.
Issued by American Flying Services Foundation, Inc.

Picture shown at 85%
WW-310   RB   .50-2.

WW-311   2.-4.

Production and the Home Front

Picture shown at 80%
WW-401   RBY   .50-2.

Picture shown at 90%
WW-402   R   .50-2.

Picture shown at 80%
WW-403   RB   .50-2.

WW-404   BrBkY   1.-3.

WW-405   MC   1.-3.

WW-406   RB   .50-2.

WW-407   MC   1.-3.

Picture shown at 90%
WW-408   RBGy   .50-2.

Patriotic, War, and Peace • 163

WW-409   RB   1.-3.

WW-410   B/Pk   .50-2.

Picture shown at 85%
WW-411   GrBk   1.-3.

Picture shown at 90%
WW-412   RB   1.-3.

WW-413   RBBk   .50-2.

WW-414   RB   .50-2.

WW-415   RB   .50-2.

WW-416   RB   .50-2.

WW-417   RB   .50-2.

WW-418   RB/Si foil   1.-3.

Picture shown at 85%
WW-419   RB   1.-3.

WW-420   RB   .50-2.

WW-421   RB   .50-2.

WW-422   Gr   .50-2.

WW-423   RB   .50-2.

WW-424   RBk   .50-2.

Picture shown at 85%
WW-425   Bk   .50-2.

WW-426   RB   .50-2.

Picture shown at 85%
WW-427   RB   .50-2.

WW-428   B   .50-2.

Picture shown at 85%
WW-429   BBk   1.-3.

WW-430   RBk   .50-2.

WW-431   BBk   .50-2.

WW-432   RBBk   .50-2.

WW-433   RB   .50-2.

WW-434   Bk   2.-4.

WW-435   RB   .50-2.

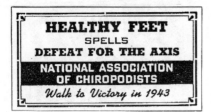

WW-436   B   .50-2.

WW-437   RBBk   .50-2.

Picture shown at 80%
WW-438   RGr   .50-2.

WW-439   .50-2.

WW-440   RB   .50-2.

WW-441   RB   .50-2.

WW-442   RB   .50-2.

WW-443   RB   .50-2.

WW-444   RB   .50-2.

WW-445   RB   .50-2.

WW-446   RB   .50-2.

Picture shown at 85%
WW-447 through WW-452

WW-447   RBk   .50-2.

WW-448   RBk   .50-2.
WW-449   RBk   .50-2.
WW-450   RBk   .50-2.

WW-451   RBk   .50-2.
WW-452   RBk   .50-2.

Letters to Soldiers

WW-501   .50-2.

WW-502   RB   .50-2.

WW-503   RB   .50-2.

WW-504   RB   .50-2.

WW-505   RB   .50-2.

WW-506   RB   .50-2.

WW-507   B   .50-2.

WW-508   R   .50-2.

Picture shown at 85%

WW-509   RGr   .50-2.

WW-510   RB   .50-2.

WW-511   RB   .50-2.

WW-512   RB   .50-2.

WW-513   RB   .50-2.

WW-514   RB   .50-2.

WW-515   RBkY   .50-2.

WW-516   RBkY   .50-2.

WW-517   RBkY   .50-2.

WW-518   RBkY   .50-2.

Army

WW-601   Bk/Go foil   .50-2.

WW-602   MC   .50-2.

WW-603   MC   .50-2.

WW-604   MC   .50-2.

WW-605   BrBk/Go foil   .50-2.

WW-606   YBk   .50-2.

WW-607   RB   .50-2.

Picture shown at 75%
WW-608   RB   1.-3.

WW-609   RB   .50-2.

WW-610   RB   .50-2.

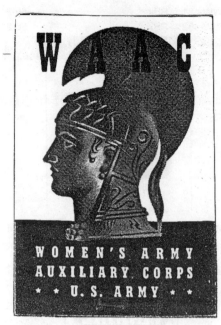

WW-611   BY   1.-3.

WW-612	MC #1	.50-1.
WW-613	MC #2	.50-1.
WW-614	MC #3	.50-1.
WW-615	MC #4	.50-1.
WW-616	MC #5	.50-1.
WW-617	MC #6	.50-1.
WW-618	MC #7	.50-1.
WW-619	MC #9	.50-1.
WW-620	MC #10	.50-1.
WW-621	MC #11	.50-1.
WW-622	MC #12	.50-1.
WW-623	MC #13	.50-1.
WW-624	MC #14	.50-1.
WW-625	MC #15	.50-1.
WW-626	MC #16	.50-1.
WW-627	MC #17	.50-1.
WW-628	MC #18	.50-1.
WW-629	MC #19	.50-1.
WW-630	MC #20	.50-1.
WW-631	MC #21	.50-1.
WW-632	MC #22	.50-1.
WW-633	MC #23	.50-1.
WW-634	MC #24	.50-1.
WW-635	MC #25	.50-1.
WW-636	MC #26	.50-1.
WW-637	MC #27	.50-1.
WW-638	MC #28	.50-1.
WW-639	MC #29	.50-1.
WW-640	MC #30	.50-1.
WW-641	MC #31	.50-1.
WW-642	MC #32	.50-1.
WW-643	MC #33	.50-1.
WW-644	MC #34	.50-1.
WW-645	MC #35	.50-1.

WW-646	MC #36	.50-1.
WW-647	MC #37	.50-1.
WW-648	MC #38	.50-1.
WW-649	MC #39	.50-1.
WW-650	MC #40	.50-1.
WW-651	MC #41	.50-1.
WW-652	MC #42	.50-1.
WW-653	MC #43	.50-1.
WW-654	MC #45	.50-1.
WW-655	MC #46	.50-1.
WW-656	MC #47	.50-1.

This is a set of forty-eight different stamps called the "Spirit of '42 Series." All of them are included here except #8 which is in the Pearl Harbor section as WW-211, #44 which is in the Air Force section as WW-809, and #48 which is the Franklin Roosevelt section as FDR-34.

Navy

WW-701　　RBY　　　　　　　　　.50-2.

WW-702　　Go foil　　　　　　　　.50-2.
Embossed.

WW-703　　MC　　　　　　　　　.50-2.

WW-704　　BW/Si foil　　　　　　.50-2.

WW-705　　RB　　　　　　　　　.50-2.

WW-706　　RB　　　　　　　　　.50-2.

WW-707　　B/Si foil　　　　　　　.50-2.

WW-708　　MC　　　　　　　　　.50-2.

WW-709　　　　　　　　　　　　.50-2.

Picture shown at 80%

WW-710　　Go foil　　　　　　　　.50-2.
Embossed.

WW-711　　BBkY　　　　　　　　.50-2.

Picture shown at 65%

WW-712　　B　　　　　　　　　　.50-2.

Air Force

WW-801　　RB　　　　　　　　　.50-2.

WW-802　　MC　　　　　　　　　.50-2.

WW-803　　RB　　　　　　　　　.50-2.

AIR SUPREMACY
MEANS VICTORY
KEEP 'EM FLYING

Picture shown at 90%
WW-804   RB   .50-2.

WW-805   RB   .50-2.

WW-806   MC   .50-2.

WW-807   MC   .50-2.

WW-808   BBk/Si foil   .50-2.

WW-809   MC   .50-1.

Marines

WW-901   MC   2.-4

WW-902   RBk   1.-3.

WW-903   RBk   .50-2.

WW-904   RB   .50-2.

WW-905   RB   .50-2.

WW-906   RB   .50-2.

WW-907   RB   .50-2.

WW-908   RB   .50-2.

WW-909   RB   .50-2.

WW-910   RB   .50-2.

WW-911   RB   .50-2.

WW-912   RB   .50-2.

WW-913   LtBDkB/Si foil   .50-2.

WW-914   MC   .50-2.

WW-915   RBGoSi   1.-3.

Coast Guard

WW-1001   B   .50-2.

WW-1002   B/Go foil   .50-2.
Embossed.

Anti-Hitler

WW-1101   RBk   3.-6.

WW-1102   RB   3.-6.

Picture shown at 60%
WW-1103   B   2.-4.

WW-1104   RB   1.-3.

WW-1105   RB   1.-3.

WW-1106   RB   1.-3.

Boycott Germany

WW-1201   Bk/Or   .50-2.

WW-1202   BkOr   .50-2.

WW-1203 LtB   .50-2.
WW-1204 DkB   .50-2.

Boycott Japan

WW-1251   .50-2.

Family Members in the Service

A flag in the window with a star on it meant that a family had a member in the armed services. Some made up stamps for the same purpose.

WW-1301 RTu   .50-2.

WW-1302 RB   .50-2.

WW-1303 RB   .50-2.

WW-1304 RB   .50-2.

WW-1305 RB   .50-2.

WW-1306 RB   .50-2.

WW-1307 RBBrY   .50-2.

WW-1308 BOr   .50-2.

WW-1309 RBrLtBDkB   .50-2.

General

Picture shown at 70%
WW-2001 MC   5.-10.

WW-2002 MC   4.-8.

WW-2003 RBY   1.-3.
WW-2004 RBY   1.-3.

WW-2005 RBY   1.-3.
WW-2006 RBY   1.-3.

WW-2007 B/B   .50-2.

WW-2008 LtGr   .50-2.
Embossed.
WW-2009 Gl foil   .50-2.
Embossed.

WW-2010   RBBkBr   1.-3.

WW-2014   RBBkBr   1.-3.

WW-2018   RB   .50-2.

WW-2011   RBBkBr   1.-3.

WW-2015   RBBkBr   1.-3.

WW-2019   RB   .50-2.

WW-2020   B   .50-2.

WW-2012   RB   1.-3.

Picture shown at 95%
WW-2016   R   .50-2

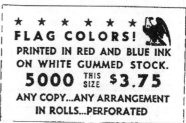

WW-2021   RB   .50-2.

WW-2013   RBBkBr   1.-3.

WW-2017   RB   .50-2.

WW-2022   MC   1.-3.

Patriotic, War, and Peace • 173

WW-2023 RB/Si foil .50-2.

WW-2024 MC 1.-3.

WW-2025 RB .50-2.

WW-2026 RB .50-2.

WW-2027 RB .50-2.

WW-2028 MC .50-2.

WW-2029 RBGo .50-2.

WW-2030 MC .50-2.

WW-2031 RBY .50-2.

WW-2032 RB .50-2.

WW-2033 OrBk/Cr .50-2.
WW-2034 GrBk/Cr .50-2.

WW-2035 RB 1.-3.

Picture shown at 90%
WW-2036 B .50-2.
WW-2037 Bk .50-2.
WW-2038 Br .50-2.
WW-2039 B/Gd .50-2.
WW-2040 Bk/Gd .50-2.
WW-2041 Br/Gd .50-2.
Individual imperforate. There may be other color combinations.

Picture shown at 85%
WW-2042 MC 2.-4.

WW-2043 B   .50-2.

WW-2044 RB   .50-2.

Picture shown at 75%
WW-2045 B/B   1.-3.
WW-2046 B/Y   1.-3.
WW-2047 BGd   1.-3.

Picture shown at 80%
WW-2048 RB   .50-2.

Picture shown at 90%
WW-2049 RB   .50-2.

WW-2050 RBYBr   .50-2.

WW-2051 R   .50-2.

Picture shown at 80%
WW-2101 MC #1   1.-3.

WW-2052 RB (pictured above)   2.-4.

WW-2053 RB   .50-2.

WW-2102 MC #2   1.-3.
WW-2103 MC #3   1.-3.
WW-2104 MC #4   1.-3.
WW-2105 MC #5   1.-3.
WW-2106 MC #6   1.-3.
WW-2107 MC #7   1.-3.
WW-2108 MC #9   1.-3.
WW-2109 MC #10   1.-3.
WW-2110 MC #11   1.-3.
WW-2111 MC #12   1.-3.
WW-2112 MC #13   1.-3.

WW-2113	MC #14	1.-3.	WW-2130	MC #31	1.-3.	WW-2147	MC #49	1.-3.
WW-2114	MC #15	1.-3.	WW-2131	MC #32	1.-3.	WW-2148	MC #50	1.-3.

WW-2113	MC #14	1.-3.	WW-2130	MC #31	1.-3.
WW-2114	MC #15	1.-3.	WW-2131	MC #32	1.-3.
WW-2115	MC #16	1.-3.	WW-2132	MC #33	1.-3.
WW-2116	MC #17	1.-3.	WW-2133	MC #34	1.-3.
WW-2117	MC #18	1.-3.	WW-2134	MC #35	1.-3.
WW-2118	MC #19	1.-3.	WW-2135	MC #36	1.-3.
WW-2119	MC #20	1.-3.	WW-2136	MC #37	1.-3.
WW-2120	MC #21	1.-3.	WW-2137	MC #38	1.-3.
WW-2121	MC #22	1.-3.	WW-2138	MC #39	1.-3.
WW-2122	MC #23	1.-3.	WW-2139	MC #40	1.-3.
WW-2123	MC #24	1.-3.	WW-2140	MC #41	1.-3.
WW-2124	MC #25	1.-3.	WW-2141	MC #42	1.-3.
WW-2125	MC #26	1.-3.	WW-2142	MC #43	1.-3.
WW-2126	MC #27	1.-3.	WW-2143	MC #45	1.-3.
WW-2127	MC #28	1.-3.	WW-2144	MC #46	1.-3.
WW-2128	MC #29	1.-3.	WW-2145	MC #47	1.-3.
WW-2129	MC #30	1.-3.	WW-2146	MC #48	1.-3.

WW-2147 MC #49   1.-3.
WW-2148 MC #50   1.-3.

This is a set of 50 different stamps called the Famous War Posters.

Vietnam

WW-3001   Gr   .50-2.

Patriotic

America First

PAT-1   RBY   3.-6.

PAT-3   RB   .50-2.

PAT-4   RDkBLtB   .50-2.

PAT-5   RB   .50-2.

PAT-6   RB   .50-2.

PAT-7   B   .50-2.

Picture shown at 90%
PAT-8   RB   .50-2.

Picture shown at 80%
PAT-9   Bk   .50-2.

PAT-2   RBGy   .50-2.

PAT-10   RB   3.-6.

PAT-11   RB   3.-6.

PAT-12   RB   3.-6.

PAT-13   RB   3.-6.

Flags

PAT-21   RB   1.-2.

PAT-22   RBGo (1917)   2.-4.

PAT-23   RB   .50-2.

PAT-24   RB   .50-2.

PAT-25   B   .50-2.

PAT-26   RB   .50-2.

PAT-27   RDkBLtB   .50-2.

PAT-28   RB   .50-2.

PAT-29   RB   .50-2.

Keep Old Glory Flying

Picture shown at 95%

PAT-30   RB   .50-2.

PAT-31   RB   .50-1.

PAT-32   RB   .50-1.

PAT-33   RB   .50-1.

PAT-34   RB   .50-1.

PAT-35   RB   .50-1.

PAT-36   RB/Si foil   .50-2.

PAT-37   RB/Si foil   .50-2.

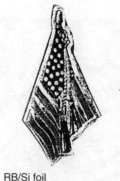

PAT-38   RB/Si foil   .50-2.

PAT-39   RB/Si foil   .50-2.

PAT-40   RBBk (1958)   .50-1.
Issued by Amvets.

PAT-41   RBBk (1959)   .50-1.
Issued by Amvets.

PAT-42   RBBk (1960)   .50-1.
Issued by Amvets.

PAT-43   RBBk (1960)   .50-2.
Issued by Amvets.

Picture shown at 90%

PAT-44   RBBk (1961)   .50-2.
Issued by Amvets.

PAT-45   MC (1962)   .50-1.
Issued by Amvets.
(The 1963 Amvets stamp is included in Chapter 4 as ACS-36.)

PAT-46   MC (1964)   .50-1.
Issued by Amvets.

PAT-47   RB (1967-73)   .50-1.
Issued by Amvets.

PAT-48   MC (1974)   .50-1.
Issued by Amvets.

PAT-49   RBBk (1975)   .50-1.
Issued by Amvets.

PAT-50   MC (1976)   .50-1.
Issued by Amvets.

PAT-51   RB   .50-2.

PAT-52   RB (1917)   2.-4.

PAT-53   BkY   .50-2.

PAT-54   MC   .50-2.
Contained on the same sheet as DMA-4.

Shields, Bells, Eagles, Ribbons, and Hats

PAT-101   RB   .50-1.

PAT-102   RB (1940)   .50-2.

PAT-103   RB   .50-2.

PAT-104   RB   .50-1.

PAT-126   MC   .50-2.

PAT-127   RB   .50-2.

PAT-128   RB   .50-2.

PAT-129   BBkPk   .50-2.

PAT-130   RB   .50-2.

PAT-131   RB "Washington"   .50-1.
PAT-132   RB "Paine"   .50-1.
PAT-133   RB "Henry"   .50-1.
PAT-134   RB "Franklin"   .50-1.
PAT-135   RB "Jefferson"   .50-1.
PAT-136   RB "Harper"   .50-1.
PAT-137   RB "Webster"   .50-1.
PAT-138   RB "Jackson"   .50-1.
PAT-139   RB "Lincoln"   .50-1.
PAT-140   RB "Cleveland"   .50-1.
PAT-141   RB "Schurz"   .50-1.
PAT-142   RB "Wilson"   .50-1.
Issued by Amvets (1960).

PAT-143   RB "Franklin"   .50-1.
PAT-144   RB "Lincoln"   .50-1.
PAT-145   RB "Paine"   .50-1.
PAT-146   RB "Washington"   .50-1.
PAT-147   RB "Henry"   .50-1.
PAT-148   RB "Webster"   .50-1.
Issued by Amvets (1967).

PAT-161   RBWGo   .50-1.

PAT-162   RB   .50-1.

PAT-163   MC   .50-2.

PAT-176   R   .50-1.

PAT-177   RB   .50-1.

Front

Back

PAT-178   RB   .50-2.
PAT-179   RB (imperf.)   .50-2.

Religious Patriotic

PAT-201   GrBkY   1.-2.
Issued by American Legion, Michigan.

PAT-202   RB   .50-2.

PAT-203   RB   .50-2.

PAT-204   RB   .50-2.

Picture shown at 90%
PAT-205   R   .50-2.

Picture shown at 85%
PAT-206   RB   .50-2.
PAT-207   R   .50-2.

PAT-208   RB   .50-2.

PAT-209   RB   .50-2.

PAT-210   RB   .50-2.

PAT-211   RB   .50-2.

PAT-212   B/Pk   .50-2.

PAT-213   RB   .50-1.

PAT-214   RB   .50-1.

PAT-215   RB   .50-1.

PAT-216   RB   1.-2.

PAT-217   MC   1.-2.

Republic/Democracy

Picture shown at 85%
PAT-301   RB   .50-2.

PAT-351   R   .50-2.

Constitution

PAT-401   RB   .50-2.

PAT-402   RB   .50-2.

PAT-403   RB   .50-2.

PAT-404   RB   .50-2.

PAT-405   RBBkGo   1.-3.
Sheets of fifty (10x5).

Tolerance and Unity

PAT-501   RB   .50-2.

PAT-502   MC (1939)   .50-2.

PAT-503   RBBk (1940-41)   .50-2.

PAT-504   MC (1941)   .50-2.

PAT-505   MC (1942-43)   .50-2.

PAT-506   MC (1943-44)   .50-2.

PAT-507   RBGy (1944-45)   .50-2.

PAT-508   MC (1945-46)   .50-2.

Fund-raising stamps have been issued by many patriotic organizations, such as the American Legion, Disabled American Veterans, and Veterans of Foreign Wars. Only those which espouse political causes are included in this book. But if you are interested in such material there are hundreds of such items available.

PAT-509 MC (1946-47) .50-2.

PAT-510 MC (1947-48) .50-2.

PAT-511 MC (1948-49) .50-2.

PAT-512 BROL (1949-50) .50-2.

PAT-513 MC (1950-51) .50-2.

PAT-514 MC (1951-52) .50-2.

PAT-515 MC .50-2.

PAT-516 RBBr (1953-54) .50-2.

PAT-517 RBBk (1954-55) .50-2.

PAT-518 MC (1955-56) .50-2.
(PAT-502 through PAT-518 were issued by the Council Against Intolerance in America.)

PAT-519 MC (1960-61) .50-2.
Issued by the Council for American Unity, perhaps a successor organization to the Council Against Intolerance in America.

PAT-520 B .50-2.

General

Picture shown at 70%

Front

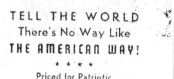

Back
Picture shown at 70%
PAT-601 RB 1.-3.

Front

TELL THE WORLD
There's No Way Like
THE AMERICAN WAY!

★ ★ ★ ★

PRICED for Patriotic
Endeavor
1000 for $1.50

★ ★ ★ ★

EVER READY LABEL CORP.
141 E. 25TH ST.   NEW YORK, N. Y.

Back

| PAT-602 | RBGy | | .50-2. |
| PAT-603 | RBGy (imperf.) | | .50-2. |

| PAT-604 | RB | | .50-2. |

| PAT-605 | RB | | .50-2. |

| PAT-606 | RBBk | | 1.-3. |

| PAT-607 | RB | | 1.-3. |

Front

PROPER
GANDER
for Americans
SPREAD IT

★ ★ ★

$1.00 for 1000
Get Prices on Quantities
Priced for Patriotic Use.

★ ★ ★

EVER READY LABEL
Corporation
141 E. 25th St. New York, N. Y.

Back

| PAT-608 | RB | | .50-2. |
Sheet of three (3x1).

| PAT-609 | RB | | .50-2. |

| PAT-610 | RBGo | | .50-2. |

| PAT-611 | RBGo | | .50-2. |

Picture shown at 90%

| PAT-612 | RB | | .50-2. |

| PAT-613 | RB | | .50-2. |
Panes of six (2x3) in booklets.

| PAT-614 | RB | | .50-2. |

| PAT-615 | Go foil | | .50-2. |
Embossed.

PAT-616   RB   .50-2.
PAT-617   RB   .50-2.
PAT-618   RB   .50-2.
PAT-619   RB   .50-2.
PAT-620   RB   .50-2.
PAT-621   RB   .50-2.

Sheets of forty (4x10) with twenty copies of PAT-616 and four copies of each of the others. Issued by the New Spirit of '76 Foundation.

Picture shown at 70%
PAT-622   RB   .50-2.

Happy we are that we live in a FREE country, that we possess an ABUNDANCE of life's necessities, that OPPORTUNITIES in education and enterprise are available to all; and it is these things that ennoble and ease human life in this greatest of all nations— AMERICA

PAT-623   RB   .50-2.

$100,000,000,000.

worth of annual business is a coming reality for . . . .

A M E R I C A

PAT-624   RB   .50-2.

invest. . .
in Solid, Solvent
A M E R I C A
and you'll never "sell short."

PAT-625   RB   .50-2.

AMERICA
Produces a major volume of World's output and supply of
METALS — COTTON
OIL — MACHINERY
and the aids to modern Living

PAT-626   RB   .50-2.

In this age of the airplane, radio and super-mechanics, we are living in the dawning of a new AMERICA—assuring real comforts and contentment to all.

PAT-627   RB   .50-2.

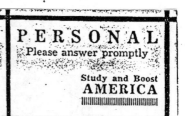

PAT-628   RB   .50-2.

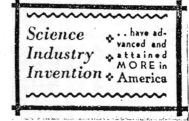

PAT-629   RB   .50-2.

PAT-630   RB   .50-2.

PAT-631   B   .50-2.

PAT-632   R   .50-2.
PAT-633   Br   .50-2.
PAT-634   Pu   .50-2.

PAT-635	RB		.50-2.	PAT-640	RB		.50-2.	PAT-645	RB		.50-2.
PAT-636	RB		.50-2.	PAT-641	RB		.50-2.	PAT-646	RB		.50-2.
PAT-637	RB		.50-2.	PAT-642	RB		.50-2.				
PAT-638	RB		.50-2.	PAT-643	RB		.50-2.				
PAT-639	RB		.50-2.	PAT-644	RB		.50-2.				

Issued by American Legion J. J. Flannery Post 827, Illinois.

To keep the subject of this book manageable it was limited to U.S. political causes. However, there are many U.S. labels supporting the rights of foreign groups or nations.

PAT-661   Bk/Go foil   1.-2.
Embossed die cut.

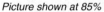
Picture shown at 85%

PAT-647	RB	.50-2.
PAT-648	RB	.50-2.
PAT-649	RB	.50-2.
PAT-650	RB	.50-2.
PAT-651	RR	.50-2.
PAT-652	RB	.50-2.
PAT-653	RB	.50-2.
PAT-654	RB	.50-2.
PAT-655	RB	.50-2.
PAT-656	RB	.50-2.
PAT-657	RB	.50-2.
PAT-658	RB	.50-2.

PAT-647 through PAT-658 shown above

PAT-660   BBk   .50-1.
Sheets of eight (4x2) and twenty (4x5).

PAT-662   RB   1.-3.
Issued by United Spanish War Veterans.

PAT-659   RBk   .50-1.
Issued by Sphinx Publishing, Clearwater, Fla.
when President Clinton bowed to Japanese
pressure to change "V-J Day" to "End of the War
Day."

Smithsonian Revisionist History

In its planned exhibit of the Enola Gay, the plane which dropped the atomic bomb on Hiroshima, the revisionist historians of the Smithsonian Institution implied that Japan was a victim of American racism and agression in World War II. The display which they designed was anti-American propaganda, dwelling upon scenes of Japanese suffering, and ignoring the atrocities Japan committed against Americans and the citizens of so many countries in Southeast Asia.

What Really Happened

Americans haven't forgotten that Japan started the war with a surprise bombing attack on unsuspecting American servicemen at Pearl Harbor. And in 1945 millions of Japanese were planning to fight an Allied invasion. Thousands of tons of bombs on Tokyo and other cities did not convince them to surrender. It took two atomic bombs before Japan finally surrendered. These bombs caused horrible suffering and thousands of deaths, but they saved hundreds of thousands of lives.

©1995 Sphinx, POB 25, Clearwater, FL 34617

Picture shown at 90%   PAT-661   BBk (souvenir sheet)   2.-4.

Hiroshima Stamp Incident

In 1994 the U.S. Postal Service announced the designs of the final ten stamps in the series of World War II commemoratives. The government of Japan immediately protested that one of the stamps pictured the bombing of Hiroshima. The postal service answered that the stamps did not celebrate the events, they only noted the anniversaries of the most important events, and that the bombing of Pearl Harbor had also been on a stamp. Not wanting to offend the Japanese, President Clinton instructed the Postal Service to redesign the stamp.

There was an immediate response from veterans groups and others who felt the U.S. should not give in to Japan's peculiar sensitivities. Over the next few months several parties produced their own versions of the stamps and these were written up by the media not only in the U.S. and Japan but throughout the world.

The author produced the first of these stamps in December and distributed over 50,000 stamps before the issue died down.

H-7 and H-8 are peel and stick labels and are included because, with these, our listing covers every stamp issued for this incident.

H-2   RBk   .50-1.
Sheets of eight (4x2) and sheets of twenty (4x5). Crude reproductions are known to exist in red ink, rouletted, rather than perforated.
H-3   RBBk   .50-1.
Sheets of eight (4x2).

H-4   RBk   .50-1.
H-4a   RBk (darker)   .50-1.
Sheets of thirty-six (6x6).
H-4a appears to be a later printing.

H-5   RBk   .50-1.
Sheets of thirty-six (6x6).

H-6   MC   .50-1.
Sheets of twenty-five (5x5).

H-7   MC   .50-1.
Sheets of twenty (4x5). Peel and stick.

H-8   MC   .50-1.
Sheets of twenty-four (6x4). Peel and stick.

Japan Surrenders, 1945

In 1937-1945 the Japanese waged a war of conquest against countries in the Pacific region. In 1945 military experts felt they would fight even more fiercely to defend their homeland and that an invasion would take months, costing tens of thousands of American lives. President Truman made the decision to use the newly-developed atomic bomb. The Japanese surrendered in a matter of days, ending the war.

United States Surrenders, 1994

In 1991-1994 the United States issued a series of postage stamps commemorating the important events of World War II. Although Americans did not object to the commemoration of the Japanese attack of Pearl Harbor, the Japanese objected to a stamp planned for 1995 depicting the atomic bomb blast over Hiroshima. President Clinton surrendered to the Japanese and ordered the Post Office not to issue the stamp.

H-1   RBk   2.-4.
Imperforate sheet (holes are printed).

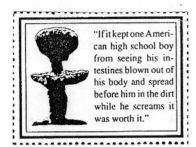

"If it kept one American high school boy from seeing his intestines blown out of his body and spread before him in the dirt while he screams it was worth it."

H-9   BkPu   .50-1.

"If it had not been for Pearl Harbor, there would not have been a Hiroshima."

H-10   BkPu   .50-1.
Sheets of twenty (4x5) alternating designs of H-9 and H-10.

| H-11 | MC gummed back | .50-1. |
| H-11a | MC peel and stick | .50-1. |

This is a copy of the original artwork for the proposed stamp which someone made into a stamp.

Anti-War & Peace

While the opposition to America's involvement in the Vietnam War was well documented, few are aware of how much opposition there was to our participation in the two World Wars. This listing of nearly 400 items will help illustrate those feelings.

World War I and World War II

AW-1   MC   5.-10.

AW-3   MC   1.-3.

AW-4   GrGy   1.-3.
Issued by Christian Women's Peace Movement.

AW-5   B (1939)   .50-2.

AW-6   Rbk (1931)   .50-2.
AW-7   BBk (1931)   .50-2.
Issued by World Peaceways.

AW-8   RTuBk (1931)   .50-2.
Issued by World Peaceways.

AW-9   MC (1931)   1.-3.
Issued by World Peaceways.

AW-10   DkGrBGo   1.-3.
Sheet of 100 (10x10).
AW-11   LtGrBGo   1.-3.
Pane of six (3x2). SE:TRB
AW-12   DkGrBY (name removed)   1.-3.
Issued by Women's International League for Peace and Freedom.

AW-2   MC (1914)   1.-3.
Issued by the Peace Stamp Society.

AW-13　　Gr　　　　　　　　1.-3.
Issued by Women's International League for Peace and Freedom.

That part of this income tax which is levied for preparation for War is paid only under Protest.

W. I. L.　　　　Sign here

AW-14　　Bk/Br　　　　　　1.-3.
AW-15　　Bk/Y　　　　　　 1.-3.
AW-16　　Bk/Gr　　　　　　1.-3.
Issued by Women's International League for Peace and Freedom.

AW-17　　LtBDkB　　　　　 1.-3.
Issued by Women's International League for Peace and Freedom.

Picture shown at 80%
AW-18　　Bk/B　　　　　　 1.-3.
Issued by Women's International League for Peace and Freedom.

Picture shown at 80%
AW-19　　BOr　　　　　　　1.-3.
Issued by National League of Women Voters.

AW-20　　RB　　　　　　　 2.-4.
Issued by the new Jersey Council on International Relations.

AW-21　　LtGrDkGr　　　　 1.-3.
AW-21a　 LtGrDkGr (imperf.)　1.-3.
Issued by the new Jersey Council on International Relations.

AW-22　　RB　　　　　　　 1.-3.
Issued by the new Jersey Council on International Relations.

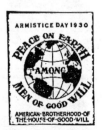

AW-23　　RBY/B (1928)　　 .50-2.
AW-24　　RBY (1928)　　　 .50-2.
AW-25　　RBGr/Y (1929)　　.50-2.
AW-26　　RB (1930)　　　　.50-2.
Issued by American Brotherhood of House of Good Will.

AW-27　　RBk/Y (1931)　　 .50-2.
Issued by American Brotherhood of House of Good Will.

AW-28　　R/Y (1932)　　　 .50-2.
Sheets of ten (5x2).
AW-29　　B/B (1932)　　　 .50-2.
Sheets of ten (5x2).
AW-30　　RPu (1934)　　　 .50-2.
Sheets of eight (4x2).
Issued by American Brotherhood of House of Good Will.
Note: the 1933 issue features a quote by Charles Evans Hughes and is listed as number CEH-5 in chapter 1.

AW-31　　PuGo　　　　　　.50-2.
Issued by World Peace Service, Chicago, Ill.

If you have any items which are not pictured in this book but should be, please send photographs to the author in care of Krause Publications, 700 E. State St., Iola, WI 54990-0001.

AW-32   GrR (1915)   2.-4.

AW-33   B   1.-3.

AW-34   Bk/R   1.-3.
Issued by The Fellowship, Seattle, WA.

AW-35   B (1914)   1.-3.

AW-36   Pu   1.-3.

AW-37   Bk   1.-3.

AW-38   Bk   1.-3.

AW-39   R/Br   1.-3.
Appears to have been made as a roll of brown
paper tape.

AW-40   Gr   1.-3.
Issued by American league Against War and
Fascism.

AW-41   B   1.-0.
Issued by American league Against War and
Fascism.

AW-42   RBk   1.-3.
issued by War Resisters' International.

AW-43   B   1.-3.

AW-44   B   .50-2.

AW-45   B   1.-3.

AW-46   RB   1.-3.
Issued by Women World War Veterans. Illegible
second phrase says "Why die for others?"

AW-47   R   .50-2.

AW-48   RGo   .50-2.

AW-49   BY   .50-2.
Issued by Catholic War Veterans.

AW-50   B   .50-2.

AW-51   RBSi   .50-2.

AW-52   RBY   1.-3.
AW-53   (smaller version)   .50-2.

AW-54   RB   1.-3.

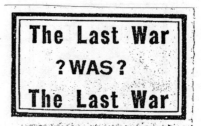

AW-55   .50-2.

AW-56   DkTu/Si foil   .50-2.

AW-57   B   .50-2.

AW-58   B   .50-2.

AW-59   RB   2.-4.
Issued by Citizens Keep America Out of War
Committee, Chicago, Ill.

AW-60   RB   2.-4.
Issued by Citizens Keep America Out of War
Committee, Chicago, Ill.

AW-61   RBGr   .50-2.
Sheets of twenty-one (7x3) die cut.

AW-62   RB (1941)   1.-3.
Sheets of twenty-five (5x5). SE:TBLR

AW-63   BkY   .50-2.
Issued by American Gold Star Mothers.

AW-64   RB (1939) (roulette)   .50-2.
AW-64a   RB (imperf.) (1939)   .50-2.
AW-65   RB larger (1939)   .50-2.

AW-66   RB   .50-2.

AW-67   RB (1940)   .50-2.
Issued by American War Mothers, Washington,
DC.

AW-68   RB   .50-2.
Sheets of 100 (10x10). Issued by American War
Mothers, Washington, DC.

AW-69   RB   .50-2.
Die cut.

Picture shown at 115%

AW-70   RB (1941)   .50-2.
AW-71   RB (1941)   1.-3.
Issued by America First Committee, Chicago, Ill.
See also numbers PAT-6 and Pat-7 in the previ-
ous section. Difference in these two items is the
address at the bottom.

AW-72   RBk   .50-2.

AW-73   RB   .50-2.

Picture shown at 85%
AW-74   RBk   .50-2.

AW-75   B   .50-2.
AW-76   R   .50-2.

Picture shown at 115%
AW-77   B   .50-2.

WAR?
Never Again!
Let them fight it
out over there!!!
"KEEP
CALM"

Picture shown at 90%
AW-78   R   .50-2.

KEEP US OUT!
We "Made the World
Safe for Democracy" once.
Once is enough!
NO MORE WAR!

Picture shown at 75%
AW-79   R   .50-2.

LET THE PEOPLE
VOTE ON WAR!!
Keep faith in our
AMERICA!
*Defend Civil
Liberties ! ! !*

Picture shown at 85%
AW-80   R   .50-2.

Let the People
Vote on War!
Who else should decide
so momentous a question
?
Write your representatives.

Picture shown at 85%
AW-81   RB   .50-2.

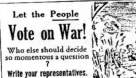

Let the PEOPLE
VOTE ON WAR!
*Who else can decide so
momentous a question?*
Write your Congressman!

Picture shown at 75%
AW-82   RB   .50-2.

KEEP U.S. OUT OF WAR
We "Made the World Safe
for Democracy" once.
Are we going to "MAKE
THE WORLD S-A-F-E
for COMMUNISM" now?

Picture shown at 70%
AW-83   R   .50-2.

DOWN
with
WAR!

Picture shown at 85%
AW-84   R   .50-2.

WAR
?
What For?
DOWN
With WAR!

Picture shown at 85%
AW-85   R   .50-2.

KEEP U. S. OUT OF WAR!
Repeal Conscription!!
"DEMOCRACY BEGINS AT HOME"
Make U.S. Impregnable in
The Democratic Way.

Picture shown at 70%
AW-86   B   .50-2.

Make America Strong

Keep U. S. Out of War!
"If I am to love my
country, it must be lov-
able; if I am to honor it,
it must be worthy of
respect."

AW-87   B   .50-2.

Make America Strong

Keep U. S. Out of War!
"If I am to love my
country, it must be lov-
able; if I am to honor it,
it must be worthy of
respect." *Wendell Phillips*

AW-88   RB   .50-2.

Make America Strong

Keep U. S. Out of War!
"If I am to love my
country, it must be lov-
able; if I am to honor it,
it must be worthy of
respect." *Wendell Phillips*

AW-89   RB   .50-2.

AMERICA FIRST
PEACE FOR U. S.!
More than four-fifths of the people want
peace! Don't let a small group of war-mon-
gering interventionists drag us into war.
Demand that the PEOPLE be allowed
to VOTE ON IT!

Picture shown at 85%
AW-90   RBk   .50-2.

AMERICA FIRST!
No Convoys — No War
A last ditch fight to keep out of Europe's
War; *Write the President, Your Represent-
atives,* TODAY.   :   :   :
PEACE FOR U. S.!

Picture shown at 85%
AW-91   R   .50-2.

AMERICA FIRST!
No Convoys — No War
A last ditch fight to keep out of Europe's War;
Write the President, Your Representatives, TODAY.
PEACE FOR U. S.!

Picture shown at 70%
AW-92   B   .50-2.

Let the People
VOTE ON WAR!
From the Democratic Party platform of 1924:
"Those who furnish the blood and bear the burdens
of war should, whenever possible, be consulted be-
fore this supreme sacrifice is required of them."

Picture shown at 90%
AW-93   R   .50-2.

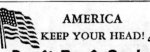

AMERICA
KEEP YOUR HEAD!
Don't Be A Sucker!!
They fooled us into "making the world safe for
democracy" once!   Don't bite twice on the
same bait!   Are you willing to lose democracy
at home to force it on the rest of the world?

Picture shown at 95%
AW-94   B   .50-2.

REPEAL
Totalitarian
Conscription!
"You can best defend democracy with
more democracy."
— AMERICAN CITIZENS UNITED AGAINST WAR —

Picture shown at 85%
AW-95　　B　　　　　　　　　　　.50-2.

God Bless America **Keep Her At PEACE**
The Flag I Love — Long may it wave!
"of the People, by the People and for the People."

AW-96　　R　　　　　　　　　　　.50-2.

NATIONAL UNITY?
Yes-
FOR PEACE!!
Help Keep
U.S. Out of War!

Picture shown at 90%
AW-97　　B　　　　　　　　　　　.50-2.

 America First!
Our interest does not lie in
controlling foreign peo-
ples; let us put our own
house in order *first*.

Picture shown at 90%
AW-98　　B　　　　　　　　　　　.50-2.

"They that can give up essential liberty to
obtain a little temporary safety deserve
neither liberty nor safety." "Mad wars destroy
in one year the works of many years of Peace."
"War is not paid for in war time; the bill comes
later." *Benjamin Franklin*

AW-99　　B　　　　　　　　　　　.50-2.

 "Government of the people,
by the people, and for the
people."
Yet we are being push-
ed into war against the
people's wishes! *WHY?*

Picture shown at 90%
AW-100　　R　　　　　　　　　　　.50-2.

 from THE DECLARATION
OF INDEPENDENCE:
*"...we hold the rest of mankind
Enemies in War, in Peace, Friends."*

Picture shown at 90%
AW-101　　B　　　　　　　　　　　.50-2.

 The Nazarene said:
"Blessed are
the peace makers."
†
HELP KEEP U.S. OUT OF WAR!

Picture shown at 90%
AW-102　　B　　　　　　　　　　　.50-2.

 "No man can serve two masters."
If in your heart you believe
in peace, no man can make
you kill, to appease the lust
of Satan.
Follow the Prince of Peace.

Picture shown at 85%
AW-103　　B　　　　　　　　　　　.50-2.

Let the PEOPLE
VOTE ON WAR!
*Who else can decide so
momentous a question?*
Write your Congressman!

AW-104　　R　　　　　　　　　　　.50-2.

**Let the PEOPLE
Vote on war!
Why Not?**

AW-105　　R　　　　　　　　　　　.50-2.

Don't Scrap The Neutrality Act!!
Will the repealer advocates dare say
this too, is "another step to help keep
U.S. out of war"?
American Citizens Unite Against War

AW-106　　Bk　　　　　　　　　　　.50-2.

Don't Scrap The Neutrality Act!!
Will the repealer advocates dare say
this too, is "another step to help keep
U.S. out of war"?
American Citizens Unite Against War

AW-107　　R　　　　　　　　　　　.50-2.

Thomas Jefferson:
I have ever deemed it fundamental for the United
States never to take an active part in the quarrels of
Europe. Their political interests are entirely distinct
from ours. Their mutual jealousies, their balance of
power, their forms and principles of government, are
all foreign to us. They are nations of eternal war.

Picture shown at 90%
AW-108　　Bk　　　　　　　　　　　.50-2.

Thomas Jefferson:
"I have ever deemed it fundamental for the United
States never to take an active part in the quarrels of
Europe. Their political interests are entirely distinct
from ours. Their mutual jealousies, their balance of
power, their forms and principles of government, are
all foreign to us. They are nations of eternal war."

Picture shown at 90%
AW-109　　B　　　　　　　　　　　.50-2.

WHOSE WAR? THE BANKERS!
"To war! Get going, you feeble-brained fools.
Kill, kill, kill until the blood of men, women and
children drown the world in blood!— to make the
world safe for bankers— but know what you do
while you slay innocents; that the world's incom-
parably worst criminals may be made safe to prac-
tice usury." *McCall.*

Picture shown at 85%
AW-110　　R　　　　　　　　　　　.50-2.

 WARNING!　　DANGEROUS!
WAR!
1 dose each 25 years; recovery not guaranteed.

Picture shown at 95%
AW-111　　B　　　　　　　　　　　.50-2.

 WAR FEVER?
R
PEACE FERVOR!

Picture shown at 90%
AW-112　　B　　　　　　　　　　　.50-2.

America! STOP!
THINK!
Why commit suicide?
Unprepared as we are today, what chance would
we have of invading Europe?
MAKE AMERICA IMPREGNABLE!
HELP KEEP U. S. OUT OF WAR!

Picture shown at 85%
AW-113　　R　　　　　　　　　　　.50-2.

 PEACE

AW-114　　B　　　　　　　　　　　.50-2.

AW-115　　B　　　　　　　　.50-2.

Picture shown at 70%
AW-116　　Br　　　　　　　.50-2.

Picture shown at 90%
AW-117　　RB　　　　　　　.50-2.
AW-118　　R　　　　　　　　.50-2.

George Washington said:

"To be **Prepared** for War is one of the most effectual means of Preserving Peace."

AW-119　　RB　　　　　　　1.-3.

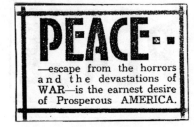

AW-120　　RB　　　　　　　1.-3.

PEACE--
—escape from the horrors and the devastations of WAR—is the earnest desire of Prosperous AMERICA.

AW-121　　RB　　　　　　　1.-3.

AW-122　　RB　　　　　　　1.-3.

AW-123　　RB　　　　　　　1.-3.

AW-124　　RBk　　　　　　　1.-3.

Issued by the National Council for the Prevention of War, Washington, DC.

AW-125　　B　　　　　　　　1.-3.

Issued by the National Council for the Prevention of War, Washington, DC.

Picture shown at 70%
AW-126　　B/B　　　　　　　1.-3.
AW-127　　Gr/Gr　　　　　　1.-3.
Sheets of ten (5x2).

Issued by the National Council for the Prevention of War, Washington, DC.

Picture shown at 90%
AW-128　　OrBBk "AGRICULTURE"　　1.-3.
AW-129　　OrBBk "ARCHITECTURE"　　1.-3.
AW-130　　OrBBk "ART"　　　　　　1.-3.
AW-131　　OrBBk "COMMERCE"　　　1.-3.
AW-132　　OrBBk "INDUSTRY"　　　1.-3.
AW-133　　OrBBk "MUSIC"　　　　　1.-3.
AW-134　　OrBBk "SCIENCE"　　　　1.-3.
AW-135　　OrBBk "TRADE"　　　　　1.-3.
AW-136　　TuBBk "AGRICULTURE"　　1.-3.
AW-137　　TuBBk "ARCHITECTURE"　　1.-3.
AW-138　　TuBBk "ART"　　　　　　1.-3.
AW-139　　TuBBk "COMMERCE"　　　1.-3.
AW-140　　TuBBk "INDUSTRY"　　　1.-3.
AW-141　　TuBBk "MUSIC"　　　　　1.-3.
AW-142　　TuBBk "SCIENCE"　　　　1.-3.
AW-143　　TuBBk "TRADE"　　　　　1.-3.
AW-144　　GoBBk "AGRICULTURE"　　1.-3.
AW-145　　GoBBk "ARCHITECTURE"　　1.-3.
AW-146　　GoBBk "ART"　　　　　　1.-3.
AW-147　　GoBBk "COMMERCE"　　　1.-3.
AW-148　　GoBBk "INDUSTRY"　　　1.-3.
AW-149　　GoBBk "MUSIC"　　　　　1.-3.
AW-150　　GoBBk "SCIENCE"　　　　1.-3.
AW-151　　GoBBk "TRADE"　　　　　1.-3.

Issued by Peace Society of America, New York, NY.

Picture shown at 80%
AW-152　　GoOrBBk "AGRICULTURE"　　1.-3.
AW-153　　GoOrBBk "ARCHITECTURE"　　1.-3.

AW-154	GoOrBBk "ART"	1.-3.
AW-155	GoOrBBk "COMMERCE"	1.-3.
AW-156	GoOrBBk "INDUSTRY"	1.-3.
AW-157	GoOrBBk "MUSIC"	1.-3.
AW-158	GoOrBBk "SCIENCE"	1.-3.
AW-159	GoOrBBk "TRADE"	1.-3.
AW-160	TuBBk "AGRICULTURE"	1.-3.
AW-161	TuBBk "ARCHITECTURE"	1.-3.
AW-162	TuBBk "ART"	1.-3.
AW-163	TuBBk "COMMERCE"	1.-3.
AW-164	TuBBk "INDUSTRY"	1.-3.
AW-165	TuBBk "MUSIC"	1.-3.
AW-166	TuBBk "SCIENCE"	1.-3.
AW-167	TuBBk "TRADE"	1.-3.
AW-168	GoBBk "AGRICULTURE"	1.-3.
AW-169	GoBBk "ARCHITECTURE"	1.-3.
AW-170	GoBBk "ART"	1.-3.
AW-171	GoBBk "COMMERCE"	1.-3.
AW-172	GoBBk "INDUSTRY"	1.-3.
AW-173	GoBBk "MUSIC"	1.-3.
AW-174	GoBBk "SCIENCE"	1.-3.
AW-175	GoBBk "TRADE"	1.-3.

Issued by Peace Society of America, New York, NY. ©1914.

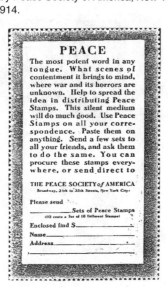

Picture shown at 90%
AW-176   TuBk   .50-2.

Picture shown at 90%
AW-177   OrBk   .50-2.

Picture shown at 125%
AW-178   DkGr   .50-2.

Picture shown at 115%
AW-179   Bk   .50-2.

AW-180   RB   .50-2.

AW-181   RB   .50-2.

AW-182   MC   2.-5.

AW-183   MC   1.-3.

AW-184   RB   2.-4.

AW-185   RB   1.-3.

AW-186   RGr   1.-3.

AW-187   Bk/Gd   1.-3.

LET US
OUTLAW WAR

BEFORE WAR
OUTLAWS US

AW-188   RB   1.-2.

AW-189   B   1.-3.

AW-190   DkBLtB   1.-3.

UPHOLD AMERICAN TRADITIONS
LIBERTY
JUSTICE
BROTHERHOOD
OPPOSE MILITARISM

AW-191   RB   1.-3.

Uphold AMERICAN Principles
PROGRESS — PROSPERITY
PEACE
NOT
WAR
WAR - IS - WASTEFUL

AW-192   RB   1.-3.

UNIVERSAL
PEACE

AW-193   LtTU   1.-3.

We believe that the time has come
when those who hate war
should definitely decide that
they will never take part in
it again.

AW-194   Bk   1.-2.

"I went into the British army
believing that if you want
peace you must prepare for
war. I believe now that if
you prepare for war you will
get war."
GEN. F. B. MAURICE.

AW-195   Bk   1.-2.

ABOLISH WAR!
If we had no war debts
hanging over us this letter
might be sent for One Cent!

AW-196   R   1.-2.

WAR IS NEVER TRULY WON
UNLESS WE ALSO
WIN THE PEACE!
NATIONAL PEACE CONFERENCE, N.Y.C.

AW-197   RB   1.-3.

FOR DAILY BREAD
FOR ALL MEN
WIN THE PEACE!
NATIONAL PEACE CONFERENCE, N.Y.C.

AW-198   RB   1.-3.

KEEP AMERICA
OUT OF WAR
BUILD HOUSES
not BATTLESHIPS

AW-199   B   1.-2.

KEEP
AMERICA
OUT OF
WAR!

AW-200   B   .50-2.

KEEP
AMERICA
OUT OF
WAR

AW-201   Bk   .50-2.

AW-202   RB   .50-2.

AW-203   RGr/Y   1.-3.

AW-204   .50-2.

AW-205   RB   .50-2.

AW-206   B/Go foil   .50-2.

AW-207   B   .50-2.

National Library Students' Peace Posters

In 1940 a sheet of 144 (12x12) different peace poster stamps was issued by the National Circulating Library of Peace Posters. Of these, 120 were posters created by students and twenty-four were text messages about the project. Some of the text stamps had one word in large white letters which made up a message with adjacent stamps. In this listing the stamps are numbered in order across the rows starting with 501 in the upper left corner and ending with 644 in the lower right corner.

Type 1

Type 1 has the word in white at the top of the stamp and is in position 529, 530, 531, and 532

Type 2

Type 2 has the word in white at the bottom of the stamp and is in position 563, 564, 565, 568, 569, and 570.

Type 3

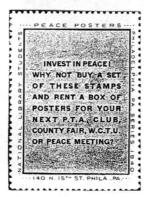

Type 3 has black text only on a blue background and is in position 541, 544, 551, 552, 557, 558, 577, 580, 589, 592, 601, 602, 603, and 604.

Type 4

Type 4 is a multicolored (in most cases) poster with the student artist's name, school, and city.

AW-501	MC Whitney	.50-2.
AW-502	MC Smellage	.50-2.
AW-503	MC Goertz	.50-2.
AW-504	MC Cross	.50-2.
AW-505	MC Nulsen	.50-2.
AW-506	MC Hendricks	.50-2.
AW-507	MC Haley	.50-2.
AW-508	MC Thain	.50-2.
AW-509	MC Button	.50-2.
AW-510	MC Albertson	.50-2.
AW-511	MC Russo	.50-2.
AW-512	MC Silberman	.50-2.
AW-513	MC Bare	.50-2.
AW-514	MC Stephenson	.50-2.
AW-515	MC Wagley	.50-2.
AW-516	MC Garasky	.50-2.
AW-517	MC Farrell	.50-2.
AW-518	MC Butt	.50-2.
AW-519	MC Jamison	.50-2.
AW-520	MC Ward	.50-2.
AW-521	MC Pantelakis	.50-2.
AW-522	MC Hollis	.50-2.

AW-523	MC Giglia	.50-2.
AW-524	MC Schaub	.50-2.
AW-525	MC Yater	.50-2.
AW-526	MC Clark	.50-2.
AW-527	MC Kraabel	.50-2.
AW-528	MC Hume	.50-2.
AW-529	BBk "NATIONAL"	.50-2.
AW-530	BBk "PEACE"	.50-2.
AW-531	BBk "POSTER"	.50-2.
AW-532	BBk "STAMP"	.50-2.
AW-533	MC Eckert	.50-2.
AW-534	MC Bush	.50-2.
AW-535	MC Sundberg	.50-2.
AW-536	MC Nishimura	.50-2.
AW-537	MC Schwarz	.50-2.
AW-538	MC Swartz	.50-2.
AW-539	MC Brown	.50-2.
AW-540	MC Hutchins	.50-2.
AW-541	BBk "Invest in…"	.50-2.
AW-542	MC Fesler	.50-2.
AW-543	MC Burke	.50-2.
AW-544	BBk "Why not…"	.50-2.
AW-545	MC Bacot	.50-2.
AW-546	MC Shirley	.50-2.
AW-547	MC Vanderlin	.50-2.
AW-548	MC Webster	.50-2.
AW-549	MC Farmer	.50-2.
AW-550	MC Alden	.50-2.
AW-551	BBk "every one…"	.50-2.
AW-552	BBk "The selection…"	.50-2.
AW-553	MC Truckenbrod	.50-2.
AW-554	MC Beam	.50-2.
AW-555	MC Wende	.50-2.
AW-556	MC Komisarow	.50-2.
AW-557	BBk "The real…"	.50-2.
AW-558	BBk "Art teachers…"	.50-2.
AW-559	MC Reed	.50-2.
AW-560	MC Perry	.50-2.
AW-561	MC Powell, D.	.50-2.
AW-562	MC Tashiro	.50-2.
AW-563	BBk "ROADS"	.50-2.
AW-564	BBk "TO"	.50-2.
AW-565	BBk "PEACE"	.50-2.
AW-566	MC Freundt	.50-2.
AW-567	MC White	.50-2.
AW-568	BBk "WHAT"	.50-2.
AW-569	BBk "PRICE"	.50-2.
AW-570	BBk "WAR"	.50-2.
AW-571	MC Fry, J.	.50-2.
AW-572	MC Zahn	.50-2.
AW-573	MC Podgorny	.50-2.
AW-574	MC Mitchell	.50-2.
AW-575	MC Tapscott	.50-2.
AW-576	MC Thomas	.50-2.
AW-577	BBk "For color…"	.50-2.
AW-578	MC Grimm	.50-2.
AW-579	MC Bixler	.50-2.
AW-580	BBk "Clubs could…"	.50-2.
AW-581	MC Barr	.50-2.
AW-582	MC Platt	.50-2.
AW-583	MC Monaco	.50-2.
AW-584	MC Chaney	.50-2.
AW-585	MC Bastian	.50-2.
AW-586	MC McConnell	.50-2.
AW-587	MC Huntley	.50-2.
AW-588	MC Martens	.50-2.
AW-589	BBk "Co-operation…"	.50-2.
AW-590	MC Snyder	.50-2.
AW-591	MD Bizzarri	.50-2.
AW-592	BBk "These stamps were…"	.50-2.
AW-593	MC Marissael	.50-2.
AW-594	MC Smith	.50-2.

AW-595	MC Cremeans	.50-2.
AW-596	MC Nusser	.50-2.
AW-597	MC Haist	.50-2.
AW-598	MC Rundell	.50-2.
AW-599	MC Hoagland	.50-2.
AW-600	MC Campbell	.50-2.
AW-601	BBk "S. S. Classes…"	.50-2.
AW-602	BBk "Good references…"	.50-2.
AW-603	BBk "Additional"	.50-2.
AW-604	BBk "These stamps have…"	.50-2.
AW-605	MC McGill	.50-2.
AW-606	MC Didier	.50-2.
AW-607	MC Boom	.50-2.
AW-608	MC Vittoz	.50-2.
AW-609	MC Larkin	.50-2.
AW-610	MC Magruder	.50-2.
AW-611	MC Halstead	.50-2.
AW-612	MC Carroll	.50-2.
AW-613	NC Shaw	.50-2.
AW-614	MC Ginsberg	.50-2.
AW-615	MC Sponsler	.50-2.
AW-616	MC Keltonic	.50-2.
AW-617	MC Mastro	.50-2.
AW-618	MC Milakovich	.50-2.
AW-619	MC Hammond	.50-2.
AW-620	MC Goerl	.50-2.
AW-621	MC Kuller	.50-2.
AW-622	MC Verner	.50-2.
AW-623	MC McBride	.50-2.
AW-624	MC Vlahos	.50-2.
AW-625	MC Kern	.50-2.
AW-626	MC Squires	.50-2.
AW-627	MC Mendelsohn	.50-2.
AW-628	MC Herderson	.50-2.
AW-629	MC Broomell	.50-2.
AW-630	MC Staples	.50-2.
AW-631	MC Mobley	.50-2.
AW-632	MC Randall	.50-2.
AW-633	MC Watson	.50-2.
AW-634	MC Fry, D.	.50-2.
AW-635	MC Courtney	.50-2.
AW-636	MC Powell, R.	.50-2.
AW-637	MC Westman	.50-2.
AW-638	MC Sharpe	.50-2.
AW-639	MC Bridge	.50-2.
AW-640	MC Pikowsky	.50-2.
AW-641	MC Wachter	.50-2.
AW-642	MC Rudo	.50-2.
AW-643	MC Margolis	.50-2.
AW-644	MC Witmer	.50-2.

Vietnam War

AW-1001   B (1965)   .50-2.

Sheets of fifty (10x5). Issued by Women Strike for Peace Organization, Los Angeles, Cal.

AW-1002   Gr   .50-2.
Issued by Women Strike for Peace Organization, Los Angeles, Cal.

AW-1003   BkYTn   .50-2.

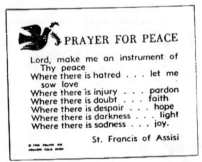

AW-1004   LtB   .50-2.

Picture shown at 65%.
AW-1005   R   .50-2.
From MAD Magazine.

AW-1006   .50-2.

AW-1007   Bk/Tu   .50-2.

How
many
Vietnamese
fought
in *our*
Civil War?

AW-1008   B   .50-2.

AW-1009   B/Y   2.-4.

Chapter 7

Miscellaneous Causes

This chapter contains stamps for causes which are not the subject of longer chapters, such as economic issues or social issues, but which can still be considered political causes.

Billboards

M-1　　Gr　　　　　　　.50-2.

FIGHT *Billboard* BLIGHT
PROTECT AMERICA'S ROADSIDES

Picture shown at 90%
M-2　　Gr　　　　　　　.50-2.

M-3　　Gr　　　　　　　.50-2.

M-4　　Gr　　　　　　　.50-2.

Busing

M-51　　Bk　　　　　　.50-1.

Calendar

M-81　　OrPuBk　　　　.50-2.

Church and State

M-101   B   .50-2.

M-121   Bk/B   .50-2.

Crime

M-151   YRBkGr   .50-2.
Issued by American Legion, Wisconsin.

M-152	Bk/Go (roulette)	.50-2.
M-153	Bk/Go (imperf.)	.50-2.
M-154	R/Go(roulette)	.50-2.
M-155	Bk/Si (roulette)	.50-2.
M-156	B/Si (roulette)	.50-2.
M-157	B/Si (imperf.)	.50-2.

M-158	Gr (imperf.)	.50-2.
M-159	Pu (imperf.)	.50-2.
M-160	B (imperf.)	.50-2.

There may be other varieties.

M-161   BkPk   .50-2.
Issued by Large Families of America, Fairfield, CT, in sheets of forty (4x10) mixed stamps of five different designs. See CEN-4 through CEN-6 and D-11.

M-162   RB   5.-10.

M-163   1.-3.

M-164   1.-3.

Gun Control

M-201   B   .50-2.

M-202   Bk   .50-2.

For A Safer America
Control Politicians
Instead Of Firearms

M-203   Bk   .50-2.

M-204   RB   .50-2.

See ACS-33 and ACS-34 for "Register Communists, not guns."

Art by Melissa Grimes for *Mother Jones* magazine

Picture shown at 80%

M-301   MC   .50-2.

Art by Victor Juhasz for *Mother Jones* magazine

Picture shown at 80%

M-302   MC   .50-2.

Art by Robert Grossman for *Mother Jones* magazine

Picture shown at 80%

M-303   MC   .50-2.

Art by Nicole Hollander for *Mother Jones* magazine

Picture shown at 80%

M-304   MC   .50-2.

Art by Richard Thompson for *Mother Jones* magazine

Picture shown at 80%

M-305   MC   .50-2.

Art by Steve Brodner for *Mother Jones* magazine

Picture shown at 80%

M-306   MC   .50-2.

Art by Lou Myers for *Mother Jones* magazine

Picture shown at 80%

M-307   BkY   .50-2.

Art by Hal Mayforth for *Mother Jones* magazine

Picture shown at 80%

M-308   MC   .50-2.

Art by Steven Guarnaccia for *Mother Jones* magazine

Picture shown at 80%

M-309   MC   .50-2.

Art by Peter de Sève for *Mother Jones* magazine

Picture shown at 80%

M-310   MC   .50-2.

Art by John Mattos for *Mother Jones* magazine

Picture shown at 85%

M-311   MC   .50-2.

Art by Mark Zingarelli for *Mother Jones* magazine

Picture shown at 80%
M-312   MC   .50-2.

STAMP OUT HANDGUN VIOLENCE!

Picture shown at 80%
M-313   RGd   .50-2.
M-301 through M-314 are from a single sheet issued by Mother Jones magazine in 1993.

Hostages

In 1979 the U.S. embassy in Tehran, Iran, was overrun and the staff taken hostage. They remained in captivity until Ronald Reagan's inauguration day in 1981.

M-401   B   .50-2.

RETURN THE HOSTAGES

M-402   RB   .50-2.

Noise

Noise abatement campaigns were most active during World War II to allow defense works to get needed rest. These labels do not refer to the war, so they are listed separately.

M-501   BBk   .50-2.

M-502   RB   .50-2.

M-601   1.-2.

M-602 GrR (shiny paper) (1977) 1.-2.
M-603 GrR (dull paper) (1977) 1.-2.
Issued by the Valley-Lode Tuberculosis and Respiratory Disease Association (Calif.).

M-604 GrR   .50-2.
M-605 GrR   .50-2.
M-606 GrR   .50-2.

M-607 GrR   .50-2.
M-608 GrR   .50-2.
M-608a (sheet of eighteen + label) 4.-6.
M-604 through M-608 are contained in a sheet of eighteen small stamps and one large label (3-3/4" x 3") issued by the National Tuberculosis and Respiratory Disease Association in 1971.

M-609 RGd (1973)   .50-1.

M-610 BR (1974)   .50-1.

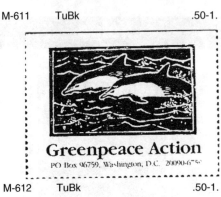

M-611 TuBk   .50-1.

M-612 TuBk   .50-1.

M-613 TuBk   .50-1.
Sheet of six (3x2) containing two of each (M-611 through M-613). SE: TBR. MIL: "Use these stamps on your letters to let your friends know you support Greenpeace Action."

M-614 Gr   .50-1.

M-615 B   .50-1.

M-616 B   .50-1.

M-617   Gr   .50-1.
Sheets of six (3x2) contain two copies each of M-614 and M-616, one copy of each of the others.

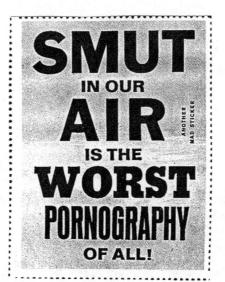

M-639   RBk   .50-2.
From MAD Magagine.

Picture shown at 70%
M-640   MC   .50-2.

M-641   BkPk   .50-1.

Sheet of M-618 through M-623

M-618	MC	.50-1.
M-619	MC	.50-1.
M-620	GdPkBk	.50-1.
M-621	MC	.50-1.
M-622	GdGrBk	.50-1.
M-623	MC	.50-1.

Sheet of M-624 through M-632

M-624	MC (text) (four in sheet)	.50-1.	M-627	MC (banner)	.50-1.	M-630	MC (kangaroo)	.50-1.
M-625	MC (dolphins)	.50-1.	M-628	MC (seals)	.50-1.	M-631	MC (boat)	.50-1.
M-626	MC (turtle)	.50-1.	M-629	MC (booth)	.50-1.	M-632	MC (penguins)	.50-1.

**Use these stamps on your letters
to show your support for
SIERRA CLUB**

SIERRA CLUB
730 Polk St., San Francisco, CA 94109

SIERRA CLUB
730 Polk St., San Francisco, CA 94109

SIERRA CLUB
730 Polk St., San Francisco, CA 94109

SIERRA CLUB
730 Polk St., San Francisco, CA 94109

SIERRA CLUB
730 Polk St., San Francisco, CA 94109

SIERRA CLUB
730 Polk St., San Francisco, CA 94109

Sheet of M-633 through M-638

M-633	MC.50-1.		M-636	MC.50-1.	
M-634	MC.50-1.		M-637	MC.50-1.	
M-635	MC.50-1.		M-638	MC.50-1.	

Sheet of six (2x3). SE: TBR. MIL: "Use these stamps on your letters to show your support for SIERRA CLUB."

Transmission

Transportation

Super Sonic Transport

M-691   RB   .50-1.

Transportation Issues

M-701   BOr   .50-1.

M-702   .50-1.

M-703   .50-1.

Picture shown at 90%
M-704   B/Or   .50-1.

M-705   B   .50-1.

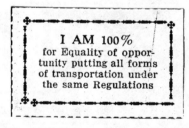

M-706   R   .50-2.

M-707   BkOl   .50-2.

M-708   BkY   .50-2.

M-709   .50-2.

United Nations/League of Nations

M-801   Or(1918)   15.-25.

M-802   B   1.-3.

M-803   B   1.-3.

210 • Miscellaneous Causes

M-804   B   1.-3.

Picture shown at 80%

M-805   B   1.-3.

M-806   B   .50-2.

M-807   B   1.-3.
M-807   B (larger)   .50-2.

M-808   B   1.-3.

M-809   RB   1.-3.

M-810   RB   1.-3.

M-811   B/Si   1.-3.
Die cut.

M-851   1.-3.

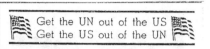

Picture shown at 80%

M-852   RB   .50-2.

> Get the US out of the UN
> Get the UN out of the US

M-853   RB   .50-2.

> **U.S. FOREVER**
> **U.N. never!**

M-854   Bk   .50-2.

Get US out!
OF THE UNITED NATIONS

M-855   1.-3.

M-1001   RB   .50-1.

M-1002   RB   .50-1.

Picture shown at 85%
M-1003   LtBDkB   .50-1.

M-1004   BkOr   .50-1.
Might be same source as M-703.

GIVE
PENNA.
LOCAL
OPTION
NOW!

M-1005   B   .50-1.

KEEP
SCHOOLS
OPEN
VOTE YES ⊠
MARCH 17

M-1006   RB   .50-1.

M-1007   RB   .50-1.
Issued by Retarded Children's Education
Project, Chicago, Illinois.

M-1008   RB   .50-1.
Issued by Retarded Children's Education
Project, Chicago, Illinois.

JOIN THE CRUSADE
to enact legislation
in behalf of
TRAINABLE RETARDED
CHILDREN

M-1009   RB   .50-1.
Issued by Retarded Children's Education
Project, Chicago, Illinois. Note: Different from M-
1008 in spacing in fourth line.

Addendum

The following items were discovered after the book had been completed. Use the extra space for new items you discover.

Theodore Roosevelt

TR-3   MC   10.-20.

Warren G. Harding

Picture shown at 90%
WGH-8   Bk   2.-6.

Calvin Coolidge

CC-10   B   R

Wendell L. Willkie

Picture shown at 90%
WLW-205 RB   2.-4.

Douglas MacArthur

DMA-12   RB   3.-6.

Dwight D. Eisenhower

DDE-43   RB   1.-2.

Gerald Ford

GF-8   RB   1.-2.

Ronald Reagan

RWR-33   RBBk   1.-3.
Sheet of twelve (5x2). SE:LTR, MIB: "Please use these stamps on your correspondence to show your support of Reagan for President. NC-PAC.
Reagan Victory Fund, 1500 Wilson Blvd., #513, Arlington, VA 22209."

The following items were discovered after the book had been completed. Use the extra space for new items you discover.

PSS-36

PSS-39

PSS-37

PSS-38

The following items were discovered after the book had been completed. Use the extra space for new items you discover.

Republican

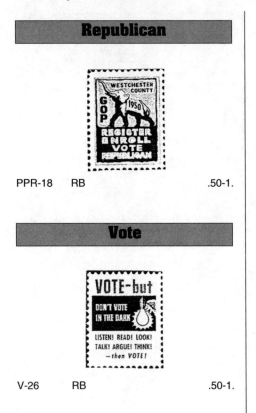

PPR-18   RB   .50-1.

Vote

V-26   RB   .50-1.

The following items were discovered after the book had been completed. Use the extra space for new items you discover.

Blacks

B-39   Bk/Y   2.-4.

B-40   RB   1.-3.

B-41   B   2.-4.

B-42   Bk/Gr   2.-4.

B-43   RGo   1.-3.

B-44   Bk/Gy   .50-2.

B-45   RB   1.-3.

B-46   .50-2.

B-47   Gr/Go foil   2.-4.

NCNW is the National Council of Negro Women.

Chapter 4: Economic Rights

The following items were discovered after the book had been completed. Use the extra space for new items you discover.

Socialist Workers Party

All
War
Funds
To The
Unemployed

SOCIALIST
WORKERS PARTY
233 S. Broadway
Rm. 312

CS-151   2.-4.

Not A Cent
Not A Man
For
Wall Street's
War

SOCIALIST
WORKERS PARTY
233 S. Broadway
Rm. 312

CS-152   2.-4.

Anti-Communism

HELP RADIO of FREE ASIA STOP COMMUNISM

RADIO OF FREE ASIA - 1028 CONN. AVE. N.W. WASH. D.C.

ACS-45   RBk   .50-1.

Communism killed Kennedy

ACS-46   B   1.-2.

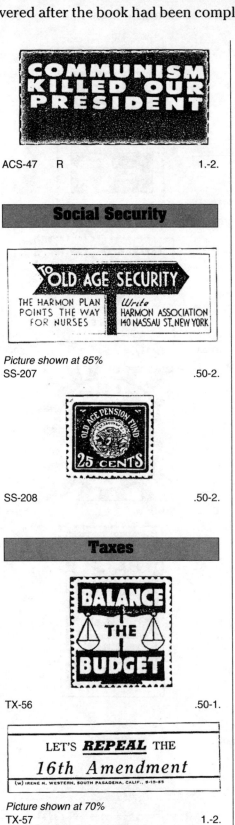

COMMUNISM KILLED OUR PRESIDENT

ACS-47   R   1.-2.

Social Security

TO OLD AGE SECURITY

THE HARMON PLAN POINTS THE WAY FOR NURSES

Write HARMON ASSOCIATION 140 NASSAU ST. NEW YORK

Picture shown at 85%
SS-207   .50-2.

OLD AGE PENSION FUND
25 CENTS

SS-208   .50-2.

Taxes

BALANCE THE BUDGET

TX-56   .50-1.

LET'S *REPEAL* THE *16th Amendment*

(w) IRENE N. WESTERN, SOUTH PASADENA, CALIF., 9-19-85

Picture shown at 70%
TX-57   1.-2.

The following items were discovered after the book had been completed. Use the extra space for new items you discover.

Drugs

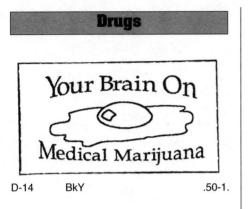

D-14   BkY   .50-1.

Chapter 6: Patriotic, War, and Peace

The following items were discovered after the book had been completed. Use the extra space for new items you discover.

WWI and WWII

War Bonds

W-55 .50-2.

General

WW-2149 MC 1.-3.

WW-2150 MC 1.-3.

This stamp is from a set of 180 which was included in the magazine *The Ladies '94 Home Journal* during World War I. Four different sheets of forty-five stamps each were issued. Some sheets of stamps were sold separately from the magazine. Those included in the magazine have text on the backs.

Patriotic

Flags

Picture shown at 80%
PAT-55   RB .50-1.

General

PAT-663   RB .50-1

The following items were discovered after the book had been completed. Use the extra space for new items you discover.

Prisoners of War

M-681   50.-1.

United Nations

M-812   .50-1.

Index

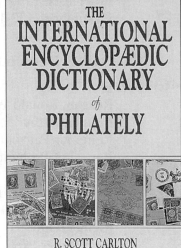
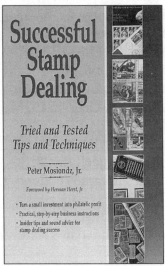
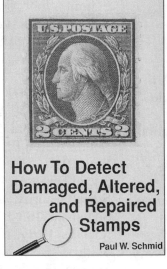